TECHNIQUES AND APPLICATIONS
FOR MOBILE COMMERCE

Frontiers in Artificial Intelligence and Applications

FAIA covers all aspects of theoretical and applied artificial intelligence research in the form of monographs, doctoral dissertations, textbooks, handbooks and proceedings volumes. The FAIA series contains several sub-series, including "Information Modelling and Knowledge Bases" and "Knowledge-Based Intelligent Engineering Systems". It also includes the biennial ECAI, the European Conference on Artificial Intelligence, proceedings volumes, and other ECCAI – the European Coordinating Committee on Artificial Intelligence – sponsored publications. An editorial panel of internationally well-known scholars is appointed to provide a high quality selection.

Series Editors:
J. Breuker, R. Dieng-Kuntz, N. Guarino, J.N. Kok, J. Liu, R. López de Mántaras,
R. Mizoguchi, M. Musen, S.K. Pal and N. Zhong

Volume 169

Recently published in this series

ISSN 0922-6389

Techniques and Applications for Mobile Commerce

Proceedings of TAMoCo 2008

Edited by

Cherif Branki
University of the West of Scotland, Scotland, UK

Brian Cross
University of the West of Scotland, Scotland, UK

Gregorio Díaz
University of Castilla La Mancha, Spain

Peter Langendörfer
ihp microelectronics GmbH, Germany

Fritz Laux
Reutlingen University, Germany

Guadalupe Ortiz
University of Extremadura, Spain

Martin Randles
Liverpool John Moores University, UK

A. Taleb-Bendiab
Liverpool John Moores University, UK

Frank Teuteberg
University of Osnabrück, Germany

Rainer Unland
University of Duisburg-Essen, Germany

and

Gerhard Wanner
University of Applied Sciences, Stuttgart, Germany

IOS

P r e s s

Amsterdam • Berlin • Oxford • Tokyo • Washington, DC

ISBN 978-1-58603-826-7
Library of Congress Control Number: 2007943352

Publisher
IOS Press
Nieuwe Hemweg 6B
1013 BG Amsterdam
Netherlands
fax: +31 20 687 0019
e-mail: order@iospress.nl

Distributor in the UK and Ireland
Gazelle Books Services Ltd.
White Cross Mills
Hightown
Lancaster LA1 4XS
United Kingdom
fax: +44 1524 63232
e-mail: sales@gazellebooks.co.uk

Distributor in the USA and Canada
IOS Press, Inc.
4502 Rachael Manor Drive
Fairfax, VA 22032
USA
fax: +1 703 323 3668
e-mail: iosbooks@iospress.com

To The Old Soldier

Mr. George Hunter

Techniques and Applications for Mobile Commerce
C. Branki et al. (Eds.)
IOS Press, 2008

Preface

Electronic business in general and mobile commerce in particular offers a new road-map for a business enterprise to gain strategic competitive advantages through up-to-date information and technology management. For mobile workers it offers a new avenue for a new knowledge-based economy, building upon the advanced hardware and software technologies.

Mobile Commerce M-Commerce comprises applications and services that are accessible from Internet-enabled mobile devices. It involves new technologies, services, and business models. While it is different from traditional e-Commerce it can also be seen as an extension of e-Commerce in the sense that it, among others, makes e-Commerce available in a modern way to new application areas and to a new set of customers.

The Internet is on its way to leave traces in all aspects of our life independently of where we are. Already today, mobile phones and PDAs become an indispensable part of our life as a source for all kinds of information and services and, especially, as our permanently available interface to our environment. Very soon they will turn into widespread intelligent assistants capable of anticipating many of our wishes and needs, such as automatically arranging for taxis to come and pick us up after business meetings or providing us with summaries of relevant news and messages left by colleagues. But, for all these changes to happen, key issues of interoperability, usability, security, and privacy still need to be addressed.

The Techniques and Applications for Mobile Commerce (TAMoCo) conference series is going to address these issues. It provides scientists, practitioners, and students a platform to discuss the latest trends in the exciting above mentioned areas.

This book is structured into three parts:

Part I: Wireless Technologies for the Extended Enterprise: Current State and Future Developments

The aim of part I is to analyse the state of the art and to stimulate discussions about future trends and technologies with respect to architectures that support business-to-employee and/or business-to-customer relations.

Nowadays, traditional office and business work is increasingly being performed in mobile environments, i.e. outside of offices, at the customer's location or on the road, where notebooks or handheld devices are used instead of PCs – often without access to high-bandwidth networks. However, users expect all services, information and tools they employ in their offices or at home to remain available to them in the mobile environment, too. Moreover, mobile solutions are expected to employ mobile technology with an added value regarding, e.g. personalization issues or context- and location-dependent information and services.

Part II: E-Service Environments: Aspect-Oriented Techniques and Mobile Devices

This part brings together approaches related to e-Services and/or mobile services and aspect-oriented techniques both from industry and academia. It provides an appropriate environment to discus the benefits of aspect-oriented techniques in e-Services systems, as well as in mobile environments, and problems and challenges that particularly arise during the practical combination of these fields.

Part III: AutoMoCo: Autonomic Computing and Mobile Commerce

Autonomic Computing is an area of research looking at imbuing software with dynamic behaviours based on its operating environment. In mobile commerce, autonomous behaviours could be used to help solve the issues of an ever-changing deployment environment, and the differing requirements for actors in commerce transactions. Since its introduction at the beginning of this millennium, autonomic computing has seen major uptakes by a range of communities including enterprise software developers, and grid computing groups to name just a few. In this part active researchers and practitioners will report on novel or ongoing research into autonomic computing and its application of mobile computing with focus on mobile commerce.

Acknowledgments

The organizers would like to express their gratitude to the authors, for submitting their work to TAMoCo 2008, and to the Program Committee, for providing very thorough evaluations of the submitted papers as well as for the discussions that followed under significant time constraints. We also would like to thank the invited speakers and the panel moderator for their efforts in contributing to the success of the conference.

On the organizational side a lot of people have been there from the start of these series and hence we thank them profusely. One of them is the Tilminator Mr. T. Bitterberg although we are not sure about his Lederhosen. Other highly supporting people include Mrs. MacDonald, Ms. Campbell, Ms. Watson, Lee, Darren and last but not least all the staff at Roderick Dhu and Ruarg.

TAMoCo Series Editors

Cherif Branki, University of the West of Scotland, Scotland, UK
Brian Cross, University of the West of Scotland, Scotland, UK
Rainer Unland, University of Duisburg-Essen, Germany
Gerhard Wanner, University of Applied Sciences, Stuttgart, Germany

TAMoCo2008 PC-Chairs

Brian Cross, University of the West of Scotland, Scotland, UK
Fritz Laux, Reutlingen University, Germany

TAMoCo2008 Symposium Chairs

Gregorio Díaz, University of Castilla La Mancha, Spain
Peter Langendörfer, ihp microelectronics GmbH, Germany
Guadalupe Ortiz, University of Extremadura, Spain
Martin Randles, Liverpool John Moores University, UK
A. Taleb-Bendiab, Liverpool John Moores University, UK
Frank Teuteberg, University of Osnabrueck, Germany

Technical Program Committee

Marco Aiello, University of Groningen, The Netherlands
Michael Amberg, University of Erlangen-Nuremberg, Germany
Jill Attewell, Learning & Skills Network, UK
Bharat K. Bhargava, Purdue University, USA
Susanne Boll, University of Oldenburg, Germany
Behzad Bordbar, University of Birmingham, England
Antonio Castello, University of Cassino, Italy
Walid Chainbi, Institut Supérieur des Sciences Appliquées et de Technologie de Sousse,
    Tunisia
Volker Coors, University of Applied Sciences, Stuttgart, Germany
Francisco Curbera, IBM Watson, USA
Gregorio Díaz, University of Castilla La Mancha
Petre Dini, Cisco Systems, USA
Giovanna Dore, Omega Generation Bologna, Italy
Frank-Dieter Dorloff, University of Duisburg-Essen, Germany
Schahram Dustdar, Technical University of Vienna
David Edgar, Glasgow Caledonian University, UK
Bernd Eichler, University of Applied Science, Dortmund, Germany
Jaafar Gaber, Université de Technologie de Belfort-Montbéliard, France
Kevin Grant, Glasgow Caledonian University, UK
Oliver Günther, Ph.D., Humboldt-University, Berlin, Germany
Juan Hernandez, University of Extremadura, Spain
Peter Heusch, University of Applied Sciences, Stuttgart, Germany
Athanassios Jimogiannis, University of Pelopennese, Greece
Ryszard Kowalczyk, Swinburne University of Technology, Australia
Ralf Kramer, University of Applied Sciences, Stuttgart, Germany
Wolfgang Kreutzer, University of Canterbury, New Zealand
Brian Lees, University of the West of Scotland, Scotland
Paulo Leitao, Polytechnic Institute of Braganca, Portugal
Heiko Ludwig, IBM TJ Watson Research Center, USA
Qusay Mahmoud, Guelph University, Canada
Katherine Maillet, Institut National des Telecommunications, France
Andreas Meissner, GMD-IPSI, Darmstadt, Germany
Andreas Meiszner, The Open University, UK/Sociedade Portuguesa de Inovação,
    Portugal
Philip Miseldine, Liverpool John Moores University, UK
Josef Noll, Telenor R&D, Norway
Guadalupe Ortiz, University of Extremadura, Spain
Kris Popat, Ultralab, UK
Key Pousttchi, University of Augsburg, Germany
Omer Rana, University of Cardiff, UK
Martin Randles, Liverpool John Moores University, UK
Kai Rannenberg, University of Frankfurt/M., Germany

Dumitru Roman, DERI Innsbruck, Austria
Stefan Sackmann, University of Freiburg, Germany
Ricardo Sanz, Universidad Politécnica de Madrid, Spain
Volker Schmitz, University of Duisburg-Essen, Germany
Eva Söderström, Ph.D., University of Skövde, Sweden
Milton Sousa, Sociedade Portuguesa de Inovação, Portugal
Geoff Stead, Cambridge Training & Development, UK
Robert Steele, University of Technology, Australia
Roy Sterrit, University of Ulster, UK
Glenn Stewart, Queensland University of Technology QUT, Australia
A. Taleb-Bendiab, Liverpool John Moores University, UK
Huaglory Tianfield, Glasgow Caledonian University, UK
John Traxler, University of Wolverhampton, UK
Christoph Tribowski, Humboldt-University, Berlin, Germany
Can Türker, Swiss Federal Institute of Technology ETH Zurich, Switzerland
Klaus Turowski, University of Augsburg, Germany
Rainer Unland, University of Duisburg-Essen, Germany
Olaf Zimmermann, IBM, Zurich
Christian Zirpins University College London, UK

Contents

Part III. AutoMoCo: Autonomic Computing and Mobile Commerce

Invited Talks

Techniques and Applications for Mobile Commerce
C. Branki et al. (Eds.)
IOS Press, 2008

ARCHITECTURAL DECISIONS IN E-SERVICES DESIGN

Olaf Zimmermann
Research Staff Member, Executive IT Architect
IBM Zurich Research Laboratory

Abstract

The design of e-services requires software architects to analyze many domain-specific requirements; the required architectural decisions recur. Many of them are motivated by cross-cutting concerns such as security, transactionality, and reliability. The decision making is driven by many forces; no single design fits all purposes. Some of these concerns can be expressed as model- and code-level aspects; others are better tackled by more conservative implementation practices. In this talk, we present architectural decision modeling as an emerging technique to transform such architectural knowledge from tacit, tribal knowledge into an explicit, manageable form. We present a three-step decision making framework, which supports the semi-automatic identification of decisions in requirements models and the injection of decisions into model and code aspects. We outline a reusable decision model for service-oriented architecture and e-services design, currently being harvested from completed projects. We conclude with a call to action for further research.

Techniques and Applications for Mobile Commerce
C. Branki et al. (Eds.)
IOS Press, 2008

THE MOBILE PAYMENT PARADOX – CURRENT RESEARCH ISSUES ON YESTERDAY'S FUTURE PAYMENT INSTRUMENT

Key Pousttchi
University of Augsburg
Business Informatics and Systems Engineering
Head research group Mobile Commerce

Since the mid-1990s, serious efforts have been made for mobile payments, the use of mobile phones for business-to-consumer payment transaction processing. Since then, customers explained their demand for m-payments. Market participants such as banks, mobile operators and specialized intermediaries attempted to make according offers. Technical problems seem to be generally solved.

However, more than ten years later m-payments are still far from being an accepted payment instrument in most markets. This result can be referred to as the m-payment paradox and attracts IS researchers throughout the world, especially as the missing m-payments are perceived to be a key enabler for the uptake of business-to-consumer m-commerce and even a possible solution for the inhibiting payment problem in business-to-consumer e-commerce on the stationary Internet.

The first m-payment efforts originated from the fact that the mobile phone – due to its specific properties, its wide distribution in the population, and its users' behavior – is especially well-suited for payment activities. Besides, the analysis of mobile banking services shows that except for account balance verification, instant payment is the strongest use case. In addition to the attractiveness of the technology, the appearance of mobile services and mobile commerce with 2.5G networks by the end of the 1990s made it essential to develop an appropriate form of settlement.

As a result, for the examination of m-payment procedures, two basic tasks must be distinguished. Inside m-commerce, payments for mobile services must be implemented in a way that ideally will be perceived by the user as a seamless part of the system. Outside m-commerce, m-payments become mobile services themselves to provide payment functionality in various scenarios. These scenarios include payments in stationary Internet/e-commerce, payments at vending machines, payments to a person acting as a merchant or service provider, and money transfer between consumers. In recent years, the latter became also an issue in the context of mobile payments in developing countries.

The keynote speech for the TAMoCo 2008 conference examines the evolution of m-payments in the last ten years, gives an overview of the IS research devoted to this area and concludes with an outlook on upcoming developments.

Part I

Wireless Technologies for the Extended Enterprise: Current State and Future Developments

Techniques and Applications for Mobile Commerce
C. Branki et al. (Eds.)
IOS Press, 2008

Surveying Users' Opinions and Trends towards Mobile Payment Issues

Iosif ANDROULIDAKIS[a], Chris BASIOS[b] and Nikos ANDROULIDAKIS[c]

[a] *NOC, University of Ioannina, Greece*
[b] *Computer Network Lab, National Technical University of Ioannina, Greece*
[c] *Nottingham Business School, Nottingham Trent University, UK*

Abstract. The current market penetration of mobile phones in conjunction with an expected growth of m-commerce offers a high potential for the growth of m-payment over the next few years. Although research analysts have predicted that m-payments will gain a significant foothold in the coming years, the requisite high-speed data services and the desirable demand will not materialize overnight. In addition, a wide variety of m-payment technologies are available today, but the value of such services is not clear yet. In order to investigate some key issues related to m-payment from a user's perspective, this paper explores and presents the mobile users' opinions and estimations about these new services via a survey conducted among 315 students in the University of Ioannina, Greece.

Keywords. Questionnaire survey, m-commerce, m-payment, security, users' preferences

Introduction

With the growing momentum of the wireless revolution and the m-commerce explosion, it is evident that mobile devices are becoming a critical component of the digital economy. The spread of mobile phones bode well for the future of m-commerce. Mobile phones have become devices for paying for merchandise [1] and as mobile markets continue to mature, the ability to pay using a mobile handset will be key for the development of next generation services.
Among various relative analysis reports, the predictions in [2] have shown that Japan, USA, Germany and UK would represent four of the largest mobile payment markets in the world by 2006 and forecast that there will be more than 200 million regular mobile payment users, spending a total of 47.2 billion Euros.
A critical factor in order to affirm the above predictions is to study the adoption criteria for the new services. Understanding the behavioral adoption requirements of mobile services, including m-payment, is important to researchers, marketers and industry players. For researchers, an important issue is how mobile end-user services differ from traditional ICT (Information and Communications Technology)-services in ways that affect their adoption. For example, the personalization, location specificity and ubiquity of these services are suggested as important characteristics making their adoption different from other ICT-services ([3], [4]).
As our main goal in this study was to evaluate the current status and adoption's criteria for m-payment in the Greek market, we have conducted a survey among one of

the most promising group of consumers; young people ranging from 18 to 24 years old. Our main concern towards this study was to compare and analyze the users' positions - concerning some key issues related with m-payment – according to their gender, a viewpoint not tested in some similar studies ([5], [6]).

1. Background

1.1 History of Surveying Mobile Services

Over the last years, some surveys assessed customer's perspectives on the mobile phone services, while some others surveys by NTT DoCoMo - which are briefly mentioned in the next lines - examined the way mobile phone owner uses their phone. A survey started at the end of year 2000 described the current trends in mobile phone usage among adolescents [7]. The next survey was conducted in April 2001, and it examined the mobile phone usage among elderly [8]. The respondents were 300 men and women in their sixties. The survey conducted in November 2000 involved 1000 subjects and investigated the use of mobile phones in every day urban life [9]. All of these surveys indicate the growing importance of mobile phones in everyday life and the increased popularity of new features such as email.

Besides the aforementioned preliminary papers, there appear quite many recent studies dealing with the acceptance of m-payment from the viewpoint of the customers [10], but it is out of the scope of this paper to enter the details mentioned in each of these papers.

1.2 M-Payment Issues

The adoption rates of a new technology are often discussed by analyzing the key factors coming out of the Diffusion of Innovation Theory. In accordance to this theory, [11] explains the adoption of the technologies necessary for mobile payment.

In the recent literature, many factors appear to shape mobile billing, in general, and m-payment, in particular [12]. A major determining factor for the success of m-commerce is service affordability - such as low access, subscription, and usage fees. What basically the customer will have to pay depends on the fact that North America's called-party-pays strategy, or Europe's calling-party-pays strategy, or a reasonable mix of both will be employed. The service charge will also have to be a function of the user's location, the time of call, the service type, the call priority, the service duration, the call frequencies (to accommodate frequent micro-payments) and the payment plans (pre-pay or on-credit) [13].

Presently, there are a great variety of mPayment technologies available globally, but significant adoption of such services is yet to come. Services launched so far have seen both success and failure with probably more of the latter. There have, also, been introduced a number of third party micro payment schemes (e.g. PayPal, which in October 2002 was acquired by eBay) that have been implemented for payments via the Internet as well as the evolution of pure mobile payment services (e.g. SimPay) and more are yet to appear.

1.2.1 Security on m-commerce

With the apparent omnipresent availability of wireless devices, m-commerce services have a very promising prospect. However, the success of m-commerce and, especially, m-payment depends much on the security of the underlying mobile technologies [14].

The growth of the various m-commerce services has dramatically increased the amount of personal information that can be potentially collected by individuals and corporations. Sharing such information with third parties is always invoking issues of privacy, especially in view of the fact that it can be done through high speed links and most often without the consumer's knowledge or consent [15].

For instance, the chargeback rate for credit card transactions on the Internet (that is for e-commerce) is about fifteen times more than that for point-of-sale credit card transactions [16]; this, in turn, points to the fact that security will always be an indispensable factor in the success of m-commerce. The m-commerce security challenges relate to the user's mobile device, the wireless access network, the wired-line backbone network, and m-commerce applications.

2. Research Analysis and Results

2.1 Methodology

Our survey was conducted using in-person delivery technique [17], with a total of 315 respondents participating in this survey. Having such a supervised survey technique ensures that each respondent understands each of the questions and answers them correctly [18]. All the respondents were students in the University of Ioannina; this is due to the fact that we wanted the participants to form a representative set that will group a certain age area (18-24), which utilizes in a major rate the current mobile services in Greece and thus has the potential to adopt newer services, like mobile payment, as well.

In our study we have used the 'gender' as the main demographic variable in order to identify some major distinctions between mobile users' preferences. 34,17% of the participants were men, while 65,83% were women. It is worth mentioning that several studies have elaborated on gender differences in the adoption of both voice and other mobile end-user services [19].

2.2 Survey Results and Analysis

In the next subsections the graphical results of all the users' answers are presented. In order to compare the contribution of its value to the total percentage, we have selected to work with the graph type of clustered columns.

2.2.1 Transaction types' usage

One topic of main concern in surveying mobile commerce, in general, and mobile payment, in particular, is the preferences that users show in certain services. Thus, we decided to ask the participants about their preferences towards various basic services ('digital goods', 'hard goods', 'voting', 'ticketing', 'other') that are related to paying via the use of their mobile. By using the word 'digital goods' we denote the download of mp3, videos and other digital content, while 'hard goods' refer to the purchase of non-digital content via the mobile phone.

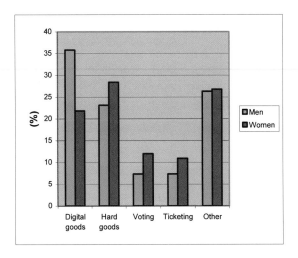

Figure 1. Usage preference among various mobile services

As the figure depicts, digital goods is the preferred and most used content type among men participants (35,79%), while most women (28,42%) seem to prefer buying hard goods via their mobile. It is however, worth mentioning, that 26,62% of all participants have widely used some other service than those mentioned in the questionnaire. This is quite reasonable, as mobile service providers have displayed too many new value-added services over the last few years (games, dating, news etc.).

2.2.2 Mobile Payment Barriers

An investigation into the impact of mobile interfaces on the usability of mobile commerce applications [20] noted that security appears to be one of the most significant barriers to user acceptance. As our study is focused on m-payment, we wanted to evaluate the participants' opinion not only about security as a major m-payment holdback, but also about other possible limitations such as 'high management cost', 'service complexity', 'device complexity', 'limited screen size', 'low processing rate'.

On a customer's perspective, security and high management cost are the most important drawbacks towards the growth of mobile payment. The figure shows that women are – among all given holdbacks – more worried about security (36,07%), while men consider management cost as the main holdback (34,74%).

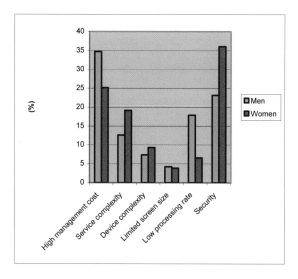

Figure 2. M-payment main holdbacks

According to another survey conducted among both users' and operators' opinions, simplicity of handsets and services is more important to users than most surveyed operators realize [21]. This is a fact operators must take into account, as both device and service complexities are two factors that, potentially, may prevent the early adoption of additional mobile services including m-payments. This is, also, shown by our survey's results, as according to them, a total of 25,54% of the participants answered that complexity (on services and devices) seems to be the main holdback for m-payment growth.

2.2.3 M-Payment Type Preference

In this subsection, we focused on the users' preference among the three generic categories of paying via a mobile phone:

- ▪ 'Pay Per View' best addresses the payment type of new services on the market, as it appears to be intuitive and predictable for customers.
- ▪ 'Pay Per Unit' is the approach commonly used for 2.5G/3G services, such as i-mode. However, end users often struggle to relate to this billing approach, as it appears difficult to predict the total cost of a browsing session or a file download.
- ▪ 'Subscription', typically, refers to a case where a consumer is charged according to a flat rate, regardless of the services' usage. This is a case to be made for operators to adopt a simplified charging model, combining access and service charges in one simple rate, similar to how fixed ISPs charge for ADSL access.

Although, this appears to be a rather generic query, we wanted to 'test' the users' attitude towards the 3 main mobile payment choices.

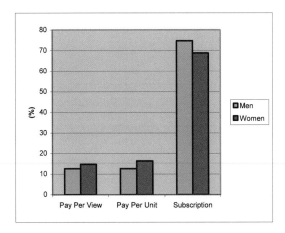

Figure 3. M-payment types' preference

According to figure 3, a total of 70,86% of the participants would prefer to pay via their mobile according to a subscription payment model. In particular, 74,74% of the men prefer the subscription type of mobile payment, while the respective proportion for women is equal to 68,85%. Such a model prevents the customers from additional and unpredictable costs coming out from a possible excessive usage on a certain service. The results' distribution between the other two preferences seems to be quite even, as 14.03% and 15,11% of all the participants would like to be charged via PPV and PPU, respectively.

2.2.4 Motivation on Adopting M-Payment

In this subsection, we focused on the main factors that can affect in a positive way the mobile users in order to adopt new m-payment services. Thus, we asked them to either select among three specific factors we consider important ('time saving', lower prices', 'payment flexibility') or choose their own possible factor (all the latter factors have been centralized as a percentage in the 'Other' column).

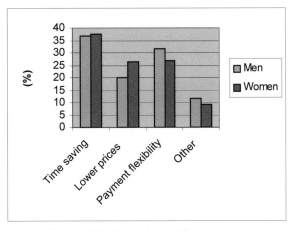

Figure 4. Main factors for adopting m-payment

As the figure shows, the main factor for adopting mobile payment seems to be the minimization of the time that users spend comparably to the current status where the consumers often need to wait in queue in order to pay for hard goods or various bills. The distribution for 'time saving' preference is quite even between the two genders; 36,84% for males and 37,7% for females. Furthermore, 24,1% of the participants selected 'lower prices' as the main motivation factor, while 28,42% of them answered that flexibility on payment seems to be a solid reason in order to use m-payment services.

2.2.5 Security

The lack of security has been a major obstacle for the success of e-commerce in the fixed line Internet environment [22] and this issue seems to remain into the current m-payments environment. Furthermore, in [23], authors conclude to the fact that the evolution of payment services has been hampered by the absence of a ubiquitous security standard.

Although consumer's lack of trust is a major barrier for the adoption of m-payment, resolving security issues will not automatically help to gain this trust. It is of more importance, however, to convince the consumers about the security of m-payment systems; this can be done with the assistance of proper marketing channels as well as advocacy from reputable institutions ([24], [25]).

In this subsection, we asked the mobile users to estimate the security levels of a possible mobile transaction. Our scope was to evaluate the users' sense about the specific issue, independently of their technical knowledge.

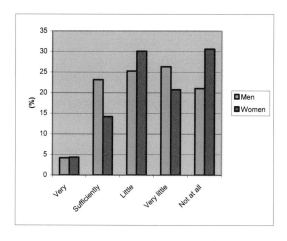

Figure 5. Estimation on m-payment's security trust levels

The figure depicts the users' estimation on the security level of a transaction, taking place via a mobile phone. A total of 28,42% of the respondents believe that the security concerning the mobile payment for services or goods is poor ("little"). More specifically, only 18,48% of women find mobile payment either "very" or even "sufficiently" secure, while the relevant proportion for men is 27,37%.

2.2.6 Interest on paying bills via mobile

Beside the willingness of mobile operators and manufacturers, the adoption of m-payment services, mainly, depends on the users' interest on paying for various services throughout their mobile phones. In order to investigate the specific topic, we asked the participants about their interest level on using their mobile phones in order to pay for their bills.

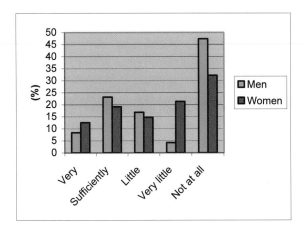

Figure 6. Estimation on m-payment's interest levels

The holdbacks and, especially, the security issues related with mobile payment are the main factors that prevent mobile users from showing the prospective interest on paying their bills via the mobile phone. Thus, almost half of the male participants (47,37%) are 'not at all' interested on such kind of payment, while the respective proportion of female participants is 32,24%. It is, however, interesting to note that 11,15% and 20,5% of all participants are 'very' and 'sufficiently' interested, respectively, on paying their bills by using their mobile phone.

3. Conclusions

A clear conclusion coming out of our survey is that both usability and security will largely determine whether users will choose to use m-payment. A test conducted by Eye-square on the relevant issue of 'Mobile Internet usability' revealed that only user-friendly mobile services enjoy a high potential of user acceptance [26], a remark that comes in accordance with our results, as both devices and m-payment services flexibility seem to be among the main factors that worry mobile users regarding m-payment usage.

Customers make their consumption choices on the basis of benefits and values that technologies enable them to achieve [27]. Thus, it is clear that providers of m-payments solutions must focus on the abilities of end-users to deliver m-payment as a service and position ongoing development with respect to consumer usage patterns [28] and the user needs [29].

Finally, it is worth mentioning that our results are in accordance with those coming out from an analytical adoption model [30], which shows that despite the fact that users have a positive attitude towards payment services, they still don't intend to use them extensively.

References

[1] Paavalainen, J. *"Mobile Business Strategies"*. Wireless Press, Addison-Wesley, 2001

[2] Wireless World Forum, *"Mobile Payment - making mobile services pay"*, Technical Report, 2002

[3] Rask, M.; and Dholakia, N. *"Next to the customer's hart and wallet: Frameworks for exploring the emerging m-commerce arena"*. AMA Winter Marketing Educator's Conference, vol. 12, pp. 372-378, 2001

[4] Watson, R.T.; Pitt, L.F.; Berthon, P.; and Zinkhan, G.M. "U-Commerce: Expanding the Universe of Marketing". *Journal of the Academy of Marketing Science*, vol. 30 (4), pp. 333-347, 2002

[5] Dahlberg, T.; Mallat, N. and Öörni, A. *"Consumer Acceptance of Mobile Payment Solutions – Ease of Use, Usefulness and Trust"*. 2nd International Conference on Mobile Business, Vienna, Austria, 2003

[6] Zmijewska, A.; Lawrence, E. and Steele, R. *"Towards understanding of factors influencing user acceptance of mobile payment systems"*. IADIS International Conference WWW/Internet, Madrid, Spain, 2004

[7] NTT DoCoMo. *"Current Trends in Mobile Phone Usage Among Adolescents"*. DoCoMo Report No. 10, 2001

[8] NTT DoCoMo. *"Mobile Phones Increasingly Popular Among the Elderly"*. DoCoMo Report No. 11, 2001

[9] NTT DoCoMo. *"The use of cell phones/PHS phones in everyday urban life: A survey of 1,000 people"*. DoCoMo Report No. 9, 2000

[10] Dahlberg, T.; Mallat, N.; Ondrus, J. and Zmijewska, A. *"Mobile Payment Market and Research – Past, Present and Future"*. Helsinki Mobility Roundtable 2006, Helsinki, Finland, 2006

[11] Fife, E. and Pereira, F. "The Diffusion of Mobile Data Applications". *Journal of Communication Network*, vol. 2(3), pp. 5-11, 2003

[12] Lee, C.; Warkentin, M.; and Choi, H. *"The Role of Technological and Social Factors on the Adoption of Mobile Payment Technologies"*. The 10th Americas Conference on Information Systems, New York City, 2004, pp. 2781-2786

[13] Sadeh, N. *"M-commerce Technologies, Services, and Business Models"*. John Wiley & Sons, 2002

[14] Siau, K. and Shen, Z. "Building Customer Trust in Mobile Commerce". *Communications of the ACM*, vol. 46(4), pp. 91-94, 2003

[15] Slyke, C.V.; and Belanger, F. *"E-Business Technologies"*, John Wiley & Sons, 2003

[16] Schwiderski-Grosche, S. and Knospe, H. "Secure mobile commerce". *Electronics and Communication Engineering Journal*, pp. 228-238, 2002

[17] Dillman, D.A. *"Mail and Internet Surveys: The Tailored Design Method"*. John Wiley & Sons, 2nd edition, November 1999

[18] Pfleeger, S.L. and Kitchenham, B.A. "Principles of Survey Research Part 1: Turning Lemons into Lemonade". *ACM SIGSOFT Software Engineering Notes*, vol. 26(6), 2001

[19] Ling, R. "We release them little by little: Maturation and gender identity as seen in the use of mobile telephony'. *Personal and Ubiquitous Computing*, vol. 5, pp. 123-136, 2001

[20] Buranatrived, J.; and Vickers, P. "*An Investigation of the Impact of Mobile Phone and PDA Interfaces on the Usability of Mobile-Commerce Applications*". IEEE International Workshop on Networked Appliances, Liverpool, pp. 90-95, 2002

[21] Aafjes, M.; Bensaou, B.; and Shaikh, J. "*Recharging mobile Innovation: Strategies to Create New Market space*". Capgemini White Paper, 2004

[22] KPMG. "*Clash of the Titans - The Future of m-Financial Services in Europe*". Press Release, 2000

[23] Baschnonga , A. "*Mobile payments*". PMN Publications, 2002

[24] Egger, F.N.; and Abrazhevich, D. "*Security & Trust: Taking Care of the Human Factor*", Electronic Payment Systems Observatory Newsletter, vol. 9, 2001

[25] Telecom Media Networks. "*Mobile Payments in M-Commerce*". TMN White Paper, 2002

[26] Duda, S., et al. "*Mobile Usability Report*", 2002

[27] Kreyer, N., et al. "*Standardized Payment Procedures as Key Enabling Factor for Mobile Commerce*". 3rd International Conference on E-Commerce and Web Technologies, 2002

[28] Wireless World Forum, "*What future mobile payments? Industry Experts speak out*", Technical Report, 2002

[29] Datamonitor. "*mPayments*", Market Research Report, 2003

[30] Pedersen, P.; Nysveen, H.; and Thorbjørnsen H. "*Adoption of Mobile Services: Model Development and Cross-Service Study*". SNF Report no. 31/02, 2002

APPENDIX

The main questions forming the questionnaire used for our survey are quoted here:

Gender:
A) Male B) Female

How interested would you be in paying your bills (credit cards, phone bill, bank) via your mobile phone?
A) Very   B) Sufficiently   C) Little D) Very little   E) Not at all

How would you like to be charged for using value-added services?
A) Pay Per View (PPV)
B) Pay Per Unit (PPU)
C) Subscription (uunlimited access for a certain time)

Which one of the followings have you paid to use or to buy or to download the most times?
A) Digital goods (mp3, ringtones, java, games etc)   B) Hard goods (books, CDs etc)
C) Voting   D) Buying tickets   E) Other

In your opinion, what is the crucial factor for the mobile operators in order to raise the accessibility in their services?

A) Usefulness   B) Speed   C) Ease of use   D) Other

In your opinion, what is the crucial factor for the mobile operators in order to accelerate the adoption of multimedia services from the users?

A) Lower cost of terminals   B) Simplification of charging models
C) Lower price of services   D) Other

In your opinion, what is the major obstacle that can hold back the evolution of m-payment?

A) High management cost   B) Services' complexity
C) Devices' complexity   D) Limited screen size
E) Low processing rate   F) Security

In your opinion, what is the major motivation for a user in order to adopt/use m-payment services?

A) Time saving   B) Lower prices
C) Payment flexibility   D) Other

Do you believe that m-payments are secure?

A) Very   B) Sufficiently   C) Little   D) Very little   E) Not at all

Techniques and Applications for Mobile Commerce
C. Branki et al. (Eds.)
IOS Press, 2008

Segmentation-Based Caching for Mobile Auctions

Stefan BÖTTCHER, Sebastian OBERMEIER, Adelhard TÜRLING, and
Jan Henrik WIESNER

University of Paderborn, Fürstenallee 11, 33102 Paderborn, Germany
{stb | so | mellow | henry}@uni-paderborn.de

Abstract. Whenever e-commerce applications want to distribute XML data over
mobile networks, the limitted battery power requires to reduce the amount of exchanged data. Therefore, we propose a technique to identify parts of the database
that are more frequently queried than other parts, to cache these parts, and to reuse
them for answering following queries.

In this paper, we present a data shipping strategy based on a segmentation of
an XML database that not only reduces the amount of transferred data within the
whole network, but also simplifies the method of testing whether an intermediate
participant that routes a query can contribute to this query. Furthermore, we use the
XMark benchmark for experimentally evaluating how the use of our segmentation
within a typical mobile auction scenario can reduce the total amount of transferred
data.

Keywords. XML Caching, Mobile Applications, XML Segmentation

1. Introduction

1.1. Motivation

Mobile devices become more and more popular and can be used for a variety of commercial activities. We focus on a mobile flea market auction scenario, where sellers use an
XML database to describe details of their offered goods, and buyers use their PDAs and
the mobile network to search for goods and buy them. Often, these networks additionally
contain gateways to the fixed-wired world, which allows participants to access databases
that reside in fixed-wired parts. In our particular application, there are gateways to the
XML database, which stores the goods offered by the participants.

Whenever remote data becomes popular and is frequently requested, the requested
data must be routed via several mobile hops for each request. This involves a lot of
energy consumption and may result in congestion within certain nodes. As sending data
consumes more energy than receiving data and both consume much more than local
computations, our contribution to reduce energy consumption is to reduce the amount of
data exchanged.

To reduce the amount of transferred data by re-using already transferred results, the
use of an efficient caching mechanism is crucial. However, current XPath caching mech-

anisms, e.g. [8, 13], limit the use of cached data to queries meeting certain conditions. Furthermore, the proposed mechanisms stress participants by finding an embedding of new queries into cached previous results.

1.2. Contributions

In comparison to other work on XML caching, our contribution combines the following advantages:

- We avoid high workload on other participants by use of caches.
- By using segmentation IDs, cache-hit testing is simplified to integer comparisons.
- Queries are forwarded only when needed.
- Transferred data segments are small-sized due to the used segmentation algorithm.
- A proven reduction of the overall data exchange in our mobile commerce auction scenario.

1.3. Paper Organization

The remainder of the paper is organized as follows. Section 2 formulates the problem statement and points out limitations of current approaches. In Section 3, we introduce a query and caching mechanism that reduces the database work load and allows the participants' caches to determine fast whether they can contribute to the query or not. Furthermore, our solution returns query results that contain additional information to assist further queries in re-using cached information. We give experimental results (Section 4), which show the benefit of our caching mechanism. We compare our approach with related work in Section 5, and finally Section 6 concludes the paper.

2. Problem Description

Whenever a client needs information that is stored in a database, it has two possibilities: *query shipping* or *data shipping*. The decision which of these two approaches should be used can be made individually for each query, however, both approaches involve limitations.

2.1. Limitation of Current Approaches

In the following, we examine *query shipping* and *data shipping* regarding their caching properties.

Query shipping means that each client C sends a given query Q_{act} to the database. Within mobile networks, the query may be routed via several intermediate participants. The database computes the result and sends it back to C, which then may cache the data. To provide the cached result of Q_{act} to other nodes, C can inspect each query Q_i that it routes and then determine whether it can answer Q_i completely. If the query Q_i is identical to Q_{act}, then Q_i does not need to be sent to the database; Q_i can be answered directly by the cache.

Besides the naive method to compare query strings, current research tries to identify when a given query can be completely answered by a cache. For example, [8] suggests to normalize both, an actual query Q_{act} and cached queries $Q_1 \ldots Q_n$, and find a homomorphism between Q_{act} and Q_n by omitting the last location step. However, there is a trade off between time and accuracy since each node that routes a query must perform these complex tests.

In addition, small missing parts of information lead to cache-misses: Assume, a node C caches the result of the following query

$$Q_{old} = \texttt{//open\_auction[./@id>30 ./@id<50]//description}$$

If another participant D issues the query Q_{act} with $Q_{act} = \texttt{//open\_auction}$ $\texttt{[./@id=45]//description,}$ and the participant C has the result Q_{old} in its cache, but lacks the information which name belongs to which id, the cache of C misses and cannot answer the query Q_{act}.

Data shipping is an approach to answer a query locally and request the data that is necessary to do so.

Although this ensures a greater amount of query-hits, e.g. Q_{act} could be answered by a cache that contains all nodes `open_auction` including their IDs and descriptions, a huge amount of data must be transferred for queries whose read-set is very large, e.g. queries that count data.

For the purpose of reducing network traffic, the data shipping approach has the following advantages: A participant can determine very fast whether it can contribute to the query, and the data shipping approach to query processing increases the number of possible cache hits. However, the disadvantage is an increase of transferred data that is not needed to answer a query.

Although both of these types have advantages and disadvantages, our goal is to combine only the advantages of both query processing approaches. Although there is a trade-off between additional data transfer and number of cache-hits, we show that our approach results in a reasonable balance of test complexity, possible cache-hits, and additional data transfer, by observing the data transfer of the whole network.

For this purpose, we provide a proof-of-concept solution, showing that it is possible to fulfill all of these criteria, within a commercial mobile auction scenario.

2.2. Data Processing Characteristics

Within our mobile auction scenario, we assume the following underlying data processing characteristics:

- The query structure is predefined by bidding and selling programs of the mobile auction application. This means, the queries are automatically generated by an application, i.e. the user does not type in arbitrary queries.

- Instead, the end-user application generates mostly point and range queries including their filters that also may include attribute comparisons.

- The auction database tracks queries in order to get information about most frequent query types and filters.

- Database updates are not part of this contribution. We focus on the content offered by a database that is not changed rapidly, e.g. text, pictures, and videos of offered goods.

- Nodes are egoistic: They do not want to spend much energy to other node's queries.

3. Solution

First, we present a general overview of our querying mechanism. Then, we explain the segmentation schema that was used in the evaluation, and its use for the concept of segmenting the XML-database into small segments.

3.1. General Overview

When we adapt the concept of data shipping to the world of XML, we have to identify all those parts of an XML document that are needed to answer a given query. We call these parts the *read-set* of a Query Q and write rs_Q. Alternatively, it is also possible to describe this read-set by a (composite) query Q_{rs}. This means that the question whether a cache node can contribute to a query is translated into an intersection test of two arbitrary XPath expressions, i.e. $Q_{rs} \cap Q_{cached} \overset{?}{=} \varnothing$. However, the complexity of such a test containing compound queries is proven to be NP-hard [9, 10]. Although techniques have been proposed to reduce this complexity by allowing only a small subset of XPath operators, namely $XP^{\{/,//,*,[]\}}$, we can restrict the kinds of queries only in particular situations. In applications like our mobile auction application where queries are composed by the program, the limitation to a small subset of XPath is often not possible.

Our idea bases on a much easier description of the read-set. Within our approach, a database that offers XML content splits this XML content into several disjoint segments $S_1 \ldots S_n$ according to a *segmentation schema*. This schema obeys the frequency of commonly asked queries and is a means of not only splitting the database, but also to determine which segments $S_i \ldots S_j$ a node needs to answer a given query. Furthermore, the concept of using this segmentation schema allows us using very simple queries to describe each segment S_i and extracting the segment data from the database. In addition, since each segment is based on the segmentation schema, we can add ID numbers to the schema in order to identify each segment with only a few bits.

Assuming the segmentation schema is known to each participant, a participant can determine which segments it needs in order to answer a query locally by itself. The participant then requests those segments $S_i \ldots S_j$ that it has not stored within its cache from the database. Intermediate participants that route the request check whether their cache contains one or more segments of $S_i \ldots S_j$, and if this is the case, they send these segments to the requesting participant. The database only sends those segments that were not found on the routing path. After receiving all requested segments, the participant merges the segments and performs the query locally. Afterwards, it stores the segments within its cache and offers them to other requesting nodes.

In the following, we describe the segmentation of the XML document, and how a client determines the required segments.

3.2. Segmentation Schema

Our segmentation schema is a hierarchical schema that consists of a sequence of split operations, each of which splits a given XML document into two or more sub-segments. During each split operation, we assign numbers $N_1, \ldots, N_k$ to each sub-segment, such that after a sequence of split operations an individual segment can be identified by a segment identifier $S_1/ \ldots /S_m$ of sub-segment numbers S_i where $S_i \in \{N_1, \ldots N_k\}$. Furthermore, the segmentation schema groups different node types and assigns to each of the groups an integer number $1, \ldots, l$, which is concatenated to the segment identifier.

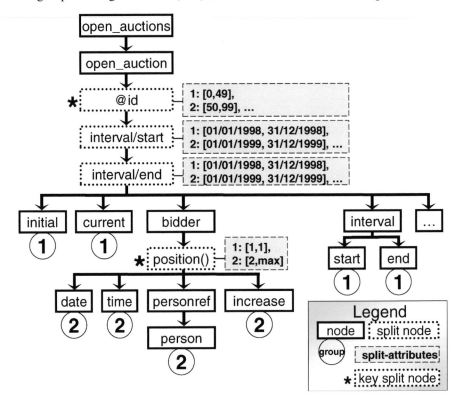

Figure 1. Segmentation Schema Graph

We first list the key operations for generating a segmentation schema and then explain the use of them by an auction database example.

A split node splits all following nodes according to the *split-attributes*

split-attributes define the criteria according to which all following nodes are split. Split-attributes may be based for example on values, ranges, times, the position within the auction XML-document, etc.

A key split node defines a split node that is as a key for all following nodes. The advantage is that only the key split node value must be added to all following nodes when segments are separately stored.

group defines which data elements are grouped together within a segment.

The example, illustrated in Figure 1 shows a part of the segmentation schema graph that was used during our experiments. It is based on the XMark benchmark [11] and contains the segmentation of the auction database.

The rectangular dashed node @id, for example, is called a *split node* since it splits all following nodes by means of the *split-attributes* of the topmost gray box. In our example, the split-node uses the attribute @id to split the data into segments, each containing 50 ids. The id-range to which each segment belongs is indicated by the index number in front of the split attributes, e.g. 2 represents the interval [50,99]. The following split nodes interval/start and interval/end split all following nodes according to their start and end date, respectively.

The circle ① indicates a *group* of node types the nodes of which are grouped together within one segment, whereas the circle ② indicates node types the nodes of which are grouped in another segment.

Since we can identify the @id attribute as a key attribute for all auctions, we call this node @id a *key split node*. The functional dependency from the key split node @id to its descendant nodes is stored in the cached segments, i.e. each segment contains the key split node @id to which it belongs. Since the id key uniquely defines the relationship of all child nodes, it is sufficient to have a single key split node.

If no key attribute can be identified, additional split nodes, like the key split node position(), group the XML document nodes according to their position.

Example 3.2.1

According to Figure 1, a segment with the identifier 2/1/2/1-2 contains the following nodes: Nodes that belong to auctions with an id in the interval 2, i.e. between 50 and 99, started in interval 1, i.e. between 01/01/1998 and 31/12/1998, ended in interval 2, i.e. between 01/01/1999 and 31/12/1999, belong to the bidder 1, i.e. the highest bidder of the corresponding open_auction *node, and are of a node type that belongs to the group 2, i.e.* date, time, personref/person, *or* increase.

```
1  <open_auction id = "65">
2   <bidder position="1">
3    <date>03/03/1998</start>
4    <time>02:02:12</end>
5    <personref>
6       <person>person12214</person>
7    </personref>
8    <increase>1.50</increase>
9   </bidder>
10  </open_auction>
11    ...
```

Listing 1: XML data for the Segment 2/1/2/1-2

A part of the corresponding XML-data can be seen in Listing 1. Each open auction contains the corresponding nodes that are in group 2 including their data.

In this case, the key attribute is the position information which is added to each `bidder` *node.*

There are different possibilities to split a schema into segments. As we have to support a mobile auction, we used a segmentation schema based on the nodes `@id`, `interval/start`, `interval/end`, and `bidder` in order to generate segments as described beforehand.

3.3. Determining Required Segments to Answer a Query

Each participant uses the segmentation schema to determine which segment IDs it needs to answer a query locally. This is done by evaluating the query Q on the segmentation schema and mark all nodes within the schema that are necessary to answer the query.

Example 3.3.1
Assume an XPath evaluator should identify the segments that are necessary to answer the query `//open_auction[@id>53][@id<120]/initial`. *It starts on the first node of the segmentation and inspects the split-node attributes for the first split node* `@id`. *Since the query contains a filter on the id attribute, the evaluator concludes that it only needs the segments belonging to the split node attributes 2 and 3. Since the query provides no information about the start and end of the auction, no reduction of the* `interval` *split nodes is possible. However, since the query returns only nodes of the type* `initial`, *we need only segments belonging to group 1. Therefore, the requested segments for the given query are 2/*/*−1 and 3/*/*−1.*

Note, that whenever a client discovers that it needs too much segments to answer the query locally, it still has the possibility to ship the query directly to the database.

4. Experimental Results

4.1. Scenario

We simulate a mobile network consisting of different mobile clients, e.g. as shown for 7 clients in Figure 2. We assume that only one client is connected via a gateway to the XML database, which provides the data that the mobile clients access. The database contains an XML document with auction data generated by the data generator of the XMark Benchmark Project [11]. We extracted the part of the benchmark dealing with `open_auctions`, resulting in an auction database size of 2.75 MByte. Within our simulation, each client has a cache of 150 kByte.

Each client sequentially executes a number of XPath queries to select information of the auctions on the basis of the unique auction IDs. Although the queries equally distributedly reference all XML node types, each query additionally contains a filter expression. 2/3 of all filter expressions are generated randomly, while 1/3 are taken from a previously fixed filter set in order to simulate a data hotspot of `open_auction` nodes that are more frequently requested than others.

Whenever the simulation selects client C to perform a query, C uses the segmentation schema in order to determine which segments are needed to answer a query locally.

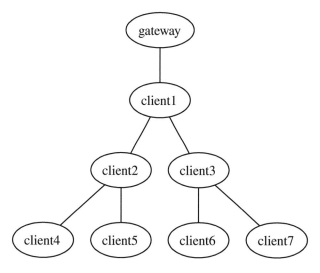

Figure 2. Topology

The request R for these segments is sent to the database. Each client C_{cache} that routes such a request checks whether it can contribute some segments to R by investigating the local cache entries. If C_{cache} can contribute some required segments S_j, C_{cache} sends these segments S_j asynchronously back to the requesting node. Furthermore, C_{cache} deletes the delivered segments from the request, i.e. it computes the remaining request $R' = R - S_j$, which requests only the still missing required segments. This modified request R' is then forwarded to the next participant on the shortest path to the database. If the remaining query R' is empty, i.e. when the query can be answered only by segments of the clients' caches, the query does not need to be further forwarded to the database.

Working with the segments produces some overhead. On the one hand because of the overlapping of segments, on the other hand because some parts of the segments selected by a query are not needed for answering the query. However, as our evaluation shows, keeping this overhead small guarantees that the caching is profitable.

In order to verify the savings that our segmentation-based data shipping solution achieves in terms of reduced data transfer, we compare our scenario with an equal scenario that does not use caching. In this scenario, the mobile network routes each XPath query on the shortest path to the database, similar to the query shipping scenario. The database sends the query result, and only the query result, back to the requesting client.

4.2. Evaluation

Figure 3 shows a comparison of the totally caused network traffic. For each participant a pair of two differently colored bars displays the amount of *sent* data. The gray bar on the left of each pair belongs to the simulation with enabled caching, whereas the black bar on the right shows the sent data within the simulation without caching.

Caching narrows the amount of data sent by every participant. Clients 4 to 7 do not have to route any messages for other clients due to their leaf position in the topology of the network. They only have to send their requests, which do not consume much data to be sent. In the scenario without caching, a request consists of the XPath query, which is

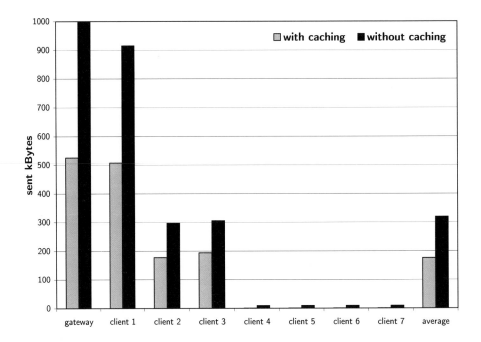

Figure 3. Network Traffic

usually smaller than the associated result. In the scenario with caching, a request consists of the IDs of segments that are required to answer the request. Those IDs are even smaller than an XPath query.

The rightmost pair of bars showing the average amount of data shipped, clearly demonstrates that on average, our segmentation based caching exchanges significantly less data than the query shipping approach that does not use caching.

The diagram in Figure 4 shows that caching also decreases the amount of messages sent within the network. Each bar is composed of two parts. The solid one represents the messages containing query results. The striped part represents messages containing requests. The database itself has not initiated any request so only a solid bar appears in the diagram. The clients 4 to 7 do not have to route any data for the other clients. So they have sent only request messages resulting in a small striped bar for each client. Clients 1 to 3 clients have sent their own requests and have to forward requests and results for the other clients. Client 1 has the only connection to the database via the gateway. Therefore, it must route the queried data on the whole network's behalf.

To summarize our experimental evaluation, our tests show that segment based caching can reduce both, the number of messages and the data volume exchanged.

5. Related Work

Our solution is related to the concept of tree patterns, which represent the tree-structure of XML query languages, e.g. XPath [5] or XQuery [3], to describe frequently occurring

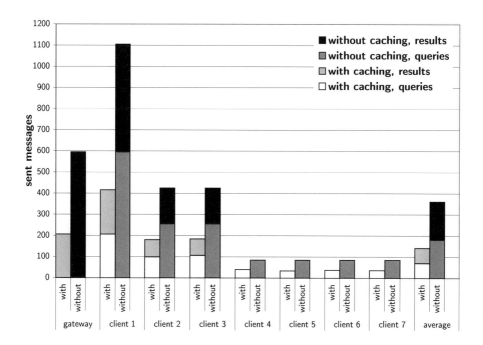

Figure 4. Total Number of Sent Messages

query patterns. However, it differs from e.g. [5] or [3], as we construct a path of segment identifiers to access data.

Several contributions focus on the question "what are frequently occurring queries" in terms of query pattern mining, e.g. [4, 7]. We follow these approaches, as we use them for identifying frequently accessed tree patterns in order to generate a database segmentation that fits many queries, as described in [12].

The concept of querying and maintaining incomplete data, presented in [1], proposes the use of incomplete data trees. These incomplete data trees relate to our segmentation schema graph since DTD based incomplete data trees also use conditions on the elements' data values. However, [1] focuses on computing missing parts of a client's cache to answer a query. In comparison, we use segmentation only to identify sets of requested segments, and we split the overall XML document a priori into several disjoint segments. A caching strategy that is based on frequently accessed tree patterns is introduced in [14]. Compared to the approach of classical patterns presented by [14], our segmentation additionally includes predicate filters, which allows defining a finer granularity for segments. Furthermore, we support cooperative caching since the use of pair-wise disjoint patterns allow multiple caches to efficiently coordinate their segment contribution to answer a single query.

A different approach for XML caching is to check whether cached data can contribute to a new request by testing the intersection of cache entries and an XPath query, and thereafter compute the data that is missing in order to execute the query locally. However, such intersection tests are NP-hard for certain XPath expressions [2, 6], and exact difference computation is known to be resource consuming. In comparison, our approach needs difference computation only a priori for generating a fitting segmentation.

Our caching strategy focuses on efficient computation and thereby requires only minimal resource consumption.

In comparison to all other approaches, our segmentation technique has been developed to support cooperative caching in mobile networks applications with a standardized set of queries, as, for example, the mobile auction application. this paper significantly extends the concept of the segmentation schema and provides experimental results using a real world application simulation.

6. Summary and Conclusion

We have presented a segmentation based caching strategy for mobile networks that combines the advantages of query shipping and data shipping. In comparison to query shipping, our caching strategy reduces the high workload that participants experience due to their close position to a fixed-wired gateway. In comparison to data shipping, only requested segments of an XML database have to be transferred. Our solution uses segmentation IDs in order to describe segments and simplifies the testing for a cache hit. Furthermore, a significant amount of queries can be answered by caches of the network without being necessarily routed to the database. We have compared both, the data transfer and the number of messages that are needed by our caching strategy with traditional query shipping within a mobile auction scenario. Our experimental evaluation has shown that the strategy of segmentation based data shipping is better than query shipping in the overall data transfer, as well as in the number of total messages.

References

[1]   S. Abiteboul, L. Segoufin, and V. Vianu. Representing and querying xml with incomplete information. *ACM Trans. Database Syst.*, 31(1):208–254, 2006.

[2]   M. Benedikt, W. Fan, and F. Geerts. Xpath satisfiability in the presence of dtds. In *PODS '05: Proceedings of the twenty-fourth ACM SIGMOD-SIGACT-SIGART symposium on Principles of database systems*, pages 25–36, New York, NY, USA, 2005. ACM Press.

[3]   S. Boag, D. Chamberlin, M. F. Fernández, D. Florescu, J. Robie, and J. Siméon. Xquery 1.0: An xml query language. W3C Recommendation, http://www.w3.org/TR/xquery/, 2001.

[4]   Y. Chen, L. H. Yang, and Y. G. Wang. Incremental mining of frequent xml query pattern. In *Proceedings of the 4th IEEE International Conference on Data Mining (ICDM 2004), Brighton, UK*, pages 343–346, 2004.

[5]   J. Clark and S. DeRose. Xml path language (xpath) version 1.0. W3C Recommendation, http://www.w3.org/TR/xpath/, 1999.

[6]   J. Hidders. Satisfiability of xpath expressions. In *Database Programming Languages, 9th International Workshop (DBPL), Potsdam, Germany*, pages 21–36, 2003.

[7]   B. Lan, B. C. Ooi, and K.-L. Tan. Efficient indexing structures for mining frequent patterns. In *Proceedings of the 18th International Conference on Data Engineering, San Jose, CA*, pages 453–462, 2002.

[8]   B. Mandhani and D. Suciu. Query caching and view selection for xml databases. In *VLDB '05: Proceedings of the 31st international conference on Very large data bases*, pages 469–480. VLDB Endowment, 2005.

[9]   F. Neven and T. Schwentick. Xpath containment in the presence of disjunction, dtds, and variables. In *ICDT*, pages 315–329, 2003.

[10] F. Neven and T. Schwentick. On the complexity of xpath containment in the presence of disjunction, dtds, and variables. *Logical Methods in Computer Science*, 2(3), 2006.

[11] A. Schmidt, F. Waas, M. Kersten, M. Carey, I. Manolescu, and R. Busse. Xmark: A benchmark for xml data management, 2002.

[12] A. Türling and S. Böttcher. Finite segmentation for xml caching. In *Mobile Information Systems, IFIP TC 8 Working Conference on Mobile Information Systems (MOBIS), Oslo, Norway*, pages 183–198, 2004.

[13] W. Xu and Z. M. Özsoyoglu. Rewriting xpath queries using materialized views. In *VLDB '05: Proceedings of the 31st international conference on Very large data bases*, pages 121–132. VLDB Endowment, 2005.

[14] L. H. Yang, M.-L. Lee, and W. Hsu. Efficient mining of xml query patterns for caching. In *VLDB*, pages 69–80, 2003.

Techniques and Applications for Mobile Commerce
C. Branki et al. (Eds.)
IOS Press, 2008

The Vehicle Routing Problem
with Real-Time Travel Times

Irena Okhrin and Knut Richter

European University Viadrina, Frankfurt (Oder), Germany

Abstract. In the paper we consider a vehicle routing problem with time windows and real-time travel time information. We assume the deployment of an information and communication system that is based on mobile technologies. It provides a real-time mobile connection between the dispatching centre and the drivers, allows localizing the vehicles on road, and gives the overview over the current traffic conditions. Therefore, we explicitly incorporate into our consideration the possibility to react to some dynamic events like traffic impediments and divert a vehicle away from its current destination. To solve the problem we develop a genetic algorithm and test its performance on the well-known benchmarks. The quality of the received solutions is between -6.48% and 2.08% with the average quality -1.5% compared to the best known published results. The negative values indicate that our solutions are better than the corresponding best known, i.e. in majority of cases we outperform them.

1 Introduction

Vehicle Routing Problems (VRPs) appear in distributing and/or collecting of goods by commercial or public transport. The aim of VRP is to determine a route and schedule of vehicles in order to satisfy customer orders and minimize operational costs. Objective is usually to minimize travel times, distances, costs or the number of used vehicles while distributing goods. In addition, many side constrains have to be satisfied, such as vehicle capacity constrains, route duration constrains, time window constrains, etc.

In the past, vehicles executing the routes and dispatchers in the control center were acting separately, without or with only little information exchange. The position of vehicles en route was not known to the dispatcher and it was not always possible to establish a good connection with drivers. The recent advances in information and communications technologies improve dramatically the quality of communication between drivers and the dispatching office. New customer orders as well as route changes can now be easily communicated to drivers, thus enhancing service quality and reducing costs. Moreover, state-of-the-art navigation systems provide real-time traffic and weather conditions allowing to escape hampered roads.

In the paper we consider a vehicle routing problem with time windows and real-time travel times. To enhance the effectiveness of operations management, we assume the deployment of an information and communication system that is based on mobile technologies. It encompasses, first of all, a real-time mobile connection between the dispatching centre and the drivers. Thus new instructions can be communicated to drivers when they have already left the depot and are heading for customers. Second, the dispatching office can localize the vehicles on road via modern global positioning system (GPS). This leads to the enhanced fleet utilization and increased productivity. And third, the modern technologies are able to provide the overview over the current traffic conditions. This enables the consideration of the time dependent travel times that are permanently updated during the day. Therefore, we consider the possibility to react to some dynamic events like traffic impediments and divert a vehicle away from its current destination. To solve the problem we develop a genetic algorithm and test its performance on the well-known benchmarks. We were able to find the solutions of the very good quality that in number of cases outperform the best known published results.

The rest of the paper is organized as follows. Section 2 outlines the application of mobile technologies to vehicle routing. Section 3 presents the literature review. Further, the VRP with real-time travel times is described in Sect. 4 and in Sect. 5 we propose the genetic algorithm to solve it. Section 6 presents the computational results and Sect. 7 concludes.

2 Mobile Technologies in Vehicle Routing

The novelty of mobile technology is in its ability to provide accurate and critical information. For the systems that are based on real-time vehicle routing, the flow of information is as important as the flow of physical assets (Cetin and List 2006). Therefore, their practical implementation is not possible without a real-time, high-bandwidth information system. The recent developments in wireless communication technologies make the exchange of information between the dispatching centre and the vehicles on-road especially cost-effective and uncomplicated. In addition, wireless technology helps to capture up-to-date traffic data which together with instructions for further actions is in real time transmitted to drivers through in-vehicle route guidance devices and advanced traveller information systems (ATIS). Thus the driver behaviour becomes more informed, as they know which route they should select under current circumstances.

Furthermore, based on the signals from satellites, the global positioning system is used to determine the current vehicle positions, dramatically improving fleet monitoring and management. GPS, together with geographic information systems (GIS), is a power tool for data integration, visualization, and analysis. Integrated GPS and GIS are a valuable source of information for the dispatching centre that can locate the vehicles on road and display their position on an electronic road map. In addition, dispatchers can determine the distance between various vehicles of the fleet as well as between a vehicle and its final destination (Küpper 2005). This improves fleet utilization, decreases reaction time, and enhances customer service quality.

Based on the used information, one distinguished several types of in-vehicle navigation systems (cf. Jahn et al. 2005). The simpler form – static route guidance systems – works with relatively static information that is not updated frequently. This encompasses extensive databases of road and transport networks, maps, existing speed limits, and so on. Otherwise, more sophisticated route guidance systems in addition to static uses also dynamic data. This includes information about congestion areas, road works, accidents and incidents, weather conditions or arrangement of specific events like football matches (Giannopoulos 2004). The collected data is in real time processed by the power back-end workstation and ready-to-use recommendations are transmitted to the drivers. Thus mobile technologies assist in making the informed decisions and have great potential to improve the operations of systems with dynamic vehicle routing.

Adoption of a mobile technology should be regarded as a usual IT project. Before implementing a mobile solution in practice, all connected with it costs and benefits should be estimated and evaluated. The company should not urgently shift its business operations to the mobile platform only because it "promises" massive costs reduction and huge efficiency gains. Instead of following the general trend of "mobilizing", every company should assess and carefully analyze all the potentials the wireless applications can bring to it. Only in this case the introduction of mobile solutions will actually be beneficial and will lead to real improvements of business operations.

To estimate the profitability of a project, the company has to compare corresponding costs and benefits. There are two problems associated with it. First, companies tend to underestimate costs connected with mobile project introduction (Potthof 1998). Not the price paid for mobile devices and hardware, but expenses for project evaluation, implementation and integration into the existing IT-infrastructure constitute the most costly part of a mobile solution launch. Second, it is very hard to convert many benefits from a mobile solution into the quantitative values and express them monetarily (Link 2003). Enhanced customer service, improved work flows or better company image contribute only indirectly to the operating profit and are intangible in the short run.

Despite all potentials and promises that mobile technology brings with it, its adoption is not as fast and smooth, as many researchers have anticipated (cf. Heng 2004). There are many things that inhibit fast growth of mobile business, the most important of which are the lack of standards, security concerns and technological limitations. In addition, immaturity of mobile infrastructure and the lack of killer application also prevent the wireless technology from quick development (Siau and Shen 2003) and make mobile business "often a highly frustrating experience" (Zhang et al. 2003). Consequently, before the mobile technology receives widespread use in the everyday business practice and wireless applications are seamlessly integrating into operations, the following limitations should be overcome (see Buellingen and Woerter 2004; Chen and Nath 2004; Siau and Shen 2003, etc.):

Lack of standards. Wide variety of hardware, software and middleware on the mobile market together with the absence of a single dominant standard creates high uncertainty among potential users. Different visions of the future IT-architecture, that could be incompatible with the current one, worsen the situation additionally. In general, lack of reliable standards essentially delays the widespread acceptance of wireless applications by businesses.

Security concerns. No single company would like to make a compromise on security issues. Lack of authentication as well as data integrity and privacy issues awakes main concerns about modern mobile solutions. Also possibility to determine users' location to within a few meters makes them very uneasy while carrying mobile devices.

Technology limitations. Limited navigation possibilities, small screens and slow connection are without doubt on the top of the restrictions list. Short battery life, insufficient memory capacity and low processing power of some devices also count to the shortcomings of modern mobile devices. Moreover, user-friendliness and man-engine interface require better solutions.

Coverage fluctuations. In addition to mobile devices imperfection, network technology also leaves much space for improvements. Network coverage in the field is usually instable and can be highly varying when moving from place to place. The connection quality depends on changing coverage conditions, geographical nature of the area and surrounding buildings. Furthermore, the quality of the signal inside buildings may be poor.

Acceptance problems. Employees that are affected by the introduction of new mobile solutions may be unwilling to accept them. They are used to the old work flows and do not want to change anything. Besides, many workers may be unfamiliar with mobile technology or desktop computer. They are afraid not to handle their work properly and, as a result, to be fired. Thus mobile applications should be easy and intuitive in use with simple and self-explanatory interface. Even employees with limited experience should be able to work with them unassisted and feel comfortable.

Integration expenses. High complexity of mobile solution development and extended efforts to integrate these applications into the company existing IT system inhibit many businesses from deploying wireless platforms. Beside this, in order to fully use all potentials of mobile technology, many business processes inside a company have to be redesigned. Unfortunately, such reorganization and transformation of established business workflows is often a very resource consuming process.

3   Literature Review

The vehicle routing problem was firstly introduced by Dantzig and Ramser (1959) in their seminal paper about the delivery of gasoline. Since that time a vast body of research was devoted to a generic problem and its numerous extensions. A variety of exact and approximate solution methods were developed for VRP. For the survey of some of them see, for example, Laporte (1992), Golden et al. (1998), Toth and Vigo (1998), Laporte et al. (2000), etc.

The majority of papers on vehicle routing make an assumption about the constant travel times that are a scalar transformation of distances. This concept, however, does not represent well the ever changing travel times of the real world. The notion of time-dependent travel times for vehicle routing was introduced by Malandraki (1989) and further investigated by Malandraki and Daskin (1992) and Malandraki and Dial (1996). The authors assumed that the travel time between the nodes changes throughout the day in an a priori known fashion. This partially captures the predictive variations of the travel time function. They divide a day into few time intervals and define the travel times variation as a step function. This function, however, does not satisfy the first-in–first-out (FIFO) assumption. That is, if two vehicles depart from the same depot and travel to the same customer using the same roads, the vehicle that left the depot later may arrive earlier to its destination compared to its rival.

The situation is improved in the subsequent papers. Ichoua et al. (2003) proposed a model for the vehicle routing problem based on the time-dependent travel speed which satisfies the FIFO property. The travel speed changes as time proceeds from one time interval to another. The work by Chen et al. (2006) also defines travel time between nodes as a step function, it is however unknown in advanced and may change if an unexpected event occurs. In addition, Jung and Haghani (2001) and Haghani and Jung (2005) consider a continuous travel time function and develop a genetic algorithm for the corresponding VRP. Finally, Donati et al. (2006) present the multi ant colony system to simultaneously optimize the number of tours and the total travel time of the time dependent VRP in urban context.

4   Problem Description

We consider a vehicle routing problem with time windows and online travel time information. The problem is defined on a complete graph $G = (V, A)$, where $V = 0, 1, \ldots, n$ is the vertex set and $A = \{(i, j) : i, j \in V, i \neq j\}$ the arc set. Vertex 0 represents a depot whilst other vertexes represent geographically dispersed customers that have to be served. A positive deterministic demand is associated with every customer. The demand of a single customer cannot be split and should be serviced by one vehicle only. Each customer defines its desired period of time when he wishes to be served. A set of K identical vehicles with capacity Q is based at the single depot. Each vehicle may perform at most one route which starts and ends at the depot. The vehicle maximum load may not exceed the vehicle capacity Q. The objective is to design routes on G such that every customer belongs to exactly one route and the total travel time of all vehicles is minimized.

The frequently considered constant travel time function, proportional to the distance between the nodes and time independent, is not realistic. It does not represent the real-world situation, where travel times vary with time and are subject to numerous factors. In practice, the link travel time function can fluctuate because of changing traffic and weather conditions like, for example, congestion during pick hours, accidents, etc. Furthermore, the available models for the dynamic vehicle routing usually imply that a vehicle en route must first reach its current destination and only after that it may be diverted from its route. Exactly on the way to its destination, however, the vehicle may encounter an unpredicted congestion or other traffic impediment. So, the vehicle has to wait unreasonably long, instead of deviating from its route and serving other customers in the meantime. Besides that, it may be difficult to satisfy the time window restrictions of the subsequent clients.

Thanks to mobile technology we can overcome the mentioned shortcomings and model vehicle routing in more realistic settings. The state-of-the-art mobile information and communication technologies can substantially facilitate the dynamic vehicle routing. First, they allow locating vehicles in real time. This gives the decision center the overview over the routes execution. Second, they enable the online communication between the drivers and the dispatching center. Thus, new instructions can be sent to drivers at any time, regardless of their location and status. And finally, mobile technologies are capable to capture the varying traffic conditions in real time and in the short run predict with high accuracy the travel time between a pair of nodes. All these enable modelling approaches that even better approximate the real-world conditions.

To construct the vehicle routes for the first time or adjust them after vehicles have already left the depot, we formulate a series of static vehicle routing problems. Each problem characterizes a particular static VRP with heterogeneous fleet at a specific point of time. We use the concept of time rolling horizon and run a re-optimization procedure to find new vehicle routes every time when the travel time between a pair of nodes is updated. For the vehicles that at time of routes adjustment are in transit to their destinations we create artificial intermediate nodes. The re-optimization algorithm is then performed on the graph that includes also the artificial intermediate nodes. Of course, no demands are associated with these nodes and the vehicles must immediately leave them.

5   Solution Algorithm

The time-dependent vehicle routing problem is a generalization of the classical travelling salesman problem (TSP) and thus belongs to the class of NP-complete problems (Lenstra and Rinnooy Kan 1981). Exact solution algorithms can solve to optimality only small instances of the problem, working unreasonably long for larger problems. Hence, to solve the described problem we implemented a genetic algorithm metaheuristics. Genetic algorithm is a global search heuristic that mimics the biological evolution to solve the problem at hand. It simulates two natural mechanisms – selection of the most vital individuals and their reproduction – to scan the solution space and produce results (Dréo et al. 2006). Genetic algorithms were successfully deployed to VRPs and have proved to produce good quality solutions (e.g. Alvarenga et al. 2007; Hanshar and Ombuki 2007; Marinakis et al. 2006; Ombuki et al. 2006, etc.).

Chromosome representation. To apply a genetic algorithm to any specific problem, first a chromosome representation should be chosen. In our approach, the information about the whole population is contained in one three-dimensional matrix. The first dimension of the matrix indexes various individuals of the population. The rows of the matrix (second dimension) correspond to different routes, whilst the columns (third dimension) to the clients visited on each route. The number of routes for each individual, the number of clients per route, and the fitness values are stored in separate arrays. Such matrix representation is very convenient, as it allows quick and efficient sorting of the solutions within the population. This is possible, since the definition of the matrix through pointers does not require the overwriting of the elements; only redirection of the pointers should be made instead of this.

Initial population. Unlike many heuristics, a genetic algorithm works with groups of solutions, instead of considering one solution at the time. Therefore, an initial population of feasible solutions has to be generated at the beginning of the algorithm performance. In the simplest case, it can be created by random permutations of customer nodes. However, it may take longer before the genetic algorithm finds a solution of a good quality if starting from such random initial population. In the paper we develop a fast and effective method to initially assign all customers to routes. At first we sort the customers by the starting time of the service window. The customer with the earliest starting time is taken as the first customer in the first route. Further customers are chosen randomly one after the other and appended to the route until the time schedule and capacity constrains are satisfied. If after 100 attempts no valid customer for the given route can be chosen, we initiate a new route. From the rest of the customers we again select the one with the earliest time window starting time and set this client as the first for the next route. The procedure is repeated until no unserved customers are left and enough individuals for the initial population are created.

Selection criteria. From every generation of individuals, one has to select a set of parents for further reproduction. As is usual for the applications of genetic algorithms to vehicle routing problems, we implement the stochastic tournament selection operator (Dréo et al. 2006, p. 88). The core of the operator is a tournament set which consists of k individuals randomly chosen from the population. In the deterministic tournament selection the fittest element from the tournament set is selected for the reproduction. In the stochastic variation of the operator, a random number $r \in [0, 1]$ is generated. If r is less than some number p, called selection pressure, then the fittest individual from the tournament set is selected for the reproduction. Otherwise, a random individual from the rest of the tournament set is selected. The selection pressure must be between 0.5 and 1 and shows the bias of the selection operator towards the fitter solution. It allows some less fit solutions to survive from generation to generation (Hanshar and Ombuki 2007). The individuals that were chosen for the tournament set are replaced in the population, as this increases the variance of the process and favours the genetic drift.

Crossover operator. We adopt the special crossover operator developed by Ombuki et al. (2006) that is particularly suitable for VRP with hard time windows. The authors carried experiments with two standard crossover operators, namely uniform order crossover and partially mapped crossover, and found the produced results unsatisfactory. Therefore, they introduced a new operator, called best cost route crossover (BCRC). The operator produces two offspring from two parents p_1 and p_2 by executing the following procedure. In the first step, a random route is selected from each parent (route r_1 is selected from parent p_1 and r_2 from p_2). Then the customers that belong to the route r_2 are removed from the parent p_1. Analogously, the customers belonging to the route r_1 are removed from parent p_2. To yield the feasible children, the removed customers should be selected randomly and re-inserted back into the corresponding solution at the least cost. For that purpose the algorithm scans all possible locations for insertion and chooses the feasible ones. The removed customer is then inserted into the place that induces the minimum additional costs. If no feasible insertion place can be found, a new route containing the removed customer alone is created and added to the offspring. Thus, from two parent solutions the BCRC operator produces two feasible offspring.

Mutation operator. Finally, a mutation operator is applied to the population to ensure that the algorithm does not converge prematurely to a local optimum. As mutation introduces a random alteration to diversify the search, it can be a relatively destructive element, deteriorating the fitness of the solution. Therefore, the mutation operator is applied to only small fraction of the offspring, determined by the mutation rate. We applied a widely-used swap mutation algorithm, exchanging two customers with similar time windows. The two windows are considered to be similar if the difference between the starting times of the corresponding windows is the smallest (Alvarenga et al. 2007). The swap operator proceeds as follows: A random customer is selected from a random tour. Then a customer with the similar time window is searched for and the two customers are exchanged. If the obtained solution is infeasible, the procedure is repeated.

Construction of a new population. In the new generation the offspring created by the sequential application of the selection, crossover, and mutation operators, completely replace the parents. Only the small number of the worst offspring are left aside and instead of them the best individuals from the old generation, called *elite*, are included into the new generation. Such strategy is called elitism (Mitchell 1996, p. 168). It ensures that the best solutions can propagate through generations without the effect of the crossover or mutation operators. Therefore, the fitness value of the best solution is monotonically nondecreasing from one generation to another (Dréo et al. 2006, p. 91). In the new generation, however, the elite individuals have to compete with the fittest offspring, forcing the algorithm to converge towards an optimum.

6   Computational Results

6.1   Benchmarks Description

To test the developed solution algorithm we used the well known Solomon's benchmark problems (Solomon 1987). The set consists of 56 instances of 100-customer problems divided into six groups depending on the geographic distribution of customers and scheduling horizon. Classes R1 and R2 contain customers with randomly generated geographic data, classes C1 and C2 contain geographically clustered customers and classes RC1 and RC2 are mixed containing both random and clustered spatial data. The index "1" indicates that the sets R1, C1 and RC1 have the short scheduling horizon, permitting only a few customers per route. The sets with index "2" have the long scheduling horizon and allow many customers to be assigned to the same vehicle. Inside a group, the geographic and demand data for customers remains the same, while the fraction of the time-constrained customers together with the tightness and positioning of the time windows differ. The distance between a pair of customers is the Euclidean distance and the travel time equals the distance. Hence, the vehicle speed is taken to equal one. The problem data are available from the Solomon's site[1].

6.2   Constant Travel Time Tests

The proposed genetic algorithm was tested in two stages: Stage one with constant travel times and stage two with variable travel times. Even though the considered problem is dynamic and time-dependent, the algorithm was initially tested on the constant travel time data to prove its efficiency. For this purpose we take the Solomon's benchmark problems with the long scheduling horizon, namely the sets R2, C2 and RC2. The test problems with the narrow horizon were discarded as during one trip a vehicle can serve only few customers. So, they are improper for the dynamic problem at hand. The algorithm was coded in C and run on a 3 GHz Intel Pentium IV machine with 1 GB memory running SuSE Linux 10.2.

    The results for the R2 and RC2 problems are presented in Table 1. They are computed for two values of tournament selection parameter $k = 3$ and $k = 4$. We considered hundred generations and take the population size that equals 300. Furthermore, the selection pressure $p = 0.8$. The column "Average TT" indicates the average travel time found over ten runs for each problem instance, whilst the column "Best TT" contains the best found solution. The two columns "Best known" state the total distance and the number of vehicles for the best known published solutions identified by heuristic methods[2]. Even though these numbers indicate the shortest travelled distance and we are minimizing the total travel time, this fact does not influence the results, as at the moment we consider the constant travel time problems and set the vehicle speed equal to one.

---

[1] http://w.cba.neu.edu/~msolomon/problems.htm, accessed 20.02.07.

[2] The prevailing majority of best known solutions identified by heuristics are taken from the article by Alvarenga et al. (2007). The results for the problems R206, R210 and RC204 are taken from the site http://w.cba.neu.edu/~msolomon/problems.htm (accessed 21.02.07.).

Table 1. Test results for the constant travel times

| Problem | k | Genetic algorithm | | | Best known | | Quality |
		Average TT	Best TT	NV	TD	NV	in %
R201	3	1200.82	1189.28	8	1165.3	8	2.06
	4	1202.28	1189.59	8	1165.3	8	2.08
R202	3	1083.56	1073.69	7	1053.9	6	1.88
	4	1081.38	1074.05	7	1053.9	6	1.91
R203	3	910.71	**897.47**	6	910.1	5	-1.39
	4	907.46	897.76	5	910.1	5	-1.36
R204	3	751.39	**739.23**	4	770.8	4	-4.10
	4	749.04	740.94	4	770.8	4	-3.87
R205	3	984.59	977.57	5	972.5	5	0.52
	4	984.95	975.01	5	972.5	5	0.26
R206	3	907.33	899.91	4	906.1	3	-0.68
	4	907.44	**897.83**	5	906.1	3	-0.91
R207	3	822.24	807.77	4	860.1	4	-6.08
	4	820.64	**804.35**	4	860.1	4	-6.48
R208	3	720.98	**709.40**	4	744.1	4	-4.66
	4	720.95	711.66	3	744.1	4	-4.36
R209	3	883.59	**867.26**	5	888.5	5	-2.39
	4	880.38	867.41	5	888.5	5	-2.37
R210	3	934.95	923.27	6	939.3	3	-1.71
	4	933.94	**921.43**	6	939.3	3	-1.90
R211	3	777.45	**763.37**	4	815.5	5	-6.39
	4	775.45	763.38	4	815.5	5	-6.39
RC201	3	1307.62	1285.32	8	1274.3	8	0.87
	4	1309.75	1278.69	8	1274.3	8	0.34
RC202	3	1128.27	1113.73	7	1119.5	7	-0.52
	4	1130.18	**1113.05**	7	1119.5	7	-0.58
RC203	3	977.00	970.70	6	958.0	5	1.33
	4	976.22	967.82	5	958.0	5	1.02
RC204	3	807.81	**796.58**	4	798.4	3	-0.23
	4	808.13	800.42	4	798.4	3	0.25
RC205	3	1178.04	1161.55	7	1154.0	7	0.65
	4	1170.81	1161.55	7	1154.0	7	0.65
RC206	3	1082.56	1066.79	6	1080.4	6	-1.26
	4	1083.47	**1062.75**	6	1080.4	6	-1.63
RC207	3	1000.79	**974.50**	5	1005.6	7	-3.09
	4	1001.11	986.50	5	1005.6	7	-1.90
RC208	3	805.71	**790.86**	5	820.5	5	-3.61
	4	802.25	794.23	5	820.5	5	-3.20

Legend: TT – travel time, NV – number of vehicles, TD – total distance

The efficiency of the developed genetic algorithm is presented in the column "Quality." The quality of our solution is defined as the relative deviation from the corresponding best known solution. The negative value means that our solution is better than the corresponding best known, while the positive value indicates that our solution is worse. As can be seen from the table, the received results are comparable with the best known so far. In fact, for eight instances of R2 problems and five instances of RC2 problems we were able to outperform the best known solutions. These solutions are emphasized in bold. Concerning the C2 problem set, the produced results are quite unsatisfactory, while the developed algorithm converges prematurely to a local optimum. Presumably, it is not suitable for the clustered problems, especially with tight time windows, or some other sets of genetic algorithm parameters have to be chosen.

To summarize, the received results for the constant travel time Solomon's benchmark problems with long scheduling horizon are very good for the random and semi-clustered problems. The quality of the obtained solutions is between -6.48% and 2.08% for the problems from R2 group and between -3.61% and 1.33% for the RC2 set with the average quality -2.11% and -0.68% respectively. Consequently, the developed genetic algorithm has proved to be efficient and can be further used to test the dynamic case with real-time travel times.

6.3   Test Results for the Real-Time Travel Times

The second stage of the computational experiments simulates the vehicle routing in more realistic settings. Here we assume that the travel time between a pair of nodes undergoes two types of disturbances. On the one hand, a link travel time depends on the time of day when a vehicle drives along this link. Thus we consider now time dependent travel times due to periodic traffic congestions. This time dependency is based on the historic data and hence is known a priori. On the other hand, we also incorporate into our investigations unpredicted random short-term fluctuations of the travel times that occur due to unexpected dynamic events like accidents. So, the main difference between the constant travel time experiments and dynamic, time dependent tests is that in the last case the dispatching centre has the real-time overview over the traffic conditions and considers the online link travel times. Based on these data it updates the optimal solution and periodically adjusts the vehicle routes in order to avoid hampered roads and be able to serve all customers at the least costs.

In practice, the actual travel times are provided by an advanced traveller information system. For our experiment, however, we have to simulate them. Similar to other authors (e.g. Chen et al. 2006; Donati et al. 2006) we divide the planning period into four intervals and define travel times as a step function. To introduce the time-dependency of travel times, we multiply the original values by the coefficients 1.1, 0.9, 1.2, and 0.8. The short-term fluctuations of travel times caused by accidents or other traffic impediments are modelled through random perturbations. They are set equal to the absolute value of a normal random variable with mean $\mu = 0$ and variation $\sigma = 9$ (cf. Potvin et al. 2006).

Table 2. Test results for the real-time travel times

Problem	Average with re-optim.	Average without re-optim.	Rejected in %	Problem	Average with re-optim.	Average without re-optim.	Rejected in %
R201	1211.06	1218.51	15	RC201	1319.02	1320.84	0
R202	1084.57	1111.92	20	RC202	1148.95	1168.27	5
R203	910.07	929.85	0	RC203	987.44	995.53	20
R204	759.15	757.26	5	RC204	817.23	829.63	10
R205	1003.64	1022.87	10	RC205	1197.12	1179.83	0
R206	910.32	915.43	15	RC206	1098.97	1130.09	15
R207	831.21	836.95	15	RC207	1021.00	1021.01	10
R208	731.18	732.54	20	RC208	825.43	834.00	5
R209	890.04	896.07	10				
R210	948.58	956.41	5				
R211	794.88	811.11	10				

The test results for the real-time case are presented in Table 2. The column "Average with re-optim." contains the average travel time value calculated over twenty runs when the routes re-optimization was undertaken after every perturbation of the travel time matrix. On the contrary, the column "Average without re-optim." states the results for the case when travel times are periodically updated but the routes are not correspondingly adjusted. Consequently, the vehicles have to follow the initial routes constructed at the beginning of the planning period. The value difference between the two columns shows that even for small perturbations of the travel times the periodic routes adjustment leads to better results. Finally, the column "Rejected" indicates the fraction of problem instances containing customers that could not be served in the case without the re-optimization. This is due to the fact that the traversed routes are definitely less-than-optimal while being determined for obsolete travel times. Hence, the vehicles arrive to the customers after the ending time of the time windows and are not able to serve them. Consequently, when solutions for the constant travel time case are deployed in the real-time settings, their optimality and even feasibility are subject to substantial changes. From these experiments we can see that if solutions computed for the constant travel times are deployed in the real-time settings, their optimality and even feasibility are subject to substantial changes. Therefore, to be able to serve all customers and decrease costs one has to make use of the modern technologies and real-time data and promptly react to the ever-changing settings of the real world.

7   Conclusions

The paper deals with a vehicle routing problem with online travel times. In particularly, we consider the case when there is a mobile connection between the drivers and the dispatching centre that allows communicating them new instructions to action in real time. Furthermore, we assume that the central office makes use of the advanced technologies to gain an overview over the variable traffic conditions and locations of vehicles on road. This fact allows us to consider the time-dependent travel times which are updated on a permanent basis. Thus we explicitly incorporate into our considerations the possibility to react to traffic impediments and divert a vehicle en route from its current destination. To solve the developed problem we implement a genetic algorithm. We perform an extensive computational study in order to prove the efficiency of the proposed algorithm on the well-known static benchmarks as well as test its performance in the dynamic settings. The achieved results are competitive with the best published solutions and prove the efficiency of the proposed solution method.

Acknowledgment

The authors would like to thank the Federal Ministry of Education and Research of Germany (BMBF) for supporting this research (reference no. 01AK060A).

References

1. Alvarenga, G.B., Mateus, G.R., de Tomi, G.: A genetic and set partitioning two-phase approach for the vehicle routing problem with time windows. Computers & Operations Research **34** (2007) 1561–1584
2. Buellingen, F., Woerter, M.: Development perspectives, firm strategies and applications in mobile commerce. Journal of Business Research **57** (2004) 1402–1408
3. Cetin, M., List, G.F.: Integrated modeling of information and physical flows in transportation systems. Transportation Research Part C **14** (2006) 139–156
4. Chen, H-K., Hsueh, C-F., Chang, M-S.: The real-time time-dependent vehicle routing problem. Transportation Research Part E **42** (2006) 383–408
5. Chen, L., Nath, R.: A framework for mobile business applications. International Journal of Mobile Communications **2** (2004) 368–381
6. Dantzig, G.B., Ramser, J.H.: The truck dispatching problem. Management Science **6** (1959) 80–91
7. Donati, A.V., Montemanni, R., Casagrande, N., Rizzoli, A.E., Gambardella, L.M.: Time dependent vehicle routing problem with a multi ant colony system. European Journal of Operational Research (2006) in press.
8. Dréo, J., Pétrovski, A., Siarry, P., Taillard, E.: Metaheuristics for Hard Optimization. Springer (2006)
9. Giannopoulos, G.A.: The application of information and communication technologies in transport. European Journal of Operational Research **152** (2004) 302–320
10. Golden, B.L., Wasil, E.A., Kelly, J.P., Chao, I-M.: Metaheuristics in vehicle routing, in: Crainic, T.G., Laporte, G. (eds.) Fleet Management and Logistics. Kluwer (1998) 33–56
11. Haghani, A., Jung, S.: A dynamic vehicle routing problem with time-dependent travel times. Computers & Operations Research **32** (2005) 2959–2986
12. Hanshar, F.T., Ombuki, B.M.: Dynamic vehicle routing using genetic algorithms. Applied Intelligence (2007) in press

13. Heng, S.: Mobile telephony – cooperation and value-added are key to further success, in: Deutsche Bank Research. E-conomics **42** (2004)
14. Ichoua, S., Gendreau, M., Potvin, J-Y.: Vehicle dispatching with time-dependent travel times. European Journal of Operational Research **144** (2003) 379–396
15. Jahn, O., Möhring, R.H., Schulz, A.S., Stier-Moses, N.E.: System-optimal routing of traffic flows with user constrains in network with congestion. Operations Research **53** (2005) 600–616
16. Jung, S., Haghani, A.: Genetic algorithm for the time-dependent vehicle routing problem. Transportation Research Record **1771** (2001) 164–171
17. Küpper, A.: Location-based Services: Fundamentals and Operation. Wiley (2005)
18. Laporte, G.: The vehicle routing problem: An overview of exact and approximate algorithms. European Journal of Operational Research **59** (1992) 345–358
19. Laporte, G., Gendreau, M., Potvin, J-Y., Semet, F.: Classical and modern heuristics for the vehicle routing problem. International Transactions in Operational Research **7** (2000) 285–300
20. Lenstra, J.K., Rinnooy Kan, A.H.G.: Complexity of vehicle routing and scheduling problems. Networks **11** (1981) 221–227
21. Link, J.: Die Klärung der Wirtschaftlichkeit von M-Commerce-Projekten, in: Link, J. (Hrsg.) Mobile Commerce: Gewinnpotenziale einer stillen Revolution. Springer (2003) 41–64
22. Malandraki, C.: Time dependent vehicle routing problems: Formulations, solution algorithms and computational experiments. Ph.D. Thesis, Northwestern University, Evanson (1989)
23. Malandraki, C., Daskin, M.S.: Time dependent vehicle routing problems: Formulations, properties and heuristic algorithms. Transportation Science **26** (1992) 185–200
24. Malandraki, C., Dial, R.B.: A restricted dynamic programming heuristic algorithm for the time dependent traveling salesman problem. European Journal of Operational Research **90** (1996) 45–55
25. Marinakis, Y., Migdalas, A., Pardalos, P.M.: A new bilevel formulation for the vehicle routing problem and a solution method using a genetic algorithm. Journal of Global Optimization (2006) in press.
26. Mitchell, M.: An Introduction to Genetic Algorithms. MIT Press (1996)
27. Ombuki, B., Ross, B.J., Hanshar, F.: Multi-objective genetic algorithms for vehicle routing problem with time windows. Applied Intelligence **24** (2006) 17–30
28. Potthof, I.: Kosten und Nutzen der Informationsverarbeitung: Analyse und Beurteilung von Investitionsentscheidungen. Deutscher Universitätsverlag (1998)
29. Potvin, J-Y., Xu, Y., Benyahia, I.: Vehicle routing and scheduling with dynamic travel times. Computers & Operations Research **33** (2006) 1129–1137
30. Siau, K., Shen, Z.: Mobile communications and mobile services. International Journal of Mobile Communications **1** (2003) 3–14
31. Solomon, M.M.: Algorithms for the vehicle routing and scheduling problems with time window constrains. Operations Research **35** (1987) 254–265
32. Toth, P., Vigo, D.: Exact solution of the vehicle routing problem, in: Crainic, T.G., Laporte, G. (eds.) Fleet Management and Logistics. Kluwer (1998) 1–32
33. Zhang, J.J., Yuan, Y., Archer, N.: Driving forces for m-commerce success, in: Shaw, M.J. (ed.) E-Business Management: Integration of Web Technologies with Business Models. Kluwer (2003) 51–76

Techniques and Applications for Mobile Commerce
C. Branki et al. (Eds.)
IOS Press, 2008

Synthetic Textures for 3D Urban Models in Pededstrian Navigation

Volker Coors

Stuttgart University of Applied Sciences, Schellingstr. 24, 70174 Stuttgart
Germany, volker.coors@hft-stuttgart.de

Abstract.

Since years the market of mobile navigation systems is growing enormously. Within this paper the goals and first results of the joint project "Mobile Navigation with 3D City Models" (MoNa3D; http://www.mona3d.de) are introduced. The project consortium consists of the University of Applied Science Stuttgart (coordinator), the University of Applied Science Mainz, the University of Bonn and the four companies Navigon, Teleatlas, GTA Geoinformatik, and Heidelberg Mobil. The aim of the project is to develop and evaluate the support of landmarks and 3D visualization in mobile navigation systems for pedestrian navigation as well as the "last mile" car navigation for instance from a parking place to the final destination. The two main goals of the project are to provide a cognitive semantic route description by using landmarks and secondly to make use of synthetic building facade textures along with a corresponding compression system for an efficient storage, transfer, and rendereing of 3D urban models. This paper focuses on the synthetic texturing and compression.

Keywords. mobile navigation, synthetic textures, 3D urban models

Introduction

There is a wide variaty of techniques to present directions and support on mobile devices ranging from spoken instructions to 3D visualization. In order to produce a coherent and cohesive presentation it is necessary to adapt a presentation to the availale technical and cognitive resources of the presentation environment. Coors et al. (2005) evaluated several means of route instructions to a mobile user. 3D visualization seems to be well suited where time and technical resources are not an issue, and where the available position information is imprecise: a 3D model of the area allows the user to search her environment visually for specific features, and then to align herself accordingly, thereby compensating for the imprecsion. 3D urban models as integrated part of a navigation system will support pedestrian navigation as well as the "last mile" car navigation from a parking place to the final destination. Especially using public transport and finding the best exit at a larger tube station for instance is a typical three-dimensional problem that is hard to solve with traditional 2D navigation support. The two main companies for navigation data, TeleAtlas and Navteq currently offer 3D landmarks of almost all big european cities. For some cities even large 3D urban models are available (Vande Velde 2005). In Germany, more and more municipalities themself build up 3D urban models. However, only a few research prototypes acually support mobile navigation with real 3D urban models on mobile devices such as smart phones (Coors & Schilling 2003, Nurminen 2006).

The aim of the project "Mobile Navigation with 3D City Models" (MoNa3D) is to develop and evaluate such a mobile navigation system. The two main goals of the project are:

- To provide a cognitive semantic route description by using landmarks in 3D, which allow context dependent personalized navigation support

- To develop an approach to create suitable building textures using image processing methods and synthetic textures along with a corresponding compression system for an efficient storage, transfer, and rendereing of 3D urban models.

The focus of this paper is on the second goal of the Mona3D Project: synthetic texturing and compression of 3D urban models.

Synthetic Textures

In photogrammetry, a 3D building model is usually created by geomerty and textures. Digital pictures of actual buildings are modified and mapped onto the building geometry. With this method very high detailed and visually photo-realistic building models can be created. However, it is a huge amount of work to create high quality models. In addition, the resulting textures are memory intensive and could not be used on mobile devides due to its memory limitations.

The aim of synthetic textures in this field is to build inexpensive and small building textures but still represent the building as close to reality as needed for navigation purposes. The goal of texture synthesis is to generate new textures that look similar to a given sample texture. Texture synthesis can be roughly subdivided in two main categories: procedural texture synthesis (Ebert et al. 1998), and texture synthesis by example (Sabha, M.et all 2007).

Procedural texture synthesis is basically an algorithm that generates the needed facade texture. Certain pattern like stone and brick walls can be analyzed and synthesized. Parish and Müller (2001) extended this approach by so-called layered grids, a semi-automatic technique based on layering and functional compostion to create procedural models of entire building facades.

Texture synthesis by example generates a novel texture that is similar to the given sample. Texture synthesis by analysis usually characterizes a sample texture by a statistic. The new texture is synthesised such that the texture statistics are maintained. Pixel- and Patch-based texture synthesis create new textures by selecting and coopying a single pixel (or a whole patch) from te sample texture, based on already synthesised pixels in the novel texture. While texture synthesis by example is usually used to generate texture for specific materials such as bricks and marble, and natural phenomena such as clouds, Sabha et al. (2007) have demonstrated an approach to generate entire building facades by using exact neighborhood matching.

Tele Atlas together with GTA Geoinformatik produce textured 3D urban models for navigation pursposes based on a texture library approach (Vande Velde 2005). Each building facade is split into components such as window and door types per storey. The used facade textures are taken from a genereic library. Prominent buildings that are used as landmarks are modeled in detail by classical photogrammetry methods.

In the Mona3D project a procedural texture synthesis approach combined with patch-based texture synthesis is used. A fassade texture is generated based on libraries of typical window, door and material images. Under the assumption that the building geometry is given as a boundary representation based on polygons, each wall of a building is represented by a least one polygon. For each of these polygons one pulse function for each dimension controls the process of texture creation. For a rectangular polygon these pulse functions px and py are fairly easy to define:

A pulse function p: [0,1] -> {0,1} is used to place features as windows and doors on a given background texture. If the product of the two pulse functions px and py is 1 the given feature image is inserted, otherwise the background image is used for texturing. To be more flexible, layers of feature textures can be used, for example one layer for windows and a second layer for doors. Each layer should make use of different pulse functions. An example is give in figure 1.

Figure 1. pulse function to generate a window pattern on a facade

The pulse functions can be mapped to any geometry using the local surface coordinate system of this geometry. On GPUs the pulse functions can easily implemented directly in the Pixel shader. The only input for generating the textures are the above mentioned puls functions and a texture library of typical facade element and background. No individual image texture will be used which saves an enourmos amout of image data.

To simplify the definition of the pulse functions a user interface has been developed. For each layer of the synthetic texture, several parameters can be specified to generate the resulting facade texture. For exaple, the position of window rows and columns and the grouping of windows can be defined. A similar model is given to define the door(s). Currently, a set of input parameters to specify the pulse functions is evaluated.

Figure 2. from left to right: User Interface to specify the pulse function for window layer, the facade generated by this pulse function with an additional layer to position a door; similar with another position of the door; variation of the window layer pulse function.

Compressed 3D urban models

The introduction and application of 3D models in distributed environemnts and mobile clients has driven the development of efficient 3D compression schemes. While general purpose compression tools such as Win-zip or Gzip achieve average compression results on 3D data, specialized algorithms that are not based on textual representation but take into account the 3D model structure of the content propose a deflation of up to 95% (Eppinger and Coors, 2005).

The de facto standard for 3D urban model data interchange, CityGML, makes use of polygonal boundary representation of terrain data as well as building data. This is also the case for visualization formats such as VRML and the *.m3g format for mobile 3D graphics (JSR 184). Each polygonal boundary representation can always be tranformed into a triangle mesh without any loss of information. A triangle mesh is usually represented by its geometry information, the vertex location of the mesh, and by its connectivity information, which describes the incidence relation between each triangle of the mesh's surface and its boundary vertices. Usually, additional attributes such as color and texture information may be part of the description. However, in the proposed approach of synthetic textures, only a few parameters are stored per polygon or triangle patch. Based on these attributes, synthetic textures are generated during rendering on the mobile device.

Geometry information of the model may in many cases be reduced by lossy compression. Basically, such techniques reduce the precision of the vertices to a level that is sufficient for the corresponding application using a combination of:

- Quantization to map the set of (floating point) coordinates to a less accurate set of values, thereby eliminating (unnecessary) precision overhead. The resulting coordinate may be represented as integer values after quantization.
- Prediction to encode small correction vectors (residues) instead of the absolute vertex coordinates
- Entropy coding such as Huffmann or Arithmetic coding to minimize the storage of the residues with variable length bit codes.

Depending on the acceptable loss of precision, which can be adjusted through quanization, this method may deflate geometry information down to approximately $1/7^{th}$ of its original size (Goodman and O'Rourke, 2004).

While geometry information may be subject to some loss without forfeiting crucial information of the model, connectivity information has to be strictly conserved. Several techniques have been proposed for the lossless compression of the connectivity of triangle meshes (Rossignac 1999, Alliez & Desbrun 2001, Coors & Rossignac 2004).

EdgeBreaker (Rossignac 1999) is known to be one of the simplest and most effective single rate compression algorithms. It traverses the mesh surface in a spiral triangle spanning tree order and generates the so called CLERS string, in which each symbol corresponds to a triangle of the mesh. The CLERS string contains all the information required by the decompression algorithm to restore the connectivity of the mesh by attaching new triangles to previously reconstructed ones. The original method guarantees 4 bit per vertex (denoted b/v for simplicity). This guaranteed upper bound was later improved to 3.60 b/v (Gumhold, 2000).

Instead of encoding the CLERS string directly, Delphi compression (Coors & Rossignac, 2004) tries to predict each CLERS symbol based on the geometry and connectivity of previously visited triangles. Just like Edgebreaker, Delphi compression traverses the mesh starting by a given seed triangle. At each step to the next triangle during this traversal, the compression algorithm encodes the identification of the tip vertex v_{tip} of the new triangle. This is accomplished by guessing an estimate location $g(v_{tip})$ using a prediction scheme, for instance parallelogram prediction. If the predicted vertex is sufficiently close to an already compressed vertex v_x of the mesh than v_x is predicted to be v_{tip}. Depending on the location of vertex v_x the next triangle is predicted as L, E, R, or S. Otherwise v_{tip} is predicted as new vertex and the corrsponding triangle as C. If the guess is correct, a single confirmation bit is written to the so called Apollo sequence, which may be seen as the predicted CLERS string. If the prediction is incorrect, additional information are added to the Apollo sequence to rectify the predicted symbol. Experiments with standard computer graphic benchmark models have shown that Delphi compresses the connectivity of a triangle mesh down to 0.4 bits per vertex, depending on the number of correct predictions, of course.

The compression scheme was tested on portions of a 3D city model of Stuttgart (LoD 2, no textures). Two different parts of the model have been chosen to represent the experiments: A small model of Stuttgart downtown with 111 buildings (11474 triangles) as shown in Figure 3 and a larger residential area with 6771 buildings (280306 triangles). Table 1 shows the mesh compression results.

Figure 3. 3D-Model of the city of Stuttgart, © Stadtmessungsamt Stuttgart.

	Stuttgart downtown	Stuttgart Residential area
Buildings	111	6771
Triangles	11474	280306
VRML file size	435 kB	13694 kB
VRML compressed (Gzip)	88 kB (20%)	1860 kB (13%)
Mesh Compression file size	31 kB (7%)	1108 kB (8%)
Compression runtime	309 ms	8078 ms
Decompression runtime	247 ms	6588 ms

Table 1: Mesh compression results. Runtime was measured on an IBM Thinkpad T41p 1700 MHz 1 GB RAM within an Eclipse development environment.

Conclusion

In this paper, two main technical challanges towards a pedestrian navigation system using 3D urban models, synthetic texturing and 3D mesh compression have been discussed and solutions have been proposed. Synthetic textures enable the effective and low-cost production of 3D urban models for navigation purposes. In addition, it also solves the problem of storing a huge amount of image data by using texture library elements. Per building facade just a few pararmeters have to be stored to generate a suited texture which leads to a very compact representation of the texture. The building geometry can be stored and transmitted very effectively by using 3D mesh compression techniques such as the proposed Delphi compression scheme. Beside the compact representation of the building geometry the mesh compression has a second advantage compared to standard text-based compression such as WinZip or Gzip. Using text-based compression, the compressed file has to be decompressed into the original text file and in a second step this usually large file is parsed to build the 3D urban model. In contrast, using mesh compression, the 3D urban model is build directly from the compressed file saving runtime for parsing the uncompressed file.

Currently, the proposed compenents are integrated into a prototype navigation system based on a service based intrastructure incuding a Web3D Service that grants access to the 3D urban models and a routing service based on the OpenLS interface. The client is implemented in Java ME using the M3G API in additon for 3D rendering on smartphones.

Acknowledgements

This work has been supported by the Germany Ministry of Education and Research (BMBF) within the project MoNa3D. Special thank to all project partners and co-workers for their valuable support and input.

References

P. Alliez, and M. Desbrun (2001): "Valence-Driven Connectivity Encoding for 3D Meshes." Eurographics 2001 Conference Proceedings.

Coors, V., Elting, C., Kray, C., and Laakso, K. (2003): Presenting Route Instructions on Mobile Devices - From Textual Directions to 3D Visualization, to appear in in Kraak, M., MacEachren, A., Dyke, J.: Geovisualization, Taylor & Francis

Coors, V., and Rossignac, J. (2004): Delphi: geometry-based connectivity prediction in triangle mesh compression In The Visual Computer, International Journal of Computer Graphics, Vol. 20, Number 8-9, Springer Verlag, Berlin Heidelberg, November 2004, pp 507 – 520.

Coors, V., and Schilling, A. (2004): 3D Maps on Mobile Devices, In: *Branki, C.; Unland, R.; Wanner, G. (Hrsg.)*: Multikonferenz Wirtschaftsinformatik (MKWI) 2004, Universität Duisburg-Essen, 9.-11. März 2004, Band 3: Mobile Business Systems, Mobile and Collaborative Business, Techniques and Applications for Mobile Commerce (TAMoCO). Essen

Ebert, D., F.K. Musgrave, D. Peachey, K. Perlin, S. Worley (2003): Texturing & Modelling. A procedural Approach. 3rd Edition, Elsevier Science

Eppinger, F. and V. Coors: Compressing 3-dimensional urban models In: Proceedings 4th Workshop on Dynamic and Multi-dimensional GIS (DMGIS 05), September 2005, International Archives of Photogrammetry and Remote Sensing, Vol XXXVI, Part 2/W29

Goodman, J.E., and J. O'Rourke (2004) Handbook of Discrete and Computational Geometry, Second Edition, volume 2, CRC press

S. Gumhold (2000), "Towards optimal coding and ongoing research", 3D Geometry Compression Course Notes, SIGGRAPH 2000.

JSR184 (2005): Java Specifiaction Request 184: Mobile 3D Graphics API, Version 1.1, June 2005; and Java Specifiaction Request 297: Mobile 3D Graphics API, Version 2.0, Early Draft, August 2007

Nurminen, A. m-LOMA - a mobile 3D city map Proceedings of the eleventh international conference on 3D web technology, 2006.

Parish, Y., and P. Müller. (2001): Procedural Modeling of Cities. In Proceedings of ACM SIGGRAPH 2001, ACM Press

J. Rossignac (1999): "EdgeBreaker: Connectivity compression for triangle meshes", IEEE Transactions on Visualization and Computer Graphics, 5(1), 47-61.

Sabha, M., P.Peers and P.Dutre (2007): Texture Synthesis using Exact Neighborhood Matching, Computer Graphics forum, Vol 2, No 2, Blackwell Publishing

Vande Velde, Linde (2005): Tele Atlas 3D navigable maps, In: Gröger / Kolbe (Eds.): Proc. 1st int. Workshop on Next generation 3D City Models, Bonn 2005, EuroSDR Publication

Techniques and Applications for Mobile Commerce
C. Branki et al. (Eds.)
IOS Press, 2008

Product-Centered Mobile Reasoning Support for Physical Shopping Situations

Wolfgang Maass, Andreas Filler, and Jan Seeburger
Research Center Intelligent Media,
Furtwangen University, Robert-Gerwig-Platz 1, 78120 Furtwangen
{wolfgang.maass, andreas.filler, jan.seeburger}@hs-furtwangen.de

Abstract. Smart products are hybrids that merge tangible products with mobile information technologies. This opens up unprecedented opportunities for product designers and marketing manager for implementing adaptive and situation-aware product interfaces that generate dynamic communication behaviour with customers during the whole life-cycle of a single product. The realisation of this vision requires, beside others, expressive and machine-readable product representations and an open product information infrastructure. With *Tip 'n Tell* we present an architecture that supports smart products. Product information is representedj by a coherent container model, called *SPDO*, that uses semantically annotated descriptions in OWL-DL format. Based on these elements we demonstrate services that allow finding multimedia content that fits to a *product in focus* based on a combination of DL-reasoning and RDF-based rule derivations. Similar products to a product in focus are determined by statistical similarity measures on feature level. Finally we present a logic-based service that determines compatible products.

Keywords: smart products, semantic technologies, electronic commerce, ambient intelligence

Introduction

Low-cost wireless identification of objects provides the basis for interactive products that can communicate with users via mobile communication devices across all product usage phases. Those *smart products* will become interactive, adaptive, context-sensitive, personalised, pro-active, business-aware and relational [24]. Integration of information and communication technologies into products anywhere and anytime enable new forms of mobile marketing in respect to situated marketing communication, dynamic pricing models and dynamic product differentiation models. As Fano and Gershman state: *"Technology enables service providers to make the location of their customers the location of their business"* (Fano & Gershman 2002).

Envisioned are products that explain themselves to customers in buying situations, discuss solutions with technicians in service situations, actively communicate with business processes, and dynamically set up relationships with other products and supporting services.

Product information is part of a product communication process. Jiang et al. argue for potentials by adaptive recommendation based on analysis of product communication on the fly [12]. Furthermore, Ariely found by empirical studies that consumers who gain more control about navigating product information show a better understanding and gain higher utilities from product information [2]. This line of thought is finalised by results presented by Urban and Hauser, who show that adaptive product communication can lead to identification of new product opportunities [23].

These results emphasise that product presentations at the point of sale can be enhanced by dynamic, dialogue-based and multimodal product-centered communication on the spot of buying decision making in the sense of "talking objects" [19].

This shift from static product presentations to adaptive product communication requires a new understanding of products. Products become interfaces that take roles and can communicate with users in their current usage situations. Hence, the centre of product communication is the product itself. Product information is not scattered by heterogeneous services across web sites, brochures, hot lines and sales personnel but is integrated into a homogeneous product interface that support users across the whole product life cycle: transaction (information, signalling, contracting, execution), training, usage (refinement, customisation, integration, configuration), support, reselling, and disposal.

In this article we will focus on information services that support shopping situations at the point of sale within the fashion domain. For making a buying decision, customers search for different kinds of information about the product, product alternatives, complementary products, e.g., accessories, and increasingly for vivid multimedia contents. Rapid changes of product portfolios in shopping environments and dynamically changing marketing strategies require adaptive mechanisms that determine product information at run-time instead of pre-configured product information at design time.

First, we will describe the *Tip 'n Tell* architecture that is used for the technical realisation of smart product interfaces. Dynamic generation of product communication is based on product descriptions that are semantically annotated. The *Smart Product Description Object* (SPDO) is introduced in following section which is a container model for machine-processible product information. Thereafter we present how reasoning mechanisms support dynamic behaviour of product communication. First, it is shown how distributed multimedia contents can be matched with media requirements stated by SPDO descriptions. This allows the integration of multimedia contents on the fly according to given constraints. We use a description logic reasoning approach based on OWL-DL. Second, we present how product alternatives are found in distributed shopping environments by statistical evaluation of product features. The last reasoning service allows the determination of complementary products, e.g. accessories based on propositional descriptions located in SPDOs. Finally, we give a summary and an outlook to further research.

Smart Product Interfaces

Tip 'n Tell architecture

A shopping situation is a medium that encompasses organisational and process components. In a simplified scenario, an individual appears by taking the role of a customer. In an advanced setting a smart product is perceived by this individual as a communication partner, i.e. role-taking actor. The goal now is that the customer intends to request product information directly from this product. We will now describe a technical architecture, called Tip 'n Tell, that supports the technical realisation of the above mentioned situation (cf. **Figure 1**).

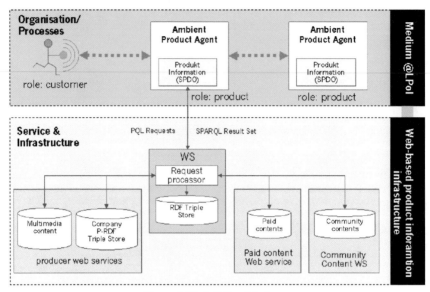

Figure 1. Tip 'n Tell architecture

Tip 'n Tell consists of an *Ambient Product Agent* that is implemented on mobile devices. A user interacts with this agent by a Natural Language interface [15]. Requests are translated into RDF-formatted requests by a SPARQL-based language.

The communication process is initialised when a customer uses a product identification device to obtain the product ID directly from a tagged product instance. In our current implementation, we use a RFID-based infrastructure. This web service (WS) collects requested information from web services that are referenced by the product ID. By this redirection logic, Tip 'n Tell can integrate any kind of product information, such provided by producers, paid content providers and Web 2.0 communities, for instance, flickr or del.icio.us. The central web service integrates RDF-based product information and sends it to the *Ambient Product Agent* which integrates this additional information into the communication process with the customer.

Semantically annotated product descriptions

Because we want to use smart products in mobile, heterogeneous and information network-aware situations we need product descriptions that can be evaluated at "run-time" but not at "design-time". Based on experience with digital products descriptions for digital goods [4], we have developed a container model for smart products, called

Semantic Product Description Object (SPDO). From the ontological viewpoint given by the foundational ontology DOLCE+ [16], a SPDO is conceptualised as a specialisation of an *information object*. The conceptual SPDO structure consists of six facets and sub-facets (cf. **Table 1**).

Table 1. Smart product description object (SPDO) model

Facets	Sub-Facets	Description
Product Description (PD)	(1) Content Classification	Connection to established meta data standards such as Dublin Core, News ML
	(2) Propositional product description	Propositional description of the functional properties of a product and rules sets for compatibility checking.
	(3) Multimedia descriptions	Propositional description of requirements for additive product information and rule sets for compatibility checking.
Presentation Description (PR)	(3) Spatio-temporal rendition	Description of how the product description is presented to users
	(4) Interaction-based rendition	
Community Description (CO)	(5) Usage tasks	Description of Plans, Tasks, Roles and Goals in the context of a community
	(6) user community	
	(7) Usage history	List of actions performed with the product during its lifecycle
Business Description (BS)	(8) Negotiation protocol	Process by which a trade will be settled
	(9) Pricing scheme	economic trading constraints
	(10) Contract	Legal constraints on the settling of a trade
Trust & Security (TS)	(11) Semantics and pragmatics of confidence in virtual goods	Authentication and certification information
Self-description (SD)	(12) The description of the SPDO's semantic structure (schema)	specification of the SPDO in machine understandable form

The main contribution of the SPDO model is that it structures different kinds of product related information categories and allows effective management of semantic product descriptions (for details cf. [14]) which is a major improvement to homogeneous approaches (e.g., [11]. The SPDO model is abstracted from implementation issues. Hence, different implementations are possible. In web-based and heterogeneous environments it improves interoperability with different product information sources if the representation format complies with web ontology representation formats. In the following, we will use an OWL-DL representation of SPDO.

To use *Tip 'n Tell* prospective buyers are equipped with a PDA (HP iPAQ Pocket PC) and a RFID-pen (Cathexis IDBlue™ RFID Pen). Products are tagged with RFID chips which carry references to product information stores. The PDA is connected to the Internet via WLAN. The whole infrastructure encompasses a *Tip 'n Tell web service* and various RDF-based product information stores. The *Tip 'n Tell web service* is realized on the basis of Jena2.0 and collects RDF-based product information from distributed product web services by *PQL requests* [14].

The communication manager provides assisted Natural Language query formulations that are translated into PQL queries [15]. Results in RDF format are passed to the *Ambient Product Agent* that generates and presents Natural Language responses.

Reasoning on products descriptions

Consumer choice theories distinguish between conscious and non-conscious decision making [5, 6]. In our work, we follow the design principle of conscious decision making which gives a more expressive means for explanation-based product reasoning. Statistical methods are used for the determination of similar and compatible products while propositional reasoning is used for searching supportive product information.

Supportive contents

Multimedia can positively influence evaluations of online products by customers [1]. Following this empirical finding, it can be assumed that multimedia contents also support buying decision making in mobile shopping situations. Because multimedia contents can be provided by an unrestricted number of services, we use a logical matching approach that compares requirements carried by a multimedia description sub-facet with descriptions of multimedia contents. Therefore, multimedia content descriptions (see below) are translated into OWL-DL representations.

```
<Video rdf:ID="Botega_Veneta_SpringSummer_2007-2008">

  (...)

  < ProductInShow>

    <Product rdf:ID="Bottega_Veneta_Dress">

      <CanBeWornBy
rdf:datatype="http://www.w3.org/2001/XMLSchema#string">
      Women</CanBeWornBy>

      <IsA>

        <Category rdf:ID="Dress"/>

      </IsA>

    </Product>

  </ ProductInShow>
```

```
<Width
rdf:datatype="http://www.w3.org/2001/XMLSchema#float">
400.0</Width>

<Height
rdf:datatype="http://www.w3.org/2001/XMLSchema#float">
400.0</Height >

(...)

</Video>
```

Sub-facet descriptions of fashion products consist of facts in OWL-Format and RDF-based rules (here Jena2 rules). Facts describe requirements, such as pixel resolution or year of a fashion show. Rules are used to combine sub-facet entities with entities used in descriptions of multimedia contents.

For instance, the following rule determines fashion multimedia contents that contain a least two distinct products. It is entailed that both products, e.g. a gown and a hand-bag, fit together. The information that both products are shown in this content it represented by predicate *IsPromotedIn* and stored in the SPDO representation of each product.

```
[fitsTogether:

(?a fcontent:ProductInShow ?b)

(?a fcontent:ProductInShow ?c)

(?b pre:IsA ?d) (?c pre:IsA ?e) notEqual(?d,?e)

->

(?b pre:FitsTo ?c) (?c pre:FitsTo ?b)

(?b mmd:IsPromotedIn ?a) (?c mmd:IsPromotedIn ?a)]
```

This rule supports transfer of information stored in multimedia content descriptions to product descriptions.

Rule systems do not check logical consistency. Therefore we integrate the SPDO model of the product in focus, results of rule evaluations and descriptions of multimedia contents in one model in OWL-DL format that is tested for consistency by a DL reasoner, (here FACT++ [21]). If the model is consistent, results of the rule evaluation on the multimedia description are stored in the multimedia description sub-facet of the product in focus.

Similarity

Statistical similarity measures are based on the assumption of additive utilities of product features. If products are only compared by binary product features, e.g., a car with or without hybrid engine, similarity is determined by *Russel&Rao (RR) coefficients* [3]. Two products are similar if their *RR coefficient* is large while smaller values indicate larger differences.

For metric product features, the *Minkowski metric* isused with $p = 2$, i.e. Euclidean metric [3]:

$$d_{rs} = \left[\sum_{j=1}^{n} \delta_j * \left| x_{rj} - x_{sj} \right|^{p} \right]^{\frac{1}{p}}$$

The values of d_{rs} represent the distance between a focused products r and alternative product s, δ_j is the weight associated with product feature j with $\delta_j > 0$ and Σ $\delta_j = 1$. If a x_{ij} value is missing for a product i then it is set to the range's mean value. Basic non-metrical dimensions are represented by metrics. For instance, colour is translated into corresponding wavelengths. The values of δ_j are assumed of being dependent of the product domain and must be empirically determined.

Two products are identical in respect to a feature set if the value is 0 while differing products have larger values depending on the metrics. Product features are considered by default but can be switched off by a customer. This is important if, for instance, price shall not be considered for similarity reasoning. With similarity values products are identified that have high resemblance with the product in focus. Customers get a ranked list of all similar products and can navigate through the distance value of each feature. Similar products are alternatives to the product in focus.

Compatibility

Descriptions of the propositional product sub-facet are used if a customer will search for products that are compatible with the product in focus. Here we use the same inference mechanism as used for supportive product information. Domain-dependent is the determination of relevant product features for compatibility testing. Within the fashion domain, we extract style related descriptions. This subset of the propositional product descriptions of the product in focus and of a retrieved product are tested for logical consistency.

For instance, within a fashion domain we assume that product 1 is an instance of category "*knee_high_leather_boot*", product 2 is an instance of cateogry "*cropped_jacket*" and product 3 is an instance of category "*miniskirt*". Furthermore assume that in the knowledge base it is defined that the style of "*knee_high_leather_boot*" fits (*GoesStyleWith*) with "*cropped_jacket*" and "*miniskirt*". With the following rule it can be inferred that also product 2 fits to product 3:

```
[ruleCompStyle:

(?a fashion:GoesStyleWith ?b)

(?a fashion:GoesStyleWith ?c)

(?d fonto:sex fonto:female)

->

(?b fashion:GoesStyleWith ?c)]
```

By applying this rule, it is concluded that product 1, 2 and 3 are compatible with one another. Sets of products that are compatible to the product in focus are presented to the customer. With this mechanism product descriptions from various product information services can be dynamically integrated, i.e. product bundles can be generated according to logical descriptions stated by rules. By changing the rules, managers gain a clear-cut control mechanism for adapting the behaviour of a product and its product differentiation model according to a defined product strategy. If a customer uses her own rule set she will be able to customise a shopping environment to her needs.

Related Work

Under the umbrella of tangible user interfaces [22] several shopping assistent systems have been recently developed. The *Mobile ShoppingAssistent* (MSA) [26] supports dialogs between users and products while focussing on multimodal communication. Earlier systems, such as *MyGrocer* (Kourouthanassis et al. 2002) and [9], venture the integration of physical objects and digital representations.

A broad field is the dynamic construction of spaces in which annotated entities and users interact. One of the first systems has been *E-Tag* [25] and *CoolTown* [13]. Recently this approach has been extended by *ELOPE* [18]. *Speakeasy* [7] investigates how patterns can support users to reduce the complexity of interactions. Furthermore, computational systems that allow annotation of physical objects increasingly become more powerful. In Smart-Its it is investigated whether this allows new methods for new product designs processes [10].

Another approach is the idea of *Invisible Media* [17] which are able to augment objects around the buyer and support him by voice-based user-system dialog. A similar approach for the interaction between users and single augmented objects has been followed in the *Reachmedia* project [8] that investigates the touch based interaction with objects based on command represented by gestures. Similarly, *Cooperative Artefacts* provide a communication and interaction framework [20]. Strohbach et al. investigated the use reasoning mechanisms for evaluating compatibilies of dangerous goods in physical situations.

These approaches use proprietary non-web-based knowledge representations and ad-hoc product ontologies. For dynamic integration of contents into heterogeneous device infrastructures has been investigated by Henrici [11]. In his approach devices and digital contents are matched on the basis of rules and formal logics (OWL-DL). The matching is realised by rule engines and inference mechanisms for description logics. Heuristic information is maintained by rules while logical information on content-device mapping is represented by formal logics. Limitations of this work are that it is only simulated on a server-based FIPA-platform. Furthermore formal representations are limited to functional attributes of contents and devices.

Conclusion and Future Work

Wireless object-identification technologies enable the development of smart product interfaces that support users through all product usage phases. With *Tip 'n Tell* we have outlined a general architecture that integrates distributed product information services and delivers semantically annotated product descriptions to the *Ambient Product Agent* in a generic format called SPDO. SPDO contains machine-processible information that supports a broad range of interaction situations, such as information search, negotiation and usage. Additional information is gathered by a RDF-based query language (PQL). In this article we have presented three services that are important during information search phases in shopping situations: (1) supportive multimedia content service, (2) similar product service and (3) complementary product service.

These three services are basic building blocks of a generic product-centered communication infrastructure. The main focus of this article is on single products. Currently we extend our approach to product bundles. Another limitation is the use of homogeneous ontologies, i.e., it is assumed that concepts and predicates are used in the same way across different product and content descriptions. In the future we will integrate ontology mapping mechanisms. On business side, smart products open up unprecedented opportunities for the implementation of dynamic product and pricing strategies that are investigated in a current BMBF project.

References

[1]   O. Appiah, *Rich Media, Poor Media: The Impact of Audio/Video vs. Text/Picture Testimonial Ads on Browsers' Evaluations of Commercial Web Sites and Online Products*, Journal of Current Issues & Research in Advertising, 28 (2006), pp. 73-86.

[2]   D. Ariely, *Controlling the information flow: Effects on consumers' decision making and preferences*, Journal of Consumer Research, 27 (2000), pp. 233-248.

[3]   K. Backhaus, B. Erichson, W. Weiber and P. R., *Multivariate Analysemethoden. Eine anwendungsorientierte Einführung*, Springer, Berlin, 2003.

[4]   W. Behrendt, A. Gangemi, W. Maass and R. Westenthaler, *Towards an Ontology-based Distributed Architecture for Paid Content*, 2005.

[5]   T. L. Chartrand, *The role of conscious awareness in consumer behavior*, Journal of Consumer Psychology, 15 (2005), pp. 203-210.

[6]   A. Dijksterhuis and P. K. Smith, *What do we do unconsciously? And how?*, Journal of Consumer Psychology, 15 (2005), pp. 225-229.

[7]   W. Edwards, M. Newman, J. Sedivy, T. Smith, D. Balfanz, D. Smetters, H. Wong and S. Izadi, *Using speakeasy for ad hoc peer-to-peer collaboration*, CSCW '02: Proceedings of the 2002 ACM conference on Computer supported cooperative work, ACM Press, New York, NY, USA, 2002, pp. 256--265.

[8]   A. Feldman, E. M. Taoa, S. Sadi, P. Maes and C. Schmandt, *Reachmedia: On-the-move interaction with everyday objects*, ISWC'05: 9th International Symposium on Wearable Computing, IEEE, 2005, pp. 52- 59.

[9]   A. Fox, B. Johanson, P. Hanrahan and T. Winograd, *Integrating information appliances into an interactive workspace*, IEEE Computer Graphics and Applications, 20 (2000), pp. 54-65.

[10]   H. Gellersen, G. Kortuem, A. Schmidt and M. Beigl, *Physical Prototyping with Smart-Its*, Pervasive Computing, 3 (2004), pp. 12-18.

[11]   S. Henrici, *Control of Adaptive Content Provisioning*, Ludwig-Maximilians-Universität Munich, Germany, 2005.

[12]   Z. Jiang, W. Wang and I. Benbazat, *Multimedia-based interactive advising technology for online consumer decision support*, Communications of the ACM, 48 (2005), pp. 93-98.

[13]   T. Kindberg, J. Barton, J. Morgan, G. Becker, D. Caswell, P. Debaty, G. Gopal, M. Frid, V. Krishnan, H. Morris, J. Schettino, B. Serra and M. Spasojevic, *People, places, things: Web presence for the real world*, WMCSA '00: Proceedings of the Third IEEE Workshop on Mobile Computing Systems and Applications (WMCSA'00), IEEE Computer Society, Washington, DC, USA, 2000, pp. 19.

[14] W. Maass and A. Filler, *Towards an Infrastructure for Semantically Annotated Physical Products*, in C. Hochberger and R. Liskowsky, eds., *Informatik 2006*, Springer, Berlin, 2006, pp. 544-549.

[15] W. Maass and S. Janzen, *Dynamic Product Interfaces: A Key Element for Ambient Shopping Environments*, 20th Bled eConference, Bled, Slovenia, 2007, pp. forthcoming.

[16] C. Masolo, S. Borgo, N. Guarino and A. Oltramari, *The WonderWeb Library of Foundational Ontologies*, WonderWeb, 2003.

[17] D. Merrill and P. Maes, *Invisible Media: Attention-sensitive informational augmentation for physical objects*, Proc. of the Seventh International Conference on Ubiquitous Computing, Tokyo, Japan, 2005.

[18] T. Pering, R. Ballagas and R. Want, *Spontaneous marriages of mobile devices and interactive spaces*, Commun. ACM, 48 (2005), pp. 53--59.

[19] B. Shneiderman and P. Maes, *Direct Manipulation vs. Interface Agents*, Interactions, 4 (1997).

[20] M. Strohbach, H. W. Gellersen, G. Kortuem and C. Kray, *Cooperative artefacts: Assessing real world situations with embedded technology*, Sixth International Conference on Ubiquitous Computing (UbiComp), 2004.

[21] D. Tsarkov and I. Horrocks, *FaCT++ description logic reasoner: System description*, Int. Joint Conf. on Automated Reasoning (IJCAR 2006), Springer, 2006, pp. 292-297.

[22] B. Ullmer and H. Ishi, *Emerging Frameworks for Tangible User Interfaces*, in J. M. Carroll, ed., *Human-Computer Interaction in the New Millenium*, Addison-Wesley, 2001, pp. 579-601.

[23] G. Urban and J. Hauser, *"Listening In" to Find and Explore New Combinations of Customer Needs*, Journal of Marketing, 68 (2004), pp. 72-87.

[24] W. Wahlster, *Towards Symmetric Multimodality: Fusion and Fission of Speech, Gesture, and Facial Expression*, in A. Günter, R. Kruse and B. Neumann, eds., *KI 2003: Advances in Artificial Intelligence. Proceedings of the 26th German Conference on Artificial Intelligence*, Berlin, Heidelberg, 2003, pp. 1 - 18.

[25] R. Want, K. P. Fishkin, A. Gujar and B. L. Harrison, *Bridging physical and virtual worlds with electronic tags*, CHI '99: Proceedings of the SIGCHI conference on Human factors in computing systems, ACM Press, New York, NY, USA, 1999, pp. 370--377.

[26] R. Wasinger and W. Wahlster, *The Anthropomorphized Product Shelf: Symmetric Multimodal Human-Environment Interaction*, in E. Aarts and J. Encarnaçao, eds., *True Visions: The Emergence of Ambient Intelligence*, Springer, Heidelberg, Berlin, New York, 2006.

Techniques and Applications for Mobile Commerce
C. Branki et al. (Eds.)
IOS Press, 2008

A service oriented loosely coupled GUI framework in the mobile context

Albrecht Stäbler

NovaTec GmbH, Dieselstrasse 18/1, 70771 Leinfelden-Echterdingen
Germany, albrecht.staebler@novatec-gmbh.de

Abstract.

This document describes the architecture of a generic GUI framework on mobile devices. In a client server system such a framework allows to display a user interface on a multitude of devices without any changes in the GUI description.

To achieve this goal an extended version of the model view controller (MVC) pattern is used in the form of a Java applet which communicates with its server via the http protocol.

The last section of this document elaborates on the special circumstances of client server applications on mobile devices.

Keywords. service oriented, GUI framework, generic client

Introduction

Business case: More and more complex business processes are required to be used on mobile platforms. The business processes are already available in backoffices of big banks, sales companies, etc.. Most of the effort of complex transactional applications is spent in building the complex GUI, because for the other tiers there are technologies like MDA, SOA, etc. available to lower the costs and reduce complexity.

Modern applications are separated in client systems using rich GUIs and the server component consisting of application servers, workflow systems, databases, etc.

A lot of effort could be minimized using a framework which allows using the already designed and accepted complex GUIs in the back offices as well on mobile platforms.

The reachable benefits are:

- Change management only for one system
- Customer satisfaction while using the same system with the usual comfort on both platforms
- Synchronous, habited behaviour of the application using distributed observer pattern
- Caching mechanisms implemented in the framework to keep the application alive and usable while having network problems

The framework described below is used in one of the biggest banks world wide to minimize the effort to bring comfortable, well known back office solutions on mobile platforms.

The effort to develop and administrate a complex, mobile application could be lowered significantly by the usage of a GUI framework providing a generic client. This generic client receives specifications of the graphical user interface out of repositories. Out of these specifications the required objects are generated using the generic mechanism. Because of this the system could be changed during runtime. Furthermore the use of a generic client offers an improved abstraction of the application.

Another effect of a generic client builds the performance enhancement during the implementation of distributed Java applications. Java applications running in web-browsers often bear the risk of low performance if a lot of classes have to be loaded via the net to visualize the requested information. E.g. a dialog including several graphical components entails the loading of all classes necessary to provide the functionality of these components.

Since the dialog-metadata is placed in a repository on the server, the network load could be lowered with the help of a generic client. This client requests the dialog-metadata from the server and generates the dialog during runtime using an interpreter. So the data transfer is reduced to a compact description of the dialog and the need to request entire classes is not given anymore.

The GUI Engine, acting as GUI technology for distributed applications, displays the graphical components on the client screen and establishes the connection to an application server. Out of the metadata send by the server the GUI Engine is able to create the application and dialogs.

Figure 1 shows an overview of such a system, while Figure2 details the communication within the GUI Engine.

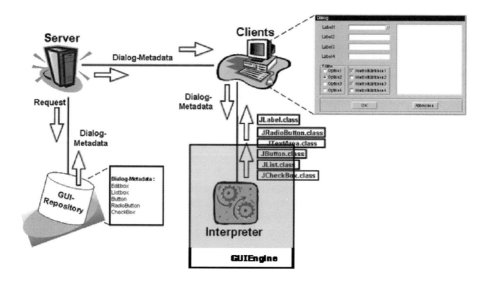

Figure 1. NovaView overview

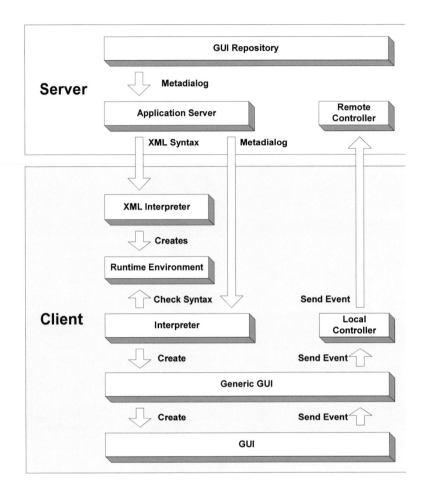

Figure 2. GUI Engine

The GUI Engine is launched by the first request of a browser to execute the servlet. At that time an applet is loaded which entails the creation of a NovaClient, an ApplicationBuilder, an ApplicationElementSpace and NovaApplication. The NovaClient starts a new application and the applet is waiting for an XML-Dialog-description. Afterwards the XML metadata is send to the parser which creates an XML-tree including all described components. This tree is interpreted by the NovaViewAssembler which leads to the generation of the corresponding generic components, LayoutConstraints, models as well as controllers with the help of specific parsers (e.g. ComponentParser, ControllerParser, ModelParser, LayoutManagerParser). The different components are connected according to the XML-metadata after the generation.

The generic GUI as construction for the user interface

We can differentiate between two layers of the GUI. The generic GUI is the connection between the controller, in the MVC design pattern, and the actual GUI, which is responsible for drawing the widgets onto the display. This decoupling allows adding and integrating additional (and unreleased) graphical libraries later without modifying the generic layer which is accessed by the controller. Every widget in the interface is mapped to exactly one corresponding generic component.

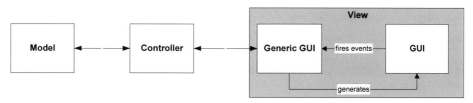

Figure 3. MVC model including Generic GUI

Creation of the graphical components is accomplished via the help of a factory. Each generic component, which is represented by a class containing the basic functionality, has a reference to an appropriate factory. This factory is called once an incoming request to create the widget is started. The second purpose of the factory is to create an Adapter object. This is necessary to map the generic information into specific one which can be used and displayed by the widgets.

The following figure illustrates the available generic component classes which are covering the basic functionality of every graphical interface.

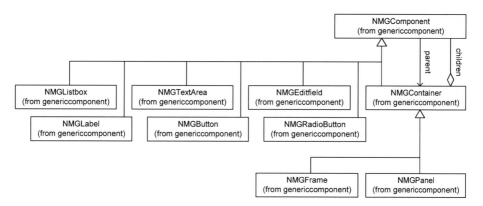

Figure 4. Overview about the generic classes

Within the scope of a bank application, classes for a frame, a button, a label, an edit field, a list box, a radio button, a text area and a panel were included.

Through the use of the generic component classes, the corresponding widget classes are created without knowing the details (with the help of the factory mentioned above). The widgets are always accessed via the generic component classes using delegation; hence they are hidden to all the other parts of the system. This access is some special form of polymorphism, called polymorphism using delegation. It differs to the "normal" form of polymorphism as it is not realized through inheritance like abstract classes.

To avoid the dependency between the widget and the generic component class, in terms of the method signature and attribute types, an adapter is put into the middle which handles the communication. The adapter has knowledge about the generic and the widget class.

The factories and adapters have to be implemented for every new graphical library which is going to be included into the whole system. This process is much easier, faster and less error-prone than implementing a new controller every time.

Figure 5 shows the adapter and factory pattern combined in a UML diagram. This model holds for every generic component and widget.

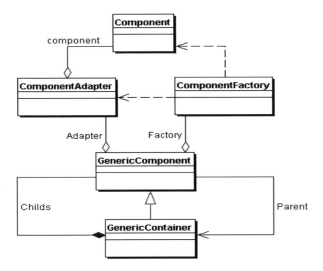

Figure 5. Application of the factory and adapter pattern

"ComponentFactory" is responsible for creating the "Component" and "ComponentAdapter" class. "ComponentAdapter" is forwarding the calls from the "GenericComponent" to the proper "Component".

Model View Controller as design pattern for the GUIEngine

Event processing gives life to dialogs. It defines the behavior of activated components; an event is thrown and forwarded to a controller or event handler.

MVC is a design pattern originated in the world of Smalltalk, its intention is to separate objects and their presentation. An architecture based on MVC consists of three elements:

- Model:
  The business logic of the application is encapsulated in the model, it responds to requests from the controller to access or modify the data it represents.
- View:
  The view renders the model into a form suitable for interaction, typically a GUI (graphical user interface). The GUI Engine generates the view on the basis of the descriptions stored in the repository. The view updates itself when the model changes.
- Controller:
  Processes and responds to events, typically user actions like usage of mouse or keyboard.

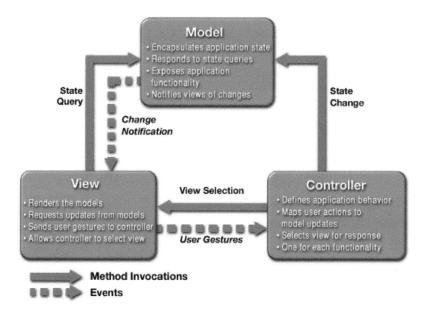

Figure 6. MVC architecture for multi-tiered enterprise J2EE applications **[SunMVC]**

Model

The Model is the representation of the attributes and the business logic of the application, for example the EditFieldModel has the attribute text and additional converters to store the data in the correct format. The model consists of this data or has to know where to find it; this means that there can exist a database or a remote connection behind this model. It is irrelevant where the data is stored, how it is stored, how administrated and of which type this data is. But there must be a defined interface so that the generic components can get access to the data. Additionally it is a big advantage that the number of generic components accessing a model is not limited. This way it is possible that the same data is used by different generic components and is displayed by many views. The problem is that all views accessing the model through the generic component, have to be notified of incoming events from the controller.

The GUI engine provides interfaces for the models in the package ‚de.novatec.genericgui.model'. These interfaces provide access to the model. Only through these interfaces generic components can gain access to the data. The concrete implementation of these interfaces has to care about where the data is stored and how it is administrated. Methods to register and deregister listeners have to be defined by the interfaces. The listeners use these methods to get informed about data changes.

Controller

The controller provides an interface for customizing. To connect the GUI Engine to a business layer it is necessary to implement specialized controllers like RMI connectors, EJB support or XML-based protocols. These controllers have to implement the interface IComponentController from the package ‚de.novatec.genericgui.genericcomponent'. Currently the GUI engine provides support for XML-based protocols.

View

The view presents the GUI to user. It works with the model objects that it gets through the services in the controller layer of the application. Neither the model nor the controller may have any references to the view, so that another view layer can be utilized without changing the rest of the application.

With the generic GUI approach it is even possible to leave large parts of the view unchanged, so that only the concrete GUI elements have to be changed, when a new view technology is to be supported.

Creation of dialogs

A formal representation is needed to successfully create the dialogs by the client in its GUIEngine. XML is selected to transport these definitions from the server to the client. The following steps are needed for the whole process:

1. Determine the parameters in the Java applet during start-up. They contain the name of the requested business process as well as some optional information about the business objects.
2. Create the XML stream which carries all information from step 1.
3. Send the XML stream to the server.
4. The server interprets the XML stream and gathers the desired business objects.
5. Start the business process on the server. The outcome of this step is the dialog description for the client.
6. Send an XML stream back to the client containing the dialog descriptions.
7. The client interprets these descriptions, creates and visualizes the corresponding dialogs.

HTML embedded tag parameter definition

Contained in the .html file, specifically in the embedded tag of the applet, are two parameters which define the business process and what business objects are needed in the server.

- ProcessName: This parameter contains the name of the business process which is going to be started on the server, e.g. Process-Name="ProcCustomeridentification"
- BOKey: This parameter is already structured in XML and contains information about the business object. The structure looks as follows: <KeyName> <KeyValueName>&<Type>-<Value>[<KeyValueName>&<Type>-<Value>]. e.g.:BOKey="<Stamm Niederlassung="TString-0230" StammKunde="TString-00100117"/>"

As HTML does not allow special characters for HTML used in the text they have to be "escaped".

Event handling

Every implementation of a generic component factory has a reference to a class handling all the registered and incoming Swing events using the observer pattern [Gamma et Al.94]. This class is named SwingEventAdapter (package de.novatec.genericgui.swingadapter). The following figure illustrates the event-handling once a button is pressed:

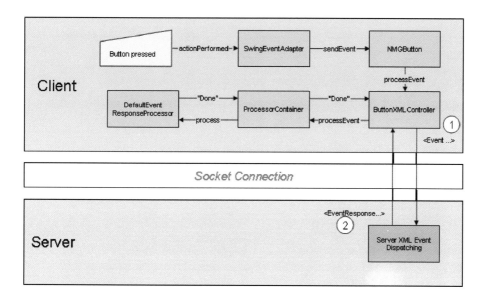

Figure 7. Order of events following a button action event

Pressing the button fires an ActionEvent which is caught by the SwingEventAdapters. The SwingEventAdapter creates a new NMGActionEvent which is sent to all the registered event handlers. As NMGButton is one of the registered event handlers, this event is passed to this class. Again, through the help of a method named processEvent, this event is passed further to the registered controller, in this case the ButtonXMLController. The controller performs a check if the event is activated at all. If this returns true, a request containing the following is sent to the server (1):

```
<?xml version="1.0" encoding="UTF-8"?>
<Event ApplicationID="0" I="93100001" EventID="NMGActionEvent">
  <EventData />
</Event>
```

The server will interpret this request and creates an appropriate event response, as seen below (2):

```
<EventResponse ApplicationID="0" I="93100001" EventID="NMGActionEvent">
  <ResponseDataList>
    <ResponseDescription/>
  <ResponseDataList>
</EventResponse>
```

This event response is processed by the XML controller in a way that the received XML string is delegated to an appropriate processor container or xml processor. In case of a button, it is sufficient to use a DefaultEventResponseProcessor, called by its process method. This processor will return "Done" and the event handling is finished.

Connection between GUIEngine (client) and server

To connect the application framework on the server with the GUIEngine on the client, it is indispensable to provide a small access point on both ends.

The following section describes the initial creation of the connection between the client and the server. The GUIEngine is presented to the user in form of a standard Java applet which is embedded in an HTML file.

Connection buildup

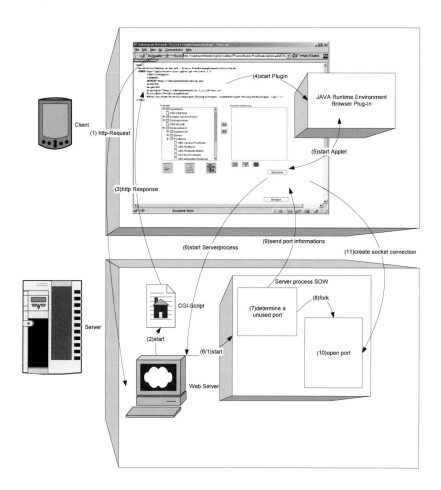

Figure 8. Architectural overview

Connection establishment through HTTP

The first steps of creating the communication in application framework is done via pure HTTP.
1. Access to a CGI script which resides in the Webserver.
2. Start the CGI script. All parameters of the transmitted URL are interpreted and included into the generated HTML stream, specifically as parameters for the applet.

3. Sending of the generated HTML stream to the client. The information for the applet is present in the embedded tag (<EMBED>). Additionally, it contains standards for the requested plugin.

Initilization of the Java environment in the browser

The browser creates and shows the incoming HTML stream, though the major work is delegated to the Java Runtime Environment (JRE).
4. Start of the Java Runtime Environment as a browser plugin
5. Start of the applet which contains the GUIEngine

Set-up of the socket communication

During starting of the applet, a socket is created which is responsible for the communication between the client and the server.
6. Start of the server process
7. Detection of an unused port which the client can use for the socket
8. Creation of an identical process with a new process id using a fork of the process. The new process is used as the future work process on the server and the existing process will transmit information about the port to the client
9. Sending of the port information to the client. Those ports will be bound on the client.
10. The server opens a port so that the client can use it. Due to security reasons, this port is only open for a particular time. When no connection is established in this timeframe, the process will close the port and terminates itself.
11. Creation of the socket by using the server-side port. To accept this connection, a sequence has to be transmitted first of all, which the client received with the socket parameters.

From this point on, the complete data communication between the client and the server is done through this socket. The webserver can then take care of other work.

Conclusion

The main advantage of a loosely coupled GUI framework is its great flexibility [WikiCoupling]. The description of the user interface elements and their behaviour is stored in a platform independent format such as XML documents.

Depending on the capabilities of the target platform it can then be rendered by native widgets. Therefore the GUI design process has to be performed only once but the GUI can be rendered on a broad range of devices. This is achieved by layout managers that can place the GUI widgets in the right context. While some GUI elements would be spread out horizontally on a large screen, on a small screen the same GUI elements would be arranged in a vertical list, but still retain their original grouping.

With the integration of scripting capabilities on the client the GUI can achieve a high degree of interactivity, aiding the user with input validation, dynamic controls and tool tips.

Another powerful concept is the utilization of the mobile device's peripheral equipment such as printers, cameras, card readers or barcode scanners.

Specialities of mobile applications

In a mobile environment it is always a distinct possibility that the network connection may fail. This can be counteracted to some amount by caching of critical data.

Displaying maps

There are several possible scenarios for displaying maps on mobile devices:
1. Low network bandwidth, low processor power: Maps should be stored locally on the mobile device as bitmap data so that only control data has to be transferred from the server. This approach possibly requires much persistent memory on the device.
2. High network bandwidth, low processor power: Maps can be rendered on the server and be sent to the client as bitmap data. The downside of this technique is that only limited interaction with the view is possible.
3. Low network bandwidth, high processor power: Vector data can be sent to the client which allows for highly interactive displays.

High network bandwidth, high processor power: Vector data and high resolution textures can be sent to the local device which allows highly interactive 3D maps with precise textures.

Outlook

As mobile devices grow more powerful the advantages of the generic GUI technology will become more and more apparent. An application that is designed with this technology today will have enhanced capabilities in the future without the need to change a single line of code.

References

Sun Microsystems [SunMVC]:
Java BluePrints: Model-View-Controller
http://java.sun.com/blueprints/patterns/MVC-detailed.html

Erich Gamma et Al. [Gamma et Al.94]:
Design Patterns: Elements of Reusable Object-Oriented Software

Addison Wesley, 1994

Wikipedia [WikiCoupling]:
Coupling (computer science)
http://en.wikipedia.org/wiki/Coupling_(computer_science)

Techniques and Applications for Mobile Commerce
C. Branki et al. (Eds.)
IOS Press, 2008
77

Using resource management games for mobile phones to teach social behaviour

Tilmann BITTERBERG, Hanno HILDMANN, Cherif BRANKI
School of Computing, University of the West of Scotland
{bitt-ic0 | hild-ci0 | bran-ci0}@uws.ac.uk

Abstract. Considerable parallels exist between what is commonly considered to constitute a good gaming or a good learning experience [8], which suggests the use of computer games in the education sector. We investigate the design of a resource management computer game (RMG) [5] to raise awareness for environmental issues. We argue that focusing on peoples attitude when investigating their behaviour is an established approach in psychology [1] and that the use of computer games in education is quickly becoming a common practice [3,2]. We present a prototype running on a mobile phone constructed to meet the identified requirements.

Keywords. mLearning, Assessment, Implementation, Pedagogical & Social issues

1. Game-based Learning

Many benefits of ascribed education aspects of games are highlighted in the literature even before the time of computer games becoming ubiquitous. Games can promote complex problem solving in training applications, promote practical reasoning skills improvement and reduce time for training and instructor load. Games can result in high sustained motivation levels and promote automaticity training where rehearsal becomes second nature. In a survey performed in 1987, it was noted that 4,600 large firms use business or experiential games in development and training.

1.1. Skill development through game playing

What then are the main benefits to game-based learning; which skills are developed and which abilities are promoted? To answer this we refer to [11] where the following (non exhaustive) list of key benefits to skill development though game playing is identified:

- Problem solving skills
- Analytical skills
- Team working skills
- Social and cultural skills
- Critical thinking skills
- Communication skills
- Discovery skills
- Negotiating skills
- Logical thinking skills
- Visualisation skills

The extend to which those skills are exercised depends on the game and some sort of preference over them is advisable when designing a game. The prototype game presented in this paper primarily targets the problem solving and social skills of the player. In addition, analytical, logical and critical thinking are required to preform well.

1.2. Stealth learning

The eLearning community and gaming sector frequently use the notion of *Stealth Learning* or *Informal Learning*. According to the definition provided by [4] stealth learning is *"where players learn subliminally or incidentally through rule structures, tasks, and activities within the game"*. Generally the reasons to play a game are to experience fun or challenges, not to learn [2]. If learning does take place is either incidental or aimed at becoming a better player. This suggests to build a game around the intended learning targets, making them implicitly deciding factors for the course of the game. For a player to improve in overall performance means to adhere to the underlying learning targets.

One noted problem with stealth learning is that it is difficult to classify or asses. Section 3.3 on assessment briefly elaborates on this aspect of our approach.

It is recognized that stealth learning or informal learning can occur through playing computer or console games: *"there is"*, for example, *"the possibility of stealth learning through using Sim City (urban planning) or Theme Hospital (health organization and purpose)"* [15]. We justify our focus on this type of learning in the next section, specifically in 2.1, by referring to the *Theory of Planned Behaviour* which provides a well established model for human decision making in the field of behavioural psychology.

1.3. Computer Games

For leisure activities computer games have increasingly replaced more traditional games. In 2007 the Entertainment Software Association reported that *"US computer and video game software sales grew six percent in 2006 to $7.4 billion - almost tripling industry software sales since 1996"*, which illustrates the magnitude of the industry involved.

Due to both the ubiquitous nature of computer games and popularity of serious games there are many of examples of educational use of games and simulations in different fields including: knowledge management, medicine and computer architecture.

A comparative study performed in 2005 and 2007 on students' motivations for playing computer games in higher education has shown that challenge, curiosity and cooperation consistently emerged as the most important motivations for using games in higher education. This implies that while computer based games enjoy an increasing attention as teaching tools their effectiveness might be even further increased when their nature as such is not immediately obvious to the students or when the intended learning outcomes are not told to the student in advance. For a detailed report on those results see [3,2].

1.4. Disadvantages

While there is a dearth of empirical evidence proving the validity of the approach [3, 2] there are also disadvantages of using (computer) games for instruction. There is a distinct lack of frameworks or guidelines for the incorporation of educational content, the incorporation of assessment or evaluation of game-based learning platforms or computer games incorporated into specific curriculums.

As game-based learning becomes increasingly accepted as a mainstream approach for learning and teaching, emphasis is placed on systems which can both provide detailed assessment information and personalise the learning experience. This is essential to enable researchers to verify their claims regarding the effectiveness of their approaches and tutors or moderators to tailor the game for individual needs of their students.

2. Pedagogical Consideration

The question what makes a good learning experience has been extensively investigated. Some learning principles of good games identified by Gee in [8,9,10] are:

- Identity
- Interaction
- Customization
- Production
- Risk Taking

- Challenge and Consolidation
- Pleasantly frustrating
- Well-Order-Problems
- System thinking
- Agency

The above listed principles are not comprehensive and given here as guidelines for following considerations, we will refer back to this in sections 4 and 5.

2.1. Theory of planned behaviour

There is a host of literature in psychology concerned with the negative effect that video games have on those that play them, especially with respect to increased automatic aggressiveness through violent computer games (e.g. [16]). The *Theory of Planned Behaviour* in psychology, i.e. a theory about the link between attitudes and behaviour, proposed by Ajzen [1] suggests that the attitude one has towards a certain behaviour influences that persons likeliness to exhibit that behaviour. This would support the aforementioned negative results found for e.g. first person shooter video games.

Attitude is a hypothetical construct that represents an individual mental predisposition either for or against some concept or idea. In accordance with the theory referenced above we suggest to target the attitude of students towards some aspect (for example environmental issues) instead of the more commonly practised approach of attempting to teach someone a desired behaviour directly. We cite e.g. [7] reporting on targeting students attitude when teaching the traditional difficult subject of responsible sexual behaviour, and quote *"There is a large volume of teaching material on health education which provides factual information. Although facts are important, other factors are also involved in bringing about attitude and behaviour change."*.

2.2. Evaluation

The immediate evaluation is simple as we see in the game whether some intended behaviour is exhibited by the players. With regard to this immediate evaluation computer games provide the perfect tool to observe or change a players' behaviour during gameplay. With respect to the long term evaluation, i.e. whether the players actually change their behaviour or attitudes in their daily lives, no immediate evaluation is possible. The full extend of the impact a game has on the player can only be evaluated through long-term investigation over years. See section 6 for proposed future work.

3. Learning Targets

Regarding the general objective of educational games two tasks are of high importance: The assessment of the player and the evaluation of the game as a learning tool. Stating the learning targets formally is a step towards providing both the means to assess the performances of the player as well as the effectiveness of the game itself.

Figure 1. Regular game events: Withdrawing cash from the bank, purchasing land, commissioning buildings

3.1. A formalism to state learning targets

In [12,13] the use of propositional logic is suggested as the basis for a language $\mathcal{L}$ to formally describe learning targets. This requires that all relevant aspects of the game are accessible as boolean values, i.e. as being either true or false. In computer games the current state of the game is completely defined at any moment as all relevant data must be represented on the computer. By the assumption that all relevant aspects are stored in variables of the type boolean this requirement is met.

As for propositional logic, sentences of the language $\mathcal{L}$ are constructed over the set Φ (the set of all atomic words) using the operators *not*, *and*, *or*, *if ... then* and *if and only if*. Consider for example the aspects `alive`, `heroic` and `happy`. The following statements could be learning targets, i.e. desirable to bring about during a game:

1. "`alive`",
2. "`alive` and `happy`",
3. "`alive` and (`happy` or `heroic`)",
4. "if not `alive` then `heroic`".

Our reason for introducing this formalism is that we want to enable game designers, teachers or supervisors to express complex aspects of a game to capture which attitude or behaviour they want to reward when their students play the game. Being able to unambiguously translate these statements into semi natural language and back allows the nontechnical user to use the formalism without having to learn propositional logic first.

Given two positive atomic learning targets `alive` and `happy` we can easily understand that the combination thereof ("`alive` and `happy`" and "`alive` or `happy`") are combined learning targets consistent with the atomic ones. The meaning of these two is also intuitively understood (both or at least one have to be true, respectively).

We can construct complex statements from them to capture rather complicated conditions. But while the meaning of the operators *not*, *and* and *or* are intuitively understood the usage '*if ... then*' is not without pitfalls. The sentence '*if* `ugly` *then* `good`' captures our intention to express that if something ugly u is true, we require the student to work on something good g to make up for it. This expresses what we want to convey, i.e. that if a certain negative event occurs we want the student to devote resources to create a specific positive counter event. On the other hand, if we want to express the

Figure 2. Bonus game events: Running for public office, newspaper interview and romantic interests

combination of two positive events, for example *'if* `good` *then it is not true that* `ugly`*'*, we encounter a problem: By the definition of the *if . . . then* construction this statement will be true in case that the condition of something positive `good` is not met. Due to this some caution and experience is required when designing learning targets using the *if . . . then* construction.

3.2. Automatic generation of learning targets

Consider that Φ contains a finite number of atomic statements and that any one of these is either true or false. This implies that the total number of different complex statements constructible over Φ, i.e. different conditions the game can be in, is finite as well ($|\Phi|^2$ to be exact). Any algorithm to enumerate all of them will suffice as a primitive generator.

To facilitate the use of games in learning environments, emphasis is placed on tools to support the teacher. The ability to automatically generate new as well as *sensible* learning targets from a set of existing ones is one of the main features of the approach presented. If adequate tools are available, no preliminary experience with propositional logic is required. However, using the properties of the underlying logic we can construct new learning targets from a set of existing ones such that the generated targets are consistent with the set. In addition, we can cluster them into groups, remove redundant ones or use them to change the dynamics, of the game. For specific implementation one task of the game designer will be to customise the algorithm producing learning targets.

3.3. Automatic evaluation & assessment

Due to the formal nature of the language in which the learning targets are stated, algorithms exist that automatically verify for any such statement whether it holds, given a specific state of the game. Such algorithms are standard and the only thing mentioned here about them is that they are computationally efficient in the sense that the time required to evaluate a statement is linear proportional to the length of the statement.

4. Resource Management Games

In [5] and [6] the authors distinguish eight principles underlying resource management games (henceforth RMG), and argue that an AI designed to play a RMG has to address those principles to the extent in which they are present in the game. We do not elaborate on the completeness of this set under all viewpoints but simply adopt them as the same competence in these levels is required of any human player playing that game.

Resource management games are games in which a player is in charge of some co-ordinated effort in some simulated world. Maybe the most famous example of this genre is SimCity. Recently this type of game is being developed both as entertainment as well as educative tools. For example Harvard's Business School uses resource management games in its student training programme. The overall goal of a RMG is to maximise the outcome of the coordinated effort. To do so the player often has to reach a number of intermediate goals. The player has a limited number of choices to attain these sub-goals while using a number of limited resources. This commonly forces some sort of tradeoff which requires the player to predict the outcome of actions in advance and to plan ahead for future actions. The 8 principles inherent to most RMGs (as identified in [5]) are:

- Dependence on resources
- Dependence on location
- Dependence on time
- Multiple objectives
- Continuity
- Non-determinism
- Competition
- Need for planning

In [14] we find a detailed account of important aspects of intrinsic motivation in the design of educational computer games. It suggests that intrinsic motivation is created by four individual factors: challenge, fantasy, curiosity and control; as well as three inter-personal factors: cooperation, competition and recognition. Interestingly, these factors also describe what makes a good game, irrespective of its educational qualities. This parallel between what makes a good gaming experience and a good learning experience is also identified by Gee [8]. We are confident that RMGs can be designed to meet these requirements and are therefore an ideal type of game for our needs because they are:

- challenging due to the restrictions or limitations of resources, location and time, the need to plan ahead and the multitude of potentially conflicting objectives.
- stimulating the fantasy by putting the player into a position one normally is not in. Through open games and non-determinism the players are also encouraged to use their fantasy to conjecture about things unknown to them.
- constantly requiring the player to control issues arising from the continuity of the game and from AI or human competition. Allowing for both cooperation and non-cooperation with the competition is yet another challenge.

5. An educational RMG: Prototype design considerations

As mentioned in the previous section the game should meet the identified important aspects of intrinsic motivation as well include as many possibly all of the principles stated above. Section 2 lists some learning principles of good games (see [8,9,10] for details) and covering these principles should be a requirement for the game designer. It stands to reason that not all skills identified in section 1.1 can be targeted efficiently by a single game so the game designer has to decide on a preference over these skills.

Figure 3. Moderator tools: Learning target design, automatic target generator, managing bonus events

In our prototype the player plays a utility tycoon, the standard game actions are to buy land or to build powerplants with the aim to corner the market (see Fig. 1). The aim of the game is to change the players attitude towards so-called *green* energy.

Underlying the game are learning targets that reward the building of solar and water power plants instead of seemingly more attractive nuclear power plants. This is not immediately obvious to the player for two reasons. The negative effect of a nuclear power plant is annulled if expensive security measures are in place and the rewarding bonus events are not occurring right away: Bonus events (see Fig. 2) are unlocked only after meeting a number of targets, making it hard for a player to deduce the causal relations.

Fig. 3 shows the modules implemented to enable a moderator to add new learning targets, choose from automatically generated targets or set the thresholds for triggering bonus events. Using the number of current targets met the moderator can easily gain insight into the players approch with respect to the intended learning outcomes. Currently these actions cannot be performed during gameplay as that requires the player to authorise the sending or receiving of data from the moderator.

The prototype was implemented using the Eclipse SDK (Version: 3.3.1) and the Java Wireless Toolkit (JWT) 2.5.2 for CLDC with the device configurations set to Connected Limited Device Configuration (CLDC) 1.1 and Mobile Information Device Profile (MIDP) 2.0. In what follows we refer to the *length* of a target as the number of atomic statements in it. All targets were exclusively constructed as conjunctions using only the AND operator, and such that no atomic statement occurred more than once. This is to ensure that evaluation and satisfiability methods are tested for the worst case scenario. The performance of the prototype was tested in the JWT environment using the above settings. For the evaluation of a targets (complexity increases linear to the length of the targets) we tested for 50 targets of length 10 and 20 and calculated the average over 50 tests, each comprised of 100 runs. The simulated phone averaged 0.019ms (length 10) and 0.025ms (length 20). When testing the targets for satisfiability we used the same targets but averaged over 50 test comprised of 10 runs each. The prototype was able to check satisfiability for all targets in 439.05ms (length 10) and 431.18ms (length 20). These results are somewhat unexpected as they do not match the relation between the targets of size 10 and 20. This is due to rounding errors, i.e. the fact that the execution was often too fast to register at all. We report these results as they show that even for unrealistic length of learning targets and large size of the set of targets checking for satisfiability will take less than half a second and is thus within acceptable parameters.

6. Conclusion / Future Work

In this paper we have shown two things. Firstly, that the use of a RMG in education is a feasible approach to teach positive social behaviour. Secondly, it is possible to use the limited capacities of a recent mobile phone to formally represent, generate and evaluate reasonable set of learning targets.

The next step is the implementation of a game on the basis of this prototype and to conduct a survey of its usability and effectiveness in an actual teaching environment. This includes the ability to quickly deploy games from a teachers' mobile to its students and the gathering of result data in return.

References

[1]   I. Ajzen. From intentions to actions: A theory of planned behavior. 1985.
[2]   T. Connolly, E. Boyle, and T. Hainey. A survey of students' motivations for playing computer games: A comparative analysis. 1st Europ. Conf. on Games-based Learning (ECGBL), Scotland, Oct. 2007.
[3]   T. Connolly, E. Boyle, M. Stansfield, and T. Hainey. The potential of online games as a collaborative learning environment. *Journal of Advanced Technology for Learning*, 2007.
[4]   S. de Castell and J. Jenson. Op-ed serious play. *Journal of Curriculum Studies*, 35(6):649–665, 2003.
[5]   S. de Jong. Hybrid ai approaches for playing resource management games. Master's thesis, University of Maastricht, The Netherlands, 2004.
[6]   S. de Jong, P. Spronck, and N. Roos. Requirements for resrource management game ai.
[7]   M. Emery. The theory and practice of behaviour change in the school context. *International journal of health education*, 23(2):116–125, 1980.
[8]   J. Gee. *What Video Games Have to Teach Us About Learning and Literacy*. Palgrave Macmillan, 2003.
[9]   J. Gee. *Situated Language and Learning: A Critique of Traditional Schooling*. Routledge, 2004.
[10] J. Gee. *Why Video Games are Good For Your Soul: Pleasure and Learning*. Common Ground, 2005.
[11] A. Healy. Does game based learning, based on constructivist pedagogy, enhance the learning experience and outcomes for the student compared to a traditional didactic pedagogy? Master's thesis, University of Paisley, Paisley, Scotland, June 2006.
[12] H. Hildmann, T. Hainey, and D. Livingstone. Psychology and logic: design considerations for a customisable educational resource management game. The Fifth Annual International Conference in Computer Game Design and Technology, Liverpool, England, November 2007.
[13] H. Hildmann and D. Livingstone. A formal approach to represent, implement and assess learning targets in computer games. 1st Europ. Conf. on Games-based Learning (ECGBL), Scotland, Oct. 2007.
[14] T. Malone and M. R. Lepper. Making learning fun: A taxonomy of intrinsic motivations for learning. *Aptitude, Learning and Instruction.*, 3: Conative and affective process analysis.:223–235, 1987.
[15] J. Sutherland, T. Connolly, and D. Livingstone. How can we build successful 3d games for learning?
[16] E. Uhlmann and J. Swanson. Exposure to violent video games increases automatic aggressiveness. *Journal of Adolescence*, 27(1):41–52, Feb 2004.

Acknowledgments

Anna Bartak (University of Amsterdam) provided indispensable advice regarding the section on planned behaviour as well as all references to the field of psychology.

Part II

E-Service Environments: Aspect-Oriented Techniques and Mobile Devices

Techniques and Applications for Mobile Commerce
C. Branki et al. (Eds.)
IOS Press, 2008

E-Services: Paving the Way for Mobile Clients

Guadalupe Ortiz

Quercus Software Engineering Group
Centro Universitario de Mérida , University of Extremadura
C/ Sta Teresa de Jornet, 38. 06800 Mérida, Spain
+34 924 387068
gobellot@unex.es

Abstract. The increasing demand for services for mobile customers has resulted in the need to develop service clients that could also be used from mobile devices and not only from PCs, which to date were the developers' main focus. In this paper we propose a model–driven development for these clients, whose platform-specific level attends to the specific requirements depending on the final device where the said client is to be installed. Furthermore, we propose the use of aspect-oriented techniques for the final implementation with the aim of facilitating the client's adaptation as a result of the particular device model characteristics and end user preferences.

Keywords. E-Services, Mobile Devices, Aspect-Oriented programming, Model-Driven Development.

Introduction

Mobile devices have acquired great prominence over the last years, with two and three times, depending on the country, more mobile users than Internet ones. The great amount of devices and its non-stop use 24 hours a day gives us a clear vision of the importance of access to mobile services [9]. This need can be observed from two points of view:

- From the point of view of the service side, the development of P2P applications in ad-hoc environments [6] has been halted particularly due to the processing and memory capacity of such mobile devices.
- Concerning the client side, service specific clients for mobile devices has been stopped due to interface limitations. In this regard, the obstacle is mainly the characterization of the client based on the final device from which the invocation is going to be pursued.

E-Service developers have focused mainly on the development of services designed to be accessible from desktop computers, creating a void in the sphere of their access from mobile clients –laptops, PDAs, mobile phones, etc.-, domain which is becoming a usual scenario. In order to meet this requirement we have to bear in mind three main factors, which are analyzed separately in the following lines:

- The type of mobile device: the developed client will vary widely depending on the target device. In this regard, there may not only be a big difference between a mobile device or a desktop computer, but also between the client developed for different types of mobile device, from a laptop to a mobile phone. We have to take into account not only the screen size, but also the available memory and runtime capacity.
- The device model: once we develop a client for a specific type of mobile device –i.e. a PDA-, we also have to account for the large differences existing between the whole assortment of PDAs in the market. The information to be provided by the client will probably not vary much from one model to another, but the way to display it will, specially depending on the screen size and shape.
- The preferences of the final user: it is also important to consider that most mobile device screen settings can be personalized based on the end-user preferences. Service clients should also take these into account, bearing in mind that the said preferences may vary over time and therefore so would the resulting settings.

In this article we outline a solution driven by models, which facilitates the adjustment of clients to the diverse mobile devices. In order to maintain the client code related to the specific device, model or end user preference decoupled from the main functionality code we propose a final aspect-oriented implementation.

The remainder of the paper is organized as follows: Section 1 provides a background on the two technologies to be used in our proposal: model-driven architecture in Section 1.1 and aspect-oriented techniques in Section 1.2. Then, Section 2 describes a motivating scenario; its proposed solution is described throughout Section 3: firstly, the adaptation to the type of device is described in Section 3.1; secondly, the dependence from the device model is tackled in Section 3.2 and, finally, final user preferences are taken into account in Section 3.3. Related proposals are examined in Section 5 and conclusions and our line of future work are provided in Section 6.

1. Background

In this section we provide a background to the two types of technology we are using in this paper; first of all we provide an introduction to model-driven development (MDD) and secondly to aspect-oriented programming (AOP*)*.

1.1 Model-Driven Development

The software engineering community is currently moving on to application development based on models rather than technologies [12]. Model-driven development allows us to focus on the essential aspects of the system, delaying the decision of which technology to use in the implementation for a later step. Models may be used from the initial system specification to its testing. Each model will address one concern, independently of the remaining issues involved in the system's development, thus allowing the separation of the final implementation technology from the business logic achieved by the system. Transformations between models enable the automated system development from the models themselves; therefore, model definition and transformation become the key parts of the process.

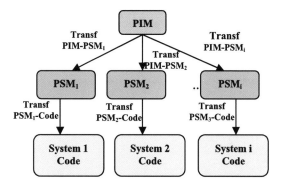

Figure 1. Model-driven process.

In this concern the programming task for developers is usually divided into three different phases (see Figure 1):

- First of all, a *Platform-Independent Model* (PIM) is proposed with the purpose of representing our system without coupling it to any specific platform or implementation language.
- Secondly, a *Platform-Specific Model* (PSM) represents our system based on a specific target platform. In fact, we may have different platform-specific models for different technologies so that we can reuse the PIM of our systems in several environments.
- Finally, *Code Layer* provides our final application code, which may be generated automatically from the platform-specific model.

1.2 Aspect-Oriented Techniques

AOP arises due to the problems detected in *Object-Oriented Programming* (OOP). OOP is supposed to permit the encapsulation and modularity of related data and methods. This should imply code organized into meaningful units and not blended at all. However, we may find it impossible to model several concerns into a unique and structured decomposition of units. We could have transversal concerns, which cannot be included in the logical code structure by functionality. As a result of these crosscutting concerns, code is scattered and tangled all over our application [4].

AOP describes five types of element to modularise crosscutting concerns: firstly, we have to define the *join point* model which indicates the points where we could include new behaviours. Secondly, we have to define a way to indicate the specific *join points* to specify in which points of the implementation the new code is to be inserted. Next, we ought to determine how we are going to specify the new behaviour to be included in the *join point* referred to [5]. We would then encapsulate the specified join points and their corresponding behaviours into independent units. Finally, a method to weave the new code with the original one has to be applied. Thus, aspects will allow us to consider the device model and user preferences in a decoupled way with respect to the main functionality of the client.

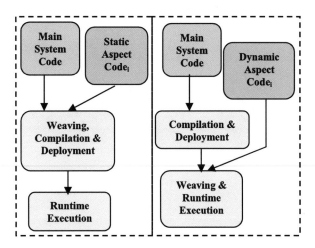

Figure 2. Static versus dynamic AOP weaving.

We can distinguish two main types of aspect-oriented techniques depending on the time the aspects are woven into the system, which are named *static* and *dynamic* AOP:

- In static AOP, represented in left side of Figure 2, aspects are woven with the primary functionality at compile-time, then the full system compilation and deployment is accomplished. Once woven, static aspects cannot be removed or reconfigured during runtime.
- In dynamic AOP, depicted in right side of Figure 2, a mechanism is provided to weave aspects after the systems' compilation and deployment, therefore aspects can be added and woven at runtime.

2. Motivating Scenario

Let us suppose we wish to invoke an e-commerce service, such as a bookstore one, which provides information on the content, availability and price of a book. Its title and author are provided for the service invocation. In the following lines we describe the facts we should take into account to implement the most suitable client for this service invocation depending on the type of device in which the client will be hosted:

1. First of all, we have to consider that diverse devices may show different results:
 - A laptop client may show the book's front cover, a summary of its content, and its index, as well as the number of available copies and its price (see left-side device in Figure 3).
 - A PDA could display a summary of the book content, but may not show the front cover and index due to the screen size. Besides, the number of copies available and its price will be shown (see device in the middle of Figure 3).
 - A mobile phone with a small screen could show the number of copies available and book price, without providing any additional information about the book's content or cover (see right-side device in Figure 3).

Figure 3. Results represented in diverse devices.

2. The second issue to consider is the device model: with device model we mean the device trademark and the different models every trademark may offer. For instance, a PDA screen size may oscillate at least between 2 and 4 inches, as represented in Figure 4. The results of the invocation we selected earlier to be shown on a PDA – summary, number of copies and price– can be displayed differently in accordance with the different size screens in order to reach prospective buyers more easily, as market studies suggest.

Figure 4. Different size devices representation

3. Finally, the end user may have selected specific setting for his device screen (such as background colour, type of font or any other more complex factor which the end-user can chose and may affect his comfort…). It is obvious that if we also consider end user tastes when showing him the information on the book he may be thinking of buying, this will contribute towards the purchase by creating a positive feeling in him. An example of the same client bearing in mind the end user preferences or not is represented in Figure 5.

Developing three different clients from beginning to end in order to achieve the different device clients does not make sense, and even more, to have to thoroughly modify them depending on the device model. Furthermore, it would be impossible to create a client to meet end user preferences beforehand. It is much more efficient to develop a unique client which works out the functionality of the service invocation and then to characterize the way to display the results depending on the type of device in a decoupled way, as explained in the following section.

Figure 5. Different end-user preferences taken into account in the client application.

3. Developing the E-Service Client Efficiently

In this section we tackle the three facts considered in the motivating scenario in order to show a more efficient way to develop e-service clients: dependences from the type of device, the device model and final user preferences are dealt with in sections 4.1, 4.2 and 4.3, respectively.

3.1. How to Tackle the Client Dependencies Resulting from the Type of Device

As previously introduced, model-driven development distinguishes between platform-independent and platform-specific models, allowing the separation of a system's business logic from the supporting platform and technologies.

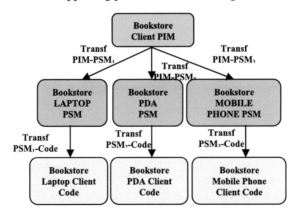

Figure 6. Using MDA to tackle client dependences resulting from the type of device

In the problem we are focusing on now, it is our purpose to define a client functionality which may be properly implemented for various types of final device. In this regard, we may initially model our PIM which represents the service invocation and client main functionality. Then, by making use of a set of transformation rules we will obtain the specific models, which will depend on the final type of device. We will normally have previously defined different set of transformation rules to convert the PIMs into different kind of specific ones. At this point, we would only have to select the type of specific model that we want to obtain and the PIM to which the transformation rules will be applied. Finally, through the use of an additional set of transformation rules which will be applied to the platform-specific model, the final code will be automatically generated. These processes are depicted in Figure 6.

In the scenario proposed in Section 3, we first of all will model our bookstore client in a platform-independent manner, which will take into account the interface offered by the specific service as well as the functionality we want to be provided by the client. Then, depending on the final type of device, we will transform this model into a PSM, specific for a client to be installed in a PC –as the approach shown in [7]-, PDA or mobile phone, respectively. Later on, departing from the PSM, we can generate the necessary code which is thus based on the final type of device.

3.2 How to Tackle the Client Dependencies Resulting from the Device's Model

Once we have developed a client specific to a type of device, there is an added constraint on the particular device model; especially for PDAs and mobile phones there is a great assortment of screen sizes, which implies that, if we want a better marketable product, we should adapt the results obtained in the invocation to the most attractive layout according to the screen size. It is not efficient to define a specific model for every device model since it would imply such huge workload at modeling stage that the advantages of MDA would not compensate the modeling effort. Besides, it would be interesting not to mix the main functionality client code with the one originated by screen size restrictions, but to have them completely separated.

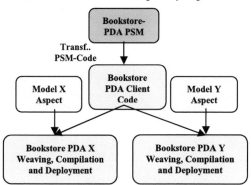

Figure 7. Using static AOP to tackle client dependences resulting from the device's model.

With this purpose we propose the use of static AOP. These will allow us to encapsulate all the code related to the characteristics specific to the device model for the correct representation of results on the screen. In this regard, we will have, on the one hand, the code obtained from the specific model according to a type of device and, on the other, the aspects which will provide us with the graphical representations of the data obtained in the invocation according to a specific device model, as represented in Figure 7. That is, what happens at runtime is that the main functionality is performed as usual and, when the invocations results are obtained, the aspect which is aware of the device model will be the one in charge of representing the answers in the device screen. Then, the complete application can be compiled and installed in the final device. Even more, we can predefine a set of aspects, specific to diverse particular device models, which can be reused for different client applications.

3.3 How to Tackle the Client Dependencies Resulting from the End User Preferences

Finally, there is a third level of specialization: the personalization based on the final user, who may define his tastes for his mobile device (font size, background colour, etc), once he is already using it. This changes may affect not only all the applications in the core software of the device, but they may also be applied to the web applications which we are interested in promoting for the possible customer. In order to change thiese elements, we would have to modify and reinstall these applications in the device or to have some code in it, mixed with the whole functionality which reads the preferences from the device and consider them in the execution.

In order to tackle this personalization and to avoid any end user-related intrusive code in the application main functionality code, which is subsequent to the installation of the client in the device, we propose the use of dynamic aspect-oriented techniques, which will permit the personalization of the client without having to recompile it and without the need to introduce intrusive code (see Figure 8). For this purpose those methods which functionality is affected by the user preferences are prepared in order to be able to be intercepted by a dynamic aspect. The particular aspects for the user preferences will be created or updated whenever the user changes his preferences. This way, an aspect will access the settings provided by the final user and will inject the necessary code in order to adapt the client's appearance accordingly on execution. As previously mentioned, this option provides us with the possibility of adapting the client to the final user preferences as a way of obtaining better product sales by applying marketing techniques-strategies.

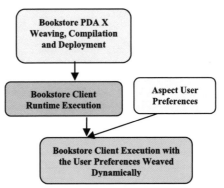

Figure 8. Using dynamic AOP to tackle client dependences resulting from the end-user preferences.

4. Discussion

This paper has depicted an approach in which MDA and AOP are used in conjunction to tackle the differences of mobile devices applications. The full process proposed is depicted in Figure 9, in which four different stages can be observed:

- Step 1 represents the definition of the platform-independent model of the system. In this regard, the application functionality is modeled independently of the final device in which it is going to be deployed.

- The system PIM is reused in stage 2 for different final type of devices in which the application is going to be deployed: the platform-specific model of the system and its corresponding code will be generated according to the final type of device (i.e for a PDA)
- Step 3 will provide us with the possibility of specialize the application for device, depending on its particular model of the device. Since the device model is known before the deployment, we have used static aspects for this purpose which will allow us to avoid the creation of intrusive code into the main application functionality due to the specific characteristics of the device model. Afterward, the main functionality and the aspects are woven, compiled and deployed in the device.
- Finally, stage 4 shows how dynamic aspects may be used in order to consider the device end-user preferences in the application, which is already deployed in device. Since the user may change his preferences once the system is already deployed, the weaving of these preferences with our application has to be done at runtime and this is the reason for using dynamic AOP.

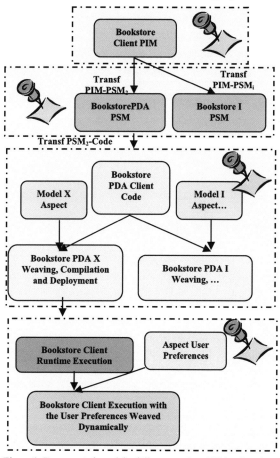

Figure 9. Representation of the full process from PIM to Runtime

Concerning the model-driven angle, MDA provides us with faster development time by automatically generating code rather than having to handwrite it, thus keeping the system well structured and modeled since the early stages of development. This implies better code consistency and maintainability, as well as an increase in the portability of the PIM across middleware vendors as we explain in the following lines:

- Reusability: A unique platform-independent model will be used for generation the platform-specific models and their code for different types of devices in which the clients want to be deployed. Besides, the predefined characteristics of several devices models may let us to create a repository of aspects ready to be weaved directly with the client generated code.
- Traceability: systems' traceability is maintained along the whole development process: the system elements can be located in every step and the device model or end user–related code is perfectly located in the aspects.
- Simplicity: as a consequence of prior statements, transformations in the model-driven development are simpler than if the specific devices or user characteristics were mixed with services at any stage, since independent elements can be generated separately.
- Maintainability: also a consequence of previous characteristics, property models and code will be easily maintainable, since they remain separated from the main functionality; therefore, it is easier to add a new model or to delete or modify user preferences without affecting the main application functionality at all.

Concerning the aspect-oriented topic, several metrics were used in order to evaluate the proposal. As a result, we can conclude that this proposal provides us with the following advantages:

- Modularity: thanks to the use of aspect-oriented techniques, both static and dynamic, we will be able to maintain our application independently of the final device model or the end user preferences, respectively. This specific code remains perfectly modularized in an aspect completely separate from the main application code.
- Encapsulation: as a consequence of the system's modularity, the influence of the specific characteristics of the model or of the user preferences in the implementation remains completely encapsulated into a meaningful unit.
- Aspect-oriented programming may lead to some overhead in the applications' performance. This belief is probably originated by the first proposals of AOP; nevertheless, AOP weavers, and specifically AspectJ ones, have evolved considerably and the latter community aims for the performance of their AspectJ implementations to be on par with the same functionality, hand-coded in Java. In spite of this assertion, the variations were under 10% of penalty, which in general can be regarded as insignificant.

5. Related Work

It was previously introduced that most e-services developers have focused their effort in applications oriented to PCs and not to mobile devices. In this regard, there is not a lot of research which can be studied in this area, but we will mention a few representative ones:

The proposal from Zhang et al. provides the possibility of reengineering PC-based systems into a mobile product line by using a meta-programming technique that uses XVCL. In their approach, systems are firstly developed for PC environments and then evolved to mobile device platforms by generating the specific components from the generic metacomponents [11].

The approach from Alvers deals with existing variations in the different mobile devices' models. He uses AOP to refactorize the variations and therefore to decouple them from the core of the mobile application [1].

The idea from Blechsschmidt et al consists of allowing the personalization of mobile device applications based on the end user profile. For this purpose user information is collected and stored in XML-format files which are precompiled with the applications' core code in order for this information to be taken into account in the application during execution.

A few works more could be mentioned, such us [3], [10], but in general, though they consider a decoupled implementation of non-functional elements, they do not conseidre the special environment of mobile devices.

Although all these proposals try to somehow deal with the characterization of the software for mobile devices, none of them approaches the problem from a wide perspective where the development of the said software is considered from initial model to ultimate implementation, and in which the device model and end user preferences are also contemplated. Besides, the notion of maintaining the personalization and graphical representation code decoupled from the core application is hardly tackled by these approaches, which also fail to provide an automated way to generate the final code of the application.

6. Conclusions and Future Work

In this paper we have proposed the use of a model-driven development for e-service clients in mobile devices, simplifying the client development and allowing the reuse of a platform-independent model of the client application for different specific types of device. Besides, the developed clients are adapted to the specific devices' models as well as end user preferences by using aspect-oriented techniques, which avoid the injection of intrusive code in our client application and allow the reuse of pre-defined configuration aspects for several applications.

Our future work consists on the extension of our developed prototype for integrating extra-functional properties in the model-driven development of web services [8] in order to support the rising ideas presented in this paper.

Acknowledgements.

This work has been developed thanks to the support of MEC under contract TIN2005-09405-C02-02.

References

[1] Alves, B. Identifying Variations in Mobile Devices. Journal of Object technology, Vol 4, N° 3, 2004.

[2] Blechsschmidt, T., Wieland, T.., Kuhmunch C, Mehrmann, L.. Personalization of End User Software on Mobile Devices. International Workshop on Mobile Commerce and Services, München (Germany), July 2005.v

[3] Duclos, F. Estubkier, J., Morat, P.Describing and Using Non-Functional Aspects in Component Based Applications. Proceedings of the 1st international conference on Aspect-oriented software development , Enschede, The Netherlands

[4] Elrad, T., Aksit, M., Kitzales, G., Lieberherr, K., Ossher, H.: Discussing Aspects of AOP. Communications of the ACM, Vol.44, No. 10, October 2001

[5] Kiczales, G. Aspect-Oriented Programming, ECOOP'97 Conference proceedings, Jyväskylä, Finland, June 1997.

[6] Nedos A., Kulpreet S., Clarke S. Mobile Ad Hoc Services: Semantic Service discovery in Mobile Ad Hoc Networks. Proc International Conference on Service-Oriented Computing, Chicago (USA), December 2006.

[7] Ortiz, G. Hernández, J. Model-Driven Extra-Functional Property Development for Web Services: a Case Study from the Service and Client Side Perspectives. Upgrade Journal Vol. VII, issue 5, October 2006

[8] Ortiz, G., Hernández J. Service-Oriented Model-Driven Development: Filling the Extra-Functional Property Gap. 4th Int. Conference on Service Oriented Computing (ICSOC 2006), Chicago, USA, December 4th-7th, 2006.

[9] Pedersen P.E., Ling. R. Modifying adoption research for mobile Internet service adoption: cross-disciplinary interactions. Proc. Hawaii International Conference on System Sciences, Hawai, 2003.

[10] Wholstadter, E., Tai, S., Mikalse, T., Roubellou, I., Devanbu, P. GlueQoS: Middleware to Sweeten Quality of Service Policy Interactions. Software Engineering, 2004. ICSE 2004. Proceedings. 26th International Conference on Software Engineering, 2004..

[11] Zhang, W., Jarzabek, S. Loughran. N. Rashid, A. Reengineering a PC-based System into the Mobile Device product Line. International Workshop on Principles of Software Evolution, Helsinki (Finland), September 2003.

[12] Model-Driven Architecture http://www.omg.org/mda/

Techniques and Applications for Mobile Commerce
C. Branki et al. (Eds.)
IOS Press, 2008
99

Enhancing the expressivity of PADL for specifying Web Services Architectures [1]

Gregorio Díaz, María-Emilia Cambronero, M. Llanos Tobarra, Valentín Valero, and
Fernando L. Pelayo

*ReTiCS group at University of Castilla-La Mancha - Escuela Politécnica Superior de
Albacete. 02071 - SPAIN,*
E-mail:[gregorio,emicp,mtobarra,valentin,fpelayo]@dsi.uclm.es

Abstract. Process Algebra Description Language, PADL in short, is a description language for describing structural components specified as individual process working in parallel with communication capabilities. This description is close to what we consider a web service except for the communication process. The PADL language is consider for synchronous communication while we need an asynchronous definition in communications terms. Then we propose in this work an extension of PADL for specifying Web Services Architectures.

Keywords. Web Services Architectures, Formal Methods, Process Algebra, WSA Modeling

1. Introduction

The Process Algebra Description Language (PADL) [8,9,7,2] has been shown, as a clear example of a formal framework applied to the description of software architectures and it has proved that it is possible to combine two different areas: software architecture and formal methods, by using a syntaxis that captures the main requirements of a software architecture by means of a component-oriented modeling.

On the other hand, an emergent programming area, web services, has become a key topic for researches all around the world. Thus, driven by the same interest, it has appeared a new concept for specifying software architectures that uses web services, which is known as Service Oriented Architecture (SOA). An important proposal for SOA specification has been the proposal of Service Component Architecture (SCA) [1] supported by international companies such as IBM and Oracle. This proposal will be our reference work in terms of concepts and assumptions for SOA.

Thus, on one hand we have the PADL that allows the description of component-oriented models and on the other hand we have SOA to specify systems that integrate web services. Then, it appears the chance to try to combine both of them, in order to provide a sound underlying foundation in the development of SOA. This is the idea developed in this work. The first task to be accomplished is the analysis of both models, in order to

---

[1] This work has been supported by the CICYT project "Description and Evaluation of Distributed Systems and Application to Multimedia Systems",TIC2003-07848-C02-02 and the UCLM project "Aplicación de Métodos Formales al Desarrollo y Verificación de Web Services"

discover the common shared points and the shortcomings detected to face the integration of both models.

The main aspect of SOA that must be analyzed in depth is the communication system. We will see that PADL describes a communication based on the idea of an unique destination or various of them in a synchronous environment, whereas Web Services basically describes a point to point communication system that normally is based on an asynchronous communication process. Therefore, we extend PADL with an asynchronous communication system by defining different types of interactions. This extension is the main contribution in this paper.

The outline of this work is as follows. The first section, deals with the related work in order to distinguish which part of our work supposes a novel contribution. The next two sections present a brief definition of SCA and a brief description of PADL. Then, an extension of the communication system of PADL with asynchronous capabilities is described. Finally, some conclusions and future work are presented.

2. Related work

In the recent years, our research group (ReTiCs) at the University of Castilla - La Mancha has studied the web services by using different formal techniques such as timed automata. The use of this formalism has allow us to use model checking to analyze web services, as is pointed out in [11,10,13]. Furthermore, we have also analyze security aspects over them as is pointed out in [15]. However, the study view point of these previous works has been from the software functionality view point. But now, we want to focuss our interests on the software architecture view point and to apply it to the web services systems. Thus, as mentioned above, we will use like our starting point two previous works each one in different fields. The first one is the SCA and the second one is PADL. SCA describes, as its name indicates, architectures implemented with components that can use services to interact among them, and, PADL describes, architectures implemented with components that interacts within a synchronous environment and provides a formal framework to work with. SCA focusses on web services, whereas PADL focusses on the description of a formal framework.

Furthermore, there are some related works as for instance [14,4], but related only to architectural design, others that perform model checking over service-oriented systems [5] and the closest one presented by Fiadeiro et all in [12] that introduces a formal approach for SCA, however, the communication mechanism specified by them introduces the definition of a large amount of operators that increase the complexity of the component diagram obtained.

3. Service Component Architecture SCA

The SCA is based in the description of Service Oriented Architectures by using components as a basic building blocks. The structure of a components is the one showed in Figure 1. These components consists of a label indicating the name and two different types of interactions with the rest of elements, services and references. The services are the functionality that the component offers to other components defined as an interface. Whereas, references are the services offered by the other components that our compo-

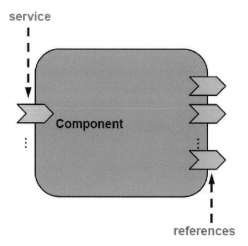

Figure 1. The component structure.

nent will use. Furthermore, SCA allows us the definition of properties that we will use in the component internal behavior.

SCA abstracts the component concept with its implementation. In fact, you can use any language that supports web service for implementing the component, such as the classical object-oriented languages like Java, C++, PHP or XML oriented languages like BPEL or even declarative languages like SQL and XQuery. This is an important feature that provides SCA.

Other important aspect that we must study is how this component can be combined or who it can be assembled with other components. To accomplish this task, SCA specifies two different environments. The first is related to the components that are closely connected within a module. And, the second environment is related to the component interaction that are loosely connected. These two different environments are tough for "programming in the large" that describes business solutions and "programming in the small" that describes fine-grained components within a close related system, respectively. In figure 2, we can see the assembly of a system, where the system consists of one or more *ModuleComponents* and potentially *EntryPoints* and *ExternalServices*, plus the *Wires* that connect them.

The last aspect, that it necessary to study, is the communication mechanism that defines SCA for SOA systems. This mechanism is an asynchronous message-oriented mechanism due to a simple synchronous call-and-return style is not appropriate. Thus, SCA provides three communication styles, *one way*, *callback* and *conversations*. **One way** can be describe as *sending a message* from the client to the service provider. **Callback** imply that calls are made in both directions between the client and provider and the timing of callback invocation is asynchronous. **Conversations**, where a series of interactions may occur over time between a service client and the service provider.

4. PADL

Process Algebra Description Language (PADL) appears due to the necessity of using a friendly component-oriented way of modeling systems with process algebra,

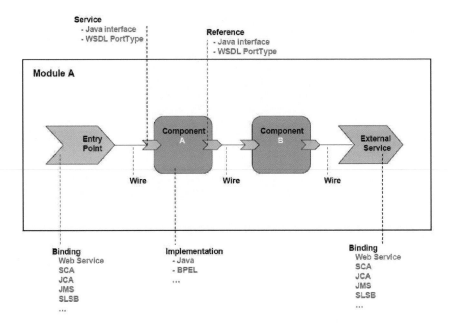

Figure 2. The system assembly in SCA.

where the designer can reason in terms of composable software units while abstracting from process algebra technicalities. Furthermore, this language will provide an efficient component-oriented way of analyzing functional and non-functional system properties with process algebra techniques, which returns component-oriented diagnostic information in case of violation.

Thus, PADL works at the architectural design level, where we do not describe algorithms and data structures but components and connectors. The objective is to obtain a document to be used in all the subsequent phases of the system development cycle, which describes the structure of the system as well as its behavior at a high level of abstraction.

The syntax of PADL is as follows:

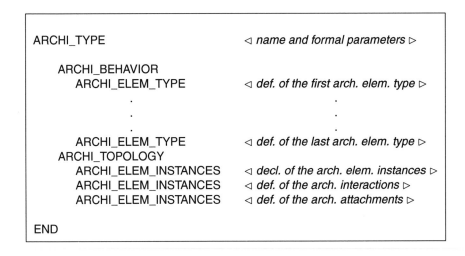

This syntax separates the behavior of each component from the topology used in the system. The behavior is defined by using components and connectors (AET - architectural element type). The topology is defined by declaring instances of these components and connectors (AEI - architectural element instance) and the way they communicate with each other (attachments).

The AET syntax consists of:

```
ARCHI_TYPE              ◁ name and formal parameters ▷
    BEHAVIOR            ◁ PA behavioral equations ▷
    INPUT_INTERACTIONS  ◁ decl. of the input interactions ▷
    OUTPUT_INTERACTIONS ◁ decl. of the output interactions ▷
```

The syntax of a behavioral equation is:

$$B(formal\_par\_list; local\_var\_list) = P$$

and the behavioral operators (**cond** is optional):

```
P        ::=      stop
         |        B(actual_par_list)
         |        cond(bool_expr) ⟶ a.P
         |        cond(bool_expr) ⟶ a?(var_list).P
         |        cond(bool_expr) ⟶ a!(var_list).P
         |        choice{P,...,P}
```

The data types supported are boolean, integer, real, list, array and record.

PADL explicitly distinguish between internal actions and the interactions between components. These interactions form the component interface and are defined as a *input versus output* in the AET definition section and *local versus architectural* in the topology section. The interactions can participate in three different forms of communications one-to-one, conjunctive one-to-one (broadcast) and disjunctive one-to-one (server-clients). They are explicitly defined in the AET definition as Uni-interactions, And-interactions and Or-interactions, respectively.

Figure 3 shows an example for a pipe-filter system composed of four identical filters connected by one pipe, where the header is:

```
ARCHI_TYPE Pipe_Filter(const integer pf_buffer_size := 10
                       const integer(0..pf_buffer_size)
                       pf_init_item_num := 0)
```

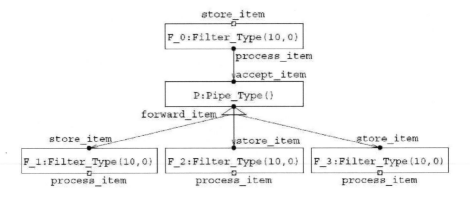

Figure 3. A PADL example for a pipe-filter system.

The filter type is:

```
ARCHI_ELEM_TYPE Filter_Type(const integer pf_buffer_size := 10
                            const integer(0..pf_buffer_size)
                            pf_init_item_num := 0)


    BEHAVIOR
        Filter(integer(0..buffer_size) item_num := init_item_num; void) =
            choice
            {
                cond(item_num < buffer_size) ⟶ store_item.Fiter(item_num + 1),
                cond(item_num > 0) ⟶ process_item.Fiter(item_num - 1),
                fail.repair.Filter(item_num)
            }
        INPUT_INTERACTIONS UNI store_item
        OUTPUT_INTERACTIONS UNI process_item
```

The pipe type is:

```
ARCHI_ELEM_TYPE Pipe_Type(void)
    BEHAVIOR
        Pipe(void; void) =
            accept_item.forward_item.Pipe()
        INPUT_INTERACTIONS UNI accept_item
        OUTPUT_INTERACTIONS OR forward_item
```

And the AEIs topology consists of:

```
ARCHI_ELEM_INSTANCES
    F_0 :   Filter_Type(pf_buffer_size,pf_init_item_num);
    P   :   Pipe_Type();
    F_1 :   Filter_Type(pf_buffer_size,pf_init_item_num);
    F_2 :   Filter_Type(pf_buffer_size,pf_init_item_num);
    F_3 :   Filter_Type(pf_buffer_size,pf_init_item_num);
ARCHI_ELEM_INTERACTIONS
    F_0.store_item;
    F_1.process_item,F_2.process_item,F_3.process_item;
ARCHI_ELEM_ATTACHMENTS
    FROM F_0.process_item TO P.accept.item;
    FROM P.forward_item    TO F_1.store.item;
    FROM P.forward_item    TO F_2.store.item;
    FROM P.forward_item    TO F_3.store.item;
```

5. Extending PADL with asynchronous communication

We have seen how we can define software architectures by using PADL and how it is possible to define software-oriented architectures by using SCA. The main difference between these two approaches is how they consider the communication process. The PADL communication is a synchronous process where the main functionality is concerned to the destination number and type. Whereas, SCA communication style is an asynchronous process where the main functionality is concerned to the duration of the communication in the sense of the communication process is only unidirectional or bidirectional.

Thus to combine this two approach it is necessary to add new capabilities to one of them. SCA describes a component-oriented diagram, while PADL describes not only a component-oriented diagram but furthermore a description language for describing behaviors. Then, we will base our proposal in the use of PADL extended with the communication system described by SCA.

Our objective is the model that we can see in Figure 4 that describes the connection of two different modules A and B. Module A consists of three connected components by inputs and output actions and Module B consists of one component. These two modules interact each other by using three different interactions. This system offers an interface that is labeled as an *Entry Point*, which consists of the services provided by one component in Module A. Furthermore, this system uses some references labeled as *External Service*, which consist of services offered by other systems.

Thus, we have seen the pursued objective and, in order to accomplish it, it is necessary to modify the PADL syntax. To start this task, we have to introduce the interface and reference concepts in the syntax. We have established that these two concepts are

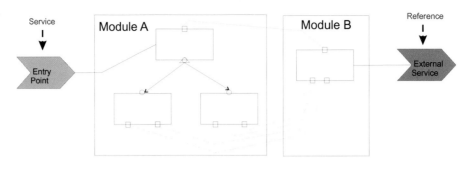

Figure 4. The combined diagram for PADL and SCA.

related to the interaction concept. Then, we must modify in the ARCHI_ELEM_TYPE: INPUT_INTERACTION and OUTPUT_INTERACTION. The reference and interface concepts works as **output versus input action**, but in an asynchronous environment. Thus we will declare the interface as input actions and the references as output actions. We will use the word INTERFACE before an input action to declare the services offered by the component and the word REFERENCE before and output action to declare the invocation of an external service.

We know how we must declare them, but the most important is to transform the communication into an asynchronous environment. Then, we have internally defined a queue that stores the external invocation that other components perform over a component interface. Thus, when a component performs an external invocation by using a "reference output action", this invocation will be stored in the queue of the receiver component and will be used by the first "interface input action" that matches the topology interaction definition. Then, the invoker component does not wait for the receiver component to process the invocation.

This environment is totally asynchronous since, only the "interface input action" is blocked waiting for the matching "reference output action". However, in some situations, it is advisable that the invoked component processes the matched "interface input action" before continuing the invoker component. Therefore, we have added the BLOCKED word before the reference declaration and this mean that the invoker component will be blocked until the invoked component synchronize to receive-process the invocation.

The use of queues for defining an asynchronous environment is not a new theory as is pointed out in [3,6] by Bergstra and Klop. And, it does not modify the operational semantic defined for PADL, but only by the inclusion of a queue for "interface input actions".

Then the invocation is defined as follow:

$$When \; o \in Interface_2 \; \wedge \; o.P_1 \; || \; P_2 \; \xrightarrow{o} \; P_1 \; || \; P_2 \; then \; o \cup Q_2$$

Then the service processing is defined as follows:

$$When \; i \in Q_2 \; \wedge \; P_1 \; || \; i.P_2 \; \xrightarrow{i} \; P_1 \; || \; P_2 \; then \; Q_2 - i$$

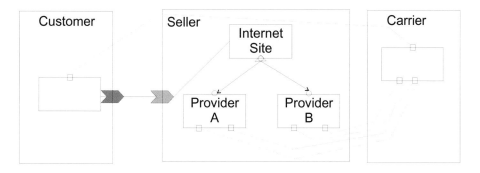

Figure 5. The Internet purchase process component diagram.

Where P_1 and P_2 are the behavior of two components. o is a "reference output action" and i is a "interface input action". $Interface_2$ is the set of "interface input actions" offered by P_2 and Q_2 is the queue that stores the "interface input actions" that are invoked by other processes.

However, when a "reference output action" is preceded by the BLOCKED word, the communication mechanism is the same defined by the interactions defined by PADL.

This definition of asynchronous communication can be used to define the three communication styles defined by SCA, **one way**, **call back** and **conversation**. One way implies the definition of an interaction over a non blocked "reference output action" and "interface input action". Call back is similar to one way but the reference output action must by blocked until the matched interface input action is performed, then the BLOCKED word must precede to the "reference output action" in its definition. Finally, conversations can be defined by using several one way and call back interactions.

In order to illustrate who it works, we will use a typical example, which consists of an Internet purchase process based on the site offered by amazon. We will have three subsystems that play three different roles: the customer, the seller and the carrier. Figure 5 shows us the component diagram that represents this example.

We will abstract the definition of the Providers A and B and the Carrier components, because we have a space limitation. Thus, we will focuss our attention on the remaining components the Internet Site and the Customer and, especially, on the communication process based on the interfaces and references. About providers and carrier, we know that they synchronize to pick up the products that must be delivered. Furthermore, The Internet Site checks, who is the provider that can provide the product that the customer has order and the carrier synchronizes with the customer in order to finally deliver the product.

The interface provided by the Internet Site as "interface input actions" are:

- List, the seller product list.
- Order, when the customer order a product.
- Status, that makes possible to know the order status.

This interface will be the one used by the customer, where are declared like references. The list and status references will be blocked references, due to the customer will need the information provided by these services in order to continue his activity.

The behavior of the Internet Site is declared as follows:

```
ARCHI_ELEM_TYPE Internet_Site_Type()
BEHAVIOR Internet_Site(void;void) =
      choice {
          send_list.Internet_Site()
          receive_order choice {
              available_prod.pick_prod.Internet_Site()
              status_prod_sent.available_prod.pick_prod.Internet_Site()
          }
      }
IMPUT_INTERACTIONS
    UNI INTERFACE send_list
    UNI INTERFACE receive_order
    UNI INTERFACE status_prod_sent
OUTPUT_INTERACTIONS
    AND request_prod
    UNI pick_prod
```

And the behavior of the customer is declared as follows:

```
ARCHI_ELEM_TYPE Customer_Type()
   BEHAVIOR Customer(void;void) =
       ask_list.order_prod
       choice
          {status_prod choice
              { status_prod.Customer()
              prod_delivered.Customer()
          }
          prod_delivered.Customer()
       }
   IMPUT_INTERACTIONS
     UNI prod_delivered
   OUTPUT_INTERACTIONS
     UNI BLOCKED REFERENCE ask_list
     UNI REFERENCE order_prod
     UNI BLOCKED REFERENCE status_prod
```

In order to finish the example, we must declare the topology that will be as follows:

```
ARCHI_ELEM_INSTANCES
        Customer_1 : Customer_Type();
        IS_1 : Internet_Site_Type();
        Prov_A : Provider_Type();
        Prov_B : Provider_Type();
        Carrier_1 : Carrier_Type()

ARCHI_INTERACTIONS
        Customer_1.ask_list; Customer_1.order_prod;
        Customer_1.status_prod; Customer_1.prod_delivered;
        IS_1.send_list; IS_1.receive_order; IS_1.status_prod_sent;
        IS_1.request_prod; IS_1.pick_prod;
        Prov_A.Available_Prod; Prov_B.Available_Prod;
        Carrier_1.pick_prod; Carrier_1.prod_delivered;

ARCHI_ATTACHMENTS
        FROM Customer_1.ask_list TO IS_1.send_list;
        FROM Customer_1.order_product TO IS_1.receive_order;
        FROM Customer_1.status_prod TO IS_1.status_prod_sent;
        FROM IS_1.request_prod TO Prov_A.Available_Prod;
        FROM IS_1.request_prod TO Prov_B.Available_Prod;
        FROM IS_1.pick_prod TO Carrier_1.pick_prod;
        FROM Carrier_1.product_delivered TO Customer_1.prod_delivered
```

This example allows different customers to ask for the product list at the same time and the Internet Site accepts orders that will process, whereas the customer can ask for the product status. The customer will be blocked waiting for the list and status, but does not wait for the Internet Site processes the order.

6. Conclusions and future work

In this work, we have enhance the expressive power of the Process Algebra Description Language PADL by extending it with an asynchronous communication, which allows us to describe the interactions specified in the Service Oriented Architectures with SCA. To accomplish it, we have declared interfaces and references, which correspond with the same elements in the SCA component diagrams. Furthermore, in the internal component behavior, we have used an internal queue in each component in order to store the output reference actions. This internal queue allows to capture an asynchronous communication mechanism. Finally, to capture whether a component can continue its activity or not, we have used a blocked attribute in the use of references.

The future work will be focus on the inclusion of the new communication mechanism inside the previous work about the different analysis and studies that it is possible to perform by using PADL, such as conformance, performance, capturing timed and stochastic behaviors, and so on.

References

[1]   SCA Consortium (2005). Building systems using a service oriented architecture. In *Whitepaper available fro www-128.ibm.com/developerworks/library/specification/ws-sca/*.

[2]   Alessandro Aldini and Marco Bernardo. On the usability of process algebra: An architectural view. *Theor. Comput. Sci.*, 335(2-3):281–329, 2005.

[3]   Jos C. M. Baeten and Jan A. Bergstra. Asynchronous communication in real space process algebra. In *FTRTFT*, pages 473–492, 1992.

[4]   Karim Baïna, Boualem Benatallah, Fabio Casati, and Farouk Toumani. Model-driven web service development. In *CAiSE*, pages 290–306, 2004.

[5]   Luciano Baresi, Reiko Heckel, Sebastian Thöne, and Dániel Varró. Modeling and validation of service-oriented architectures: application vs. style. In *ESEC / SIGSOFT FSE*, pages 68–77, 2003.

[6]   Jan A. Bergstra, Jan Willem Klop, and J. V. Tucker. Process algebra with asynchronous communication mechanisms. In *Seminar on Concurrency*, pages 76–95, 1984.

[7]   Marco Bernardo and Edoardo Bontà. Generating well-synchronized multithreaded programs from software architecture descriptions. In *WICSA*, pages 167–176, 2004.

[8]   Marco Bernardo and Francesco Franzè. Exogenous and endogenous extensions of architectural types. In *COORDINATION*, pages 40–55, 2002.

[9]   Marco Bernardo and Paola Inverardi, editors. *Formal Methods for Software Architectures, Third International School on Formal Methods for the Design of Computer, Communication and Software Systems: Software Architectures, SFM 2003, Bertinoro, Italy, September 22-27, 2003, Advanced Lectures*, volume 2804 of *Lecture Notes in Computer Science*. Springer, 2003.

[10] Gregorio Díaz, María-Emilia Cambronero, M. Llanos Tobarra, Valentin Valero, and Fernando Cuartero. Analysis and verification of time requirements applied to the web services composition. In *WS-FM*, pages 178–192, 2006.

[11] Gregorio Díaz, Juan José Pardo, María-Emilia Cambronero, Valentin Valero, and Fernando Cuartero. Automatic translation of ws-cdl choreographies to timed automata. In *EPEW/WS-FM*, volume 3670 of *Lecture Notes in Computer Science*, pages 230–242. Springer, 2005.

[12] José Luiz Fiadeiro, Antónia Lopes, and Laura Bocchi. A formal approach to service component architecture. In *WS-FM*, pages 193–213, 2006.

[13] M. E. Cambronero V. Valero G. Diaz, J. J. Pardo and F. Cuartero. Verification of web services with timed autoamata. In *In proceedings of First International Workshop on Automated Specification and Verification of Web Sites*.

[14] Quan Z. Sheng and Boualem Benatallah. Contextuml: A uml-based modeling language for model-driven development of context-aware web services. In *ICMB*, pages 206–212, 2005.

[15] M. Llanos Tobarra, Diego Cazorla, Fernando Cuartero, and Gregorio Díaz. Application of formal methods to the analysis of web services security. In *EPEW/WS-FM*, pages 215–229, 2005.

Techniques and Applications for Mobile Commerce
C. Branki et al. (Eds.)
IOS Press, 2008

111

Applying Usability Patterns in e-Commerce Applications

Francisco Montero, Víctor López-Jaquero

and José Pascual Molina

LoUISE Research Group, I3A

Campus Universitario s/n, 02071, Albacete, Spain

{fmontero, victor, jpmolina}@dsi.uclm.es

Abstract: The exigencies and the particular characteristics of website development are a great challenge for designers and developers. There are many differences between typical software application development and website development. In website development, the presentation component; visual and graphical, plays an important role, which is not that important for not web applications. This component can be documented by using patterns, and particularly usability patterns. Traditionally, guidelines have been used to deal with it. These patterns should be written so that they can be used by users, designers and developers. Thus, users will be able to make proposals, user interface designers will be able to imagine and developers will be able to build the application.

Keywords: usability patterns, user interfaces

1 Introduction

The growth of Internet is evident. Nowadays, almost everybody is concerned about new economy, new business, information society, information technology, the Internet and e-commerce, e-business, and so on. Seminars, forums, conferences and debates are being constantly organized, both on public and private level, to discuss the risks and opportunities of this challenge. Currently, websites development is different to traditional software applications. The differences that makes differ these two development processes are related with contents, flexibility, adaptability and plasticity (Montero et al, 2003) requirements.

Web is changing, at the beginning, it was basically textual and interaction possibilities were quite limited. However, at this moment, Web has become mostly graphical, and although information to be shown could be the same, now we want to provide additional web services and task support.

Like in traditional software application development process, software engineering discipline can provide many solutions; modeling, specification or programming languages, methodologies, software architectures, guidelines and patterns, are some of them. Patterns, which is the focus of this work, were not first introduced in computer sciences, they were inspired by architectural patterns introduced by (Alexander et al., 1997), an architect. His patterns gathered experience about city layouts, buildings and ornamental details. These patterns are organized into several levels and they suggest requirements for living our lives with the so called *quality without name*.

In website development we have a similar requirement, we need to provide quality, but, in our case, this quality is an usability and accessibility-centered one. In this context, usability patterns can be used to gather experience in web application development. We are aimed to provide usable environments with ornamental elements appropriate to achieve user's commodity when he is visiting our website.

This paper is organized as follows: first, we shall speak about related work on pattern topic, on its use and how they can be applied to web development. Then, the challenges for using patterns, their problems and their advantages are introduced. And finally, an e-shop study case will be presented to illustrate our ideas.

2   Related Work

Pattern concept was introduced quite late in computer science. Curiously, this term was first used in computer science for gathering experience in user interfaces development using Smalltalk programming language. Later, the book *Design Patterns* (Gamma et al, 1995) provided experience in object-oriented development. This book and workshops, international conferences and other different events have given an important dimension to this topic.

Nowadays, we face great challenges in human-computer interaction. We have new devices, new interaction mechanisms and many languages and methodologies to develop applications. But these elements are not enough, the final user must be considered. Without the user, the final developed application will not be successful, and probably our application will be neither used nor visited.

Under a user-centered design philosophy, user plays a really meaningful role. The final user decides when the application is ready. Satisfaction is an important element of usability, and it is a subjective factor that depends on the user. We need to know user's characteristics, his tasks and goals when we want to develop any software application. If we know this information, the possibilities to create a successful software tool will be greatly increased. Our main objective as designers or developers is to provide solutions to problems under a context of use, and a pattern is basically that. A pattern is a tupla of three elements: a problem, a context and a solution. Many patterns have been proposed for many different computer science fields. For example in Graphical User-Interface (GUI) development, (Tidwell, 1999), (Welie, 2003) or (Borchers, 2001) are meaningful references, and in web development (Percel et al., 1999), (Tidwell, 2002), (Welie, 2003), (Van Duyne et al., 2002), (Rossi et al., 12), or (Montero et al., 2002b) (Montero et al, 2002c) can be cited.

Tidwell's collection (Tidwell, 1999) is organized according the following criteria: Whole UI, Page Layout, Forms and Input, Tables, Direct Manipulation and Miscellaneous. These patterns are intended to be read by people who have some knowledge of UI design concepts and terminology: dialogs, selection, comboboxes, navigation bars, whitespace, branding, and so on. Nevertheless, it does not identify some widely accepted techniques such as wizards. Welie's patterns (Welie, 2003) are organized according to the different sorts of applications.

Patterns have proved to be a useful tool for software development. However, they have some problems, mostly related with their structure and presentation. Patterns are introduced using natural language, so ambiguity and flexibility appear. Specifically with usability patterns, we find another problem, the way solution is specified. Code, using an object-oriented language like C++ or Java, can be associated with the solution proposed in a design pattern. But usability patterns have no language associated, maybe an XML-based declarative language could be used, but at this moment no collection is using such a language to specify the solution.

The use of usability patterns introduce yet another problem, we have no tool in order to make easier the collection, compilation and later use of patterns. However, we have some prototypes with this intention. We can make reference to Damask (Lin et al, 2003), that is a tool for early-stage design and prototyping of multi-device user interfaces. Damask is not a tool to create final UIs, so designers are allowed to modify the generated user interface design. The Concurrent Task Tree Environment (Paternò, 1999) is a tool realized by the Human Computer Interaction Group - CNUCE (Pisa). With this editor we can build a task model and generate an interactor-based architectural model. MOUDIL (Gaffar et al., 2003) is an integrated pattern environment. This environment is a service for UI designers and software engineers. Besides, it is a research forum to understand how patterns are really discovered, validated, used and perceived. MOUDIL has a pattern ontology editor, a pattern navigator and a pattern viewer available to make easier working with our patterns. Finally, UPADE (Usability Patterns-Assisted Design Environment (Seffah et al., 2002)) is a project, where patterns are documented using an XML-based notation.

3   A Study Case: e-shop Web site

This workshop proposed as a particular study case e-shop patterns. Under this topic several collections of patterns can be cited:

- (Welie, 2003): SHOPPING CART, LOGIN, REGISTERING, PRODUCT COMPARISON, PRODUCT COMFIGURATOR, PRODUCT ADVISOR, PREMIUM CONTENT LOCK, NEWSLETTER, PRINTER-FRIENDLY PAGE or CASE STUDY.

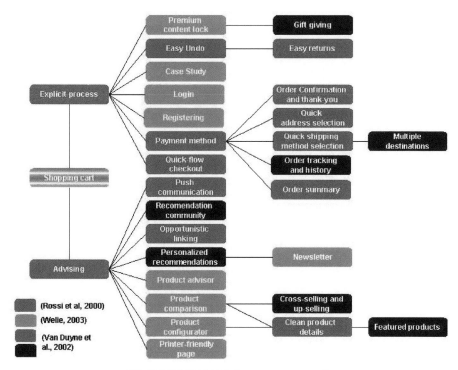

Figure 1: Relationships between e-commerce patterns

- (Rossi et al., 2000): where we can find several patterns like: OPPORTUNISTIC LINKING, ADVISING, EXPLICIT PROCESS, EASY UNDO or PUSH COMMUNICATION.
- (Van Duyne et al., 2002). We find two groups of patterns:
  - **Basic E-commerce**: QUICK-FLOW CHECKOUT, CLEAN PRODUCT DETAILS, SHOPPING CART, QUICK ADDRESS SELECTION, QUICK SHIPPING METHOD SELECTION, PAYMENT METHOD, ORDER SUMMARY, ORDER CONFIRMATION AND THANK-YOU, EASY RETURNS.
  - **Advanced E-commerce**: FEATURED PRODUCTS, CROSS-SELLING AND UP-SELLING, PERSONALIZED RECOMMENDATIONS, RECOMMENDATION COMMUNITY, MULTIPLE DESTINATIONS, GIFT GIVING and ORDER TRACKING AND HISTORY.

Before these patterns are gathered and presented, in Figure 1 we can see the relationships between these patterns, that we have found. A hierarchical structure is presented to organize them, where more general patterns are located first in the structure. From these patterns, and following the relationships identified, the solution is enriched. Inside a concrete collection there are more relationships, but this ones are not displayed in Figure 1 for the sake of legibility. These relationships can be found in the associated references.

All patterns were introduced using natural language. The authors did not use any programming language, declarative or procedural.

Examples of using these patterns are provided when each pattern is introduced.

In these proposals there are many curiosities, for example, all the pattern collection authors' are writing e-commerce patterns but only a pattern: SHOPPING CART pattern, is appearing in all collections. Then, all proposed patterns are different and complementary. It is shown in the Figure 1. In an activity like e-commerce, users need to have the easy things, he needs an EXPLICIT PROCESS, and this is achieved following an STEP BY STEP process (Tidwell, 1998a) or WIZARD one (Welie, 2000). This process consist of several steps, REGISTERING / LOGIN, SHOPPING CART, QUICK-FLOW CHECKOUT and a PAYMENT METHOD. In these activities an EASY UNDO should be provided. EASY UNDO and EASY RETURNS are very similar patterns, we are considering that EASY UNDO is more general that EASY RETURNS in Figure 1. We think that this last pattern only refers to the navigational situation, but the former involves edition or acceptation tasks that user want to avoid.

Other task that we have to provide when we are designing or developing an e-shop web site should be ADVISING. This task is a typical one for a salesman, they provide information about several products, and then clients have to choose. PRODUCT ADVISOR, PRODUCT COMPARISON, PRODUCT CONFIGURATOR or PERSONALIZED RECOMMENDATIONS are related with advising tasks.

Then we can ask if these collections or pattern languages are complete and fully functional. We have three collections and between theirs patterns we can establish relationships.

Other question could be: How should we use this pattern collection? We should follow these steps:

1. Read the resumed list of patterns.

2. Scan down the list, and find the pattern, which best describes the overall scope of the project or the problem that you want to solve.

3. Read the starting pattern. Tick all of the low order patterns and ignore all the high order patterns.

4. Turn to each pattern and now tick only relevant low order patterns.

5. Keep going like this, until you have ticked all the patterns you want for your project.

6. Adjust the sequence by adding your own material where you haven't found a corresponding pattern.

7. Change any patterns where you have a personal version, which is more relevant.

Obviously, our problem is to develop an e-shop web site. This web should have usability characteristics; natural mapping, consistency, accessibility, feedback, explicit user control, error management, guidance, adaptability or minimize cognitive load. Many of these patterns are related with these features of usability. We can see relationships between usability properties and e-shop patterns in the following table.

Usability Property	e-shop Patterns
Natural Mapping	SHOPPING CART, EXPLICIT PROCESS,
Consistency	EASY UNDO, EASY RETURN, PRINTER-FRIENDLY PAGE, PRODUCT ADVISOR,
Accessibility	*WAI guidelines, Section 508*, PERSONALIZED RECOMMENDATIONS, NEWSLETTER, PRINTER-FRIENDLY PAGE,
Feedback	PREMIUM CONTENT LOCK, GIFT GIVING, OPPORTUNISTIC LINKING,
Explicit user control	EASY UNDO, EASY RETURN, MULTIPLE DESTINATIONS, ORDER TRACKING AND HISTORY, ORDER SUMMARY, ORDER CONFIRMATION AND THANK-YOU, PUSH COMMUNICATION,
Error Management	CASE STUDY, EXPLICIT PROCESS, ADVISING,
Guidance	CASE STUDY, PAYMENT METHOD, QUICK ADDRESS SELECTION, QUICK SHIPPING SELECTION, PRODUCT ADVISOR, PRODUCT COMPARISON, PRODUCT CONFIGURATOR, ADVISING, EXPLICIT PROCESS,
Adaptability	LOGIN, REGISTERING, PERSONALIZED RECOMMENDATIONS, PRINTER-FRIENDLY PAGE,
Minimize cognitive load	SHOPPING CART, EXPLICIT PROCESS, ADVISING

Reference	Name	Problem	Solution
(Welie, 2003)	Shopping cart	Users want to buy a product	Introduce a shopping cart where users can put their products in before they actually purchase them.
	Login	The users need to identify themselves so that stored data about/of them can be used in the process they are in	When needed, ask the users to login using a combination of an email-address and a password
	Registering	The users repeatedly need to (re)enter a large amount of personal data	Offer users to possibility to store their personal information for later use
	Product comparison	The users need to compare similar products	Show a matrix of products and features
	Product configurator	Users want to configure the product they may intend to buy	Allow users to configure a product using a direct and visual version of the configured product
	Product advisor	Users want advice on selecting the best product for them among a set of products	Advise users on product based on constraints, preferences and needs users have
	Premium content lock	Users need to know which content is for free and which is not	Show previews of premium content and mark it visually
	Newsletter	Users want to be regularity informed or updated.	Send users a newsletter regularly
	Printer-friendly page	User may need to print content of the page they are viewing	Place a link to a print-ready version of the page the users are viewing.
	Case study	Users need to know how a certain real-life problem was solved in order to decide whether the problem-solvers could do the same for them	Describe a case by describing the problem, the solution and the value of that solution
(Rossi et al, 2000)	Opportunistic linking	Keep the user interested in the site. Seduce him to navigate in the site even when he has already found what he was looking for	Improve the linking topology by suggesting new products to explore from a giver one
	Advising	Help the user find a product in the store. Assist him according to his wishes	Build specific functionality for advising about products
	Explicit process	Help the user understand the buying process when it is not atomic	Give the user a perceivable feedback about the process by keeping him up to date about which steps he has already accomplished
	Easy Undo	Provide safe undoing capabilities in a complex process	Provide the user with Undo facilities avoiding him to use navigation facilities for this purpose
	Push Communication	Simplify the searching process for customer-selected areas or products	Combine the usual Web pull model with a push-based communication

(Van Duyne et al. , 2002)	**Quick-flow checkout**	An e-commerce shopping experience will not be enjoyable, or worse, a purchase might not be completed, if the checkout process is cumbersome, confusing, or error prone	Follow a simple four step approach so that customers can complete their orders: 1. In a secure area of the site, allow customers to check out without storing their information, or let them create or use a customer identifier so that they do not need to reenter information. Set expectations by giving an overview of the process and providing answers to common questions. 2. Gather shipping and handling information and shipping methods so that you can tabulate the total cost of the order, including taxes, at the next step. 3. Show the total cost of the order along with the order summary so that customers can verify that the information is correct. 4. Confirm that funds for the order are currently available, and give the customer a final opportunity to confirm the order. When the order is complete, provide a printable receipt and invite the customer to return
	Clean product details	When shopping, customers want to see product details to help inform their buying decisions. They must also trust a seller before deciding to make a purchase. Many sites do not provide enough in-depth information about their products, or they project an untrustworthy image	Provide in-depth information in a grid layout. Keep important items that every customer will needed above the fold, such as general navigation, product thumbnails, need-based descriptions, prices, an options pick list or a link to a configuration page, product ratings and delivery time frame, the Add to Cart action button, and links to more detailed information, even if the information is farther down on the page. Put secondary items, such as a full product description reviews, related products, and a product comparator if possible, below the fold
	Shopping cart	Customers want to collect and purchase several items in one transaction. Online shopping carts can provide much more than their offline namesakes, such as making it easy to change the quantity of an item in the cart. However making shopping carts simple and useful requires restraint	Give customers easy access to the shopping cart from every page of your site
	Quick address selection	Entering addresses need not be cumbersome, especially if customers are ordering from a site for a second time	At the top of the page, provide a link to the area where a new address can be entered
	Quick shipping method selection	Customers resent hidden shipping and handling charges, and they want to pick the best shipping option for their situation	Provide a pick list or radio buttons for selecting shipping options. Give a high level description of the delivery time frames and the associated costs. Calculate the shipping costs on the basis of size and weight of the products being shipped. Provide links to more in-depth information about shipping issues, including international requirements and insurance

Pattern	Problem	Solution
Payment method	When it comes to paying for an order, people demand security and simplicity	Dispel any concerns that customers might have about security by addressing them up front with a link to your security or privacy policy. A pick list or radio buttons help customers select the billing options. Create a new credit card form that is quick and easy to read: with labels right-aligned and input fields, left aligned along the same vertical grid line, using a minimum of fields, minimal instructions, and a Use this card action button. If storing multiple billing addresses, above the new address form include a list of all previously stored addresses with a Use this address action button next to each one
Order summary	When finalizing orders, customers want to see everything related to what they're ordering; the specific products, all the charges, and the billing methods, as well as where, how, and approximately when packages will be delivered. If any one of these elements is missing from an order summary, customers might abandon their purchases	First, let the customer know that the order still has not been placed, and provide high-visibility action buttons for completing the order. Second, show the items being purchased and all the information that the customer entered: address, payment method, and shipping selections. Provide action buttons to edit these items in case they are incorrect. Third, calculate and present the total costs, including shipping and taxes.
Order confirmation and Thank-you	After they complete their orders, if customers do not get confirmation or a receipt indicating that the order has gone through, they will be unsure of their order status and have to work to find confirmation evidence	Provide a thank-you on a printable page that displays the order number, the order date, and all the order information, including items purchased, quantities, prices, shipping prices, tax, total and shipping and billing information. Give customers an action button to continue shopping and cross-sell them on other products they might be interested in purchasing
Easy returns	When items that are accidentally ordered, damaged during delivery, or just not wanted can be returned quickly and easily, customers are more likely to order. But making returns easy is not simple	Put the return policy on all product and checkout pages, including a link to a return process. If customers throw away a return label, give them the ability to print another one, and use the label to track returns as they arrive
Featured products	Customers find value when sites identify specific products as recommended or featured. Otherwise product lists can appear bland and tedious	To give people a better sense of what's on your site, build category pages that highlight special featured products and editorialize in the product recommendations. Provide different kinds of recommendations, choosing different categories, such as top sellers, editor's choice, and so on. Let visitors explore by highlighting as many areas of interest as possible
Cross-selling and up-selling	When choosing a product in stores, people appreciate hearing about related products that are complementary to or better than the products they have chosen. Doing the same thing online requires prudence and planning	In a subtle and careful way, cross-sell and up-sell related products by indicating the benefit they provide to your customers. Customers will be seduced and will not need to go far to make a purchase if you make it quick and easy to add a related product to a shopping cart without leaving the context of the current page. Make a visual distinction between these promotions and the order content on the page. Sell the related products again later in the checkout process, in case customers missed them the first time

Personalized recommendations	Personalized recommendations can provide customers with a better sense of what's useful and what isn't. But if they require too much effort on the customer's part, or if they are based on what customers perceive as scant evidence, they will fail	Avoid using pure inference data to make product recommendations because it will not necessarily reflect real customer choices. Start by offering product and category recommendations based on previous purchases by other customers. Then add recommendations based on past purchases, ratings, and interviews completed by the customer. Integrate this data into your site on product pages, category pages, and personalized recommendation pages. Provide feedback about why a recommendation was made. Provide multiple recommendations, including those that customers have seen before, to help people gauge the quality of the recommendations. Address privacy concerns and how the personalization data will be used
Recommendation Community	Recommendations from other customers are valuable, but the process of making sure the community system is not abused is time-consuming and littered with obstacles	Provide a two-step process to write a review: (1) Have customers enter review title and text of the review, and any numerical rating. The text must follow the guidelines of the site. (2) Let customers see the recommendation as it will appear in the site, and allow them to edit it. Filter the title and text for profanity and HTML that might link to another site. Staff an editor to review customer-written recommendations and remove them if they are offensive or libellous. Once the review has been posted, provide a mechanism for other customers to rate the review, giving it a meta-rating. Finally, offer an incentive for customers to write the first review, to get people to use the community features
Multiple destinations	Customers sometimes want to ship to multiple addresses once they have chosen their items to purchase. Making this process simple requires changes throughout the checkout process	Provide a Send to multiple addresses action button at the top of the quick address selection page. If the customer clicks it, show a new page with an Add new address action button, a list of all the products in the order, and a pick list next to each product. The pick list provides all the destination options. If there are no existing addresses, as in the case of first-time customers, immediately go to a new-address page
Gift giving	When ordering gifts online, customers want to write notes to the recipients and to be assured that the price sill not be disclosed. If a site does not offer these conveniences, customers will be less likely to order gifts	Give customers clear indications early in the shopping process that the site has gift-giving options, so that they can shop for that reason. On the checkout page, provide a button that takes customers to a form where they can enter notes and select gift-wrapping options. And on this form, provide a button that takes customers back to the order summary page, where they can review their whole order, including gift options. Then they're done, the order confirmation page will list the entire order, including gifts, in case customers want to the information for their records
Order tracking and history	Then customers place online orders, the details about order status and shipping become important. If this information is not easily available online, the cost of processing customer inquires increases dramatically	Require customers to sign in to review their orders and modify them. Give them access to an order history that categorizes orders as pending, shipped or completed. Display the selected orders chronologically, listing the order number, as well as the contents of the order if the list is not too long. For pending orders, indicate each item's availability, and allow modification of everything from shipping and billing to products and options. For orders you have already shipped, allow order tracking by interfacing with the shipper's database and displaying the shipment way-station history

4   Challenges and Advantages of Available Patterns

Several problems and advantages derived from using patterns can be identified in the available literature. We are considering that usability patterns are generally presented as the ideal medium for gathering and disseminating user experiences and UI design practices.

The narrative format used to document patterns makes them similar to design guidelines (Seffah et al., 2002). However, one question arises: have the patterns been elaborated for users, graphical designers or developers?. If the final user needs to be involved in the design and development process, natural language will be needed, so that the user can identify his problems in an easier way. Furthermore, our patterns address usability and interaction issues. If we use a formal notation to specify the solution, probably we will loose generality, and the graphical design can be too limited, because, from our point of view, design patterns are oriented to internal characteristics as modularity or reuse, but usability patterns try to get external facilities related with satisfaction and ease of use. Therefore, providing a concrete solution in a particular language for each usability pattern is not clearly a good idea.

In addition, which language is the best one?, there are many platforms, many devices and many languages and, the modeling languages such as UML have limited capabilities when describing user interfaces.

The final success of a pattern collection depends on different aspects, for instance, Alexander's patterns have a good structure, and relationships between patterns is rigorous (Montero et al., 2002a), so when a architectural problem is identified we know which patterns can provide a solution. In other collections, for example GoF's patterns (Gamma et al., 1995), we have a more reduced number of patterns, and the problems are programming ones, more objective that usability or interaction problems. It is well-known that usability itself is already a subjective quality.

Providing usability pattern-oriented tools is difficult, we have not a clear language or notation, patterns are disseminated and the relationships between them are not clearly defined. Perhaps, at this moment, the pattern collections introduced can be used as a checklist where designers can verify prototypes or applications, as a heuristic usability evaluation method.

5   Conclusions

Designing interactive systems is difficult and designers need effective tools that are usable themselves. Guidelines have since long been used to capture design knowledge and to help designers in designing user interfaces. Patterns can be more powerful than guidelines as a tool for designers, however, there are a lot of suggestions, drawbacks and possibilities that need further work. In this paper we have done an overview on usability patterns, the tools that support them, the problems that appear when applying those patterns and the challenges we will have to face in a near future to include usability patterns in daily software development.

Acknowledgements

This work is supported in part by the Spanish PBC-03-003 grant.

References

Alexander, C., Ishikawa, S., Silverstein, M., Jacobson, M., Fiksadhl-King, I., and Angel, S.. A Pattern Language: Towns, Buildings, Construction. New York: Oxford University Press, 1977.

Borchers, J.. A Pattern Approach to Interaction Design. John Wiley & Sons. 2001.

Gaffar, A., Sinnig, H., Javahery, H., Seffah A.. MOUDIL: A Comprehensive Framework for Disseminating and Sharing HCI Patterns. Whorkshop at CHI 2003, Fort Lauderdale, Florida, USA. Perspectives on HCI patterns: concepts and tools. 2003.

Gamma, E., Helm, R., Johnson, R. and Vlissides, J. Design Patterns: Elements of Reusable Object-Oriented Software. Addison-Wesley, 1995.

Lin, J., Landay, J.. Damask: A Tool for Early-Stage Design and Prototyping of Cross-Device User Interfaces. Whorkshop at CHI 2003, Fort Lauderdale, Florida, USA. Perspectives on HCI patterns: concepts and tools. 2003.

Montero, F., López-Jaquero, V., Molina, J.P., González, P.. Approach to develop User Interfaces with Plasticity. Design, Specification and Verification of Interactive Systems. DSV-IS03. Madeira. Portugal. LNCS to appear. 2003.

Montero, F., González, P., Lozano, M.. Patrones de interacción. Taxonomía y otros problema. Congreso Internacional de Interacción. Leganés. Madrid. España. 2002a

Montero, F., Lozano, M., González, P., Ramos, I.. Design Websites by Using Patterns. Second Latin American conference on Pattern Languages of Programming. SugarLoafPLoP02. Itaipava. Rio de Janeiro. Brasil. ISBN: 85-87837-07-9. pp. 209 – 224. 2002b.

Montero, F., Lozano, M., González, P., Ramos, I.. A First Approach to Design Websites by Using Patterns. First Nordic Conference on Pattern Languages of Programs. VikingPLoP02. Hojstrupgard Slot. Dinamarca. ISBN: 87-7849-769-8.pp. 137 – 158. 2002c

Paternò, F.. Model-based Design and Evaluation of Interactive Applications. Springer Verlag, 1999.

Perzel, K., Kane, D.. Usability Patterns for Applications on the World Wide Web. PloP'99. http://jerry.cs.uiuc.edu/~plop/plop99/proceedings/Kane/perzel_kane.pdf. 1999.

Rossi, G., Lyardet, F., Schwabe, D.. Patterns for e commerce applications. Proceedings EuroPLoP'2000. whttp://www.inf.puc-rio.br/~schwabe/papers/Europlop00.pdf. 2000

Seffah, A., Javhery, H. On the Usability of Usability Patterns. Workshop entitled Patterns in Practice, CHI 2002. Minneapolis, 2002.

Tidwell, J. (a) Common Ground: A pattern language for HCI design. http://www.mit.edu/~jtidwell/interaction_patterns.html. Updated 1999. (b) UI Patterns and Techniques. http://time-tripper.com/uipatterns/. Updated 2002.

Van Duyne, D. K., Landay, J. A., Hong, J.I.. The Design of Sites. Patterns, principles, and processes for crafting a customer-centered web experience.2002

Welie, M. Interaction Design Patterns. http://www.welie.com/patterns/. Updated 2003.

Techniques and Applications for Mobile Commerce
C. Branki et al. (Eds.)
IOS Press, 2008

Adapting educational web service to mobile devices

Slim Khélifi[a], Mona Laroussi[a], Xavier Le Pallec[b]

[a]*INSAT Centre Urbain Tunis Nord BP 676 CEDEX 1080 Tunis TUNISIA*

[b]*Université des Sciences et Technologies de Lille 59655 Villeneuve d'Ascq cedex – France*

Abstract:

The users became more and more mobile. By mobility, we mean free communication through various and different devices. This new way of communication generates a new fashion of learning. We add the notion of on any devices to the traditional concept of E-learning which is being free to learn any time and on any device. To carry out courses in E-Learning environment, we use LMS (Learning management Systems). LMS are now numbrous and more and more available. Our research team develops a new LMS based on the Use of Web Services entitled SOLEIL. This paper deals with the adaptation of educational Web Services to mobile devices.

KeyWords: Mobility, E-learning, Web services, M-Services.

Introduction

Mobile Computing encompasses any technology that enables people to access information and supports them in daily workflows independent of location [1]. Actually, it is remarkable that many of the Mobile Computing research results and breakthroughs come from the Human-Computer Interaction (HCI) field [2]. This phenomenal growth of Mobile Computing [3] has an impact in the E-learning field. That's why complete independence of both location and time is often emphasized as the main advantage of E-Learning [4].

The last few years has seen a significant increase of the diversity of mobile devices used to access the Internet by learners. However, in the traditional E-Learning the Personal Computer (PC) is still a requirement, yetan absolute independence in location is not provided, because a real independency in time and location means learning wherever and whenever a person wants to have access to learning material. Mobile learning (M-Learning) is the next generation of E-Learning. It's a field which combines mobile computing and e-learning [5].

This rush in the field of wireless and mobile technologies introduces certainly new dimensions of adaptation [6] especially for Learning Management Systems (LMS). The goals of the different LMS can differ and so the functionalities offered by them[5]: the educational needs and goals of an industrial company are different from those of a university institution. These functionalities can be grouped in four categories: resources (data), specific e-learning services, common services and presentation.

The new generation of Learning management Systems (LMS) are based on the Web Services.

So, the relevant questions which need to be answered are :

How can we adapt LMS based on Web Services to mobility?

And equally how can we adapt Web Services to Mobile Devices?

In this paper we will present a framework of adaptation of an LMS based on the Web Services and this framework assembles different adaptation dimensions (user's model, user's context, devices and connectivity) [6] and the functionalities offered by LMS [5] as Web services and the functionalities offered by the adapted LMS as M-Services. Then, we propose an approach of adaptation of Web Services. This framework and this approach will be used in the adaptation of a LMS based on Web Services « SOLEIL » to mobility.

The paper is arranged as follows: Section 2 deals with the Use of web service in E-learning, Section 3 presents Mobile Web Services (M-Services) and their Use of M-Services (Section 4), Section 5 our Objective, Section is dedicated to the proposed framework and our proposition (Section 6), followed by the realization (Section 7), conclusions (Section 8) finally references and netographie.

1. Use of web service in E-learning

An e-learning system may store the personal data of a learner in a database while other e-learning system will store some information about the cognitive style of the same learner. Using Web Services allow us to make a search for this federated data (personal data + cognitive style) in each of the participant system in the environment[7]. A third participant may use this information to improve his learner model. To make this exchange possible, an interchange standard must be created to identify data through the different participant, a learning environment, so that all federation participants can "understand" in the same way the fragments of the stored information. In this work the information in the learner model is composed of two parts: information supplied by the learner and information collected through the learner's behavior using the e-learning system.

The solution resides in an efficient security mechanism that allows safe and secured data distribution and communication. Web Services allow implanting various security related services, such as authentication, access policies and cryptography, which can be used isolated or collectively. The users accessing the service must be identified in order to establish roles, permissions or access, therefore, restrict the access to data and services offered.

1.1 What are the Web Services?

Web services are Internet-based [8], distributed modular applications that provide standard interfaces and communication protocols aiming at efficient and effective service integration. These services start to show their usefulness in a wide variety of domains.

Typical Web service applications include business-to-business integration, business process integration and management, e-sourcing and content distribution. Web service interfaces and bindings are defined, described and discovered by XML artifacts. There target is to support direct XML message-based interactions with other services and applications via Internet-based protocols like SOAP [9]. Standards for service lookup and discovery such as the Universal Description Discovery and Integration (UDDI) [10] specification are designed to function in a fashion similar to white pages or yellow pages, where businesses and services can be looked up by name and/or by standard service taxonomy. UDDI provides a first framework for the description of basic business and service information and offers a simple and extensible mechanism to provide detailed service access information on the basis of the Web Services Description Language (WSDL) [11].

1.2 Why Web Services?

Web services hold out a lot of promise [12]. They leverage existing investments in Web infrastructure and create a framework that can be used in any application domain, including e-commerce, enterprise resource planning, and e-learning. This should make it easier for applications from one domain to use services from another domain. For instance, an e-learning system might use an external authentication service to offer a single log in, or it might access learner management services that encompass a human resources or student information system.

In terms of architecture, Web services also offer some advantages that could make computing enterprise more reliable and more effective. Creating a Web service requires a good model of business processes. That needs to if be self-contained, so that if can we reduce the problems arising from technical cross-dependencies. Using Web protocols to connect enterprise applications should also improve reliability and eliminate problems caused by the fact of having multiple protocols, especially proprietary ones.

Although the solutions, the independence of platform and interoperation already exist, the main advantage of the Web Services technology is the use of Web protocols to exchange messages instead of the proprietary standards, such as RMI[7]. The Web Services technology was used at this level as a consequence of the standardized functionalities it offers. Besides, the SOAP protocol may operate over HTTPS, yet the learner's information cannot be observed without advanced hacking techniques providing a good level of data privacy.

2. Mobile Web Services (M-Services)

With the quick growth of mobile technologies, we are beginning to see a variety of mobile applications using mobile web services (m-services).

The concept of *m-service* extends the web services to the wireless environment [13]. It refers to requesting and running web services on wireless devices. M-services should offer new opportunities to users of wireless devices]. An application component is considered as an M-service if it is: 1) transportable through wireless networks; 2) flexible in term of composition with other M- services; 3) adaptable according to the computing features of mobile devices; 4) runnable on mobile devices.

There are a number of emerging technologies and protocol enhancements designed to extend online services to users of mobile devices. Emerging protocols such as WAP (Wireless Application Protocol) gives us the oppurtunity to design miniature websites specifically for mobile phones with small display screens and limited network bandwidth. The Wireless Application Protocol (WAP) together with Wireless Markup Language (WML) constitute an open architecture for mobile Web services. They make it possible to provide markup-language based on services for different mobile devices equipped with WAP browsers [14].These services need to be integrated as web services in order to provide interoperability [15].The wireless application environment (WAE) allows interaction between wireless protocols (e.g., WAP and iMode), web applications, and wireless devices equipped with browsers capable of rendering web pages encoded in wireless markup languages such as WML and cHTML.

3. Use of M-Services

There are a variety of M-services applications [15]. A number of benefits can be gained from m-services, including getting access to real-time information anytime and anywhere; providing faster responses to customer queries and needs, thus increasing customer satisfaction and reducing the cost; triggering business events and initiating business transactions from mobile devices to shorten the cycle time of core business processes; and enabling mobile access to obtain up-to-date intranet and extranet content and prevent data inconsistency.

These are mainly applications [16] :

The first class of applications we consider, is derived by looking at physical things people carry in their daily lives and see if they can be replaced with M-Services. So, credit cards, debit cards, keys, identification cards, frequent flier numbers, etc., can be provisioned as Web Services on a mobile device carried by the user.

Another class of M-Services could be related to services that can be provided by the mobile device that the user is carrying. Examples could include providing location, time, data from wearable sensors, context information around the user, dictionary or translation services, transcoding content, renting information including songs, etc.

Yet another class of services includes providing data about the person carrying the mobile device. One example
is the skills possessed by the owner of the mobile device.

The above classes of services can be combined and aggregated among themselves, and with services from the infrastructure to build more complex and useful services.

On the Learning Field, there is a big potential in the Mobile Web Services there are some disadvantages and problems that should be overcome [5]. In fact, One of them is the loss of network connectivity – the service is not available if there is no connection and the problem is how a system should recover from a failed web service stays open. It is also not clear how the services are discovered in peer-to-peer networks and how to manage the resources of the devices. These issues are the objective of research like Microsoft Marlin project (http://research.microsoft.com/research/sv/Marlin: Mobile Access to Resources Living In .NET).

4. Our Objective

Our objective is to present a practical solution to adapt Educational web Service to mobility, and make them accessible by all the users anywhere and anytime and especially for the mobile users.

The architecture will be based on a Web services system of standardization including/understanding WSDL for the description of the service, SOAP for transmission of messages between distant objects and UDDI for the localization of the service.

We will introduce the Soleil system "SOLEIL Service Oriented Loading Environment for Interactive Learn." SOLEIL [17] is a platform of mobile training collaborative based on the Web services. The Principal objectives of the platform is to manage interactions personalized between the system, composed of services, and the user who could use various devices and achieve various modes of learning (collaborative learning for example).

The Figure 1 shows the architecture of SOLEIL.

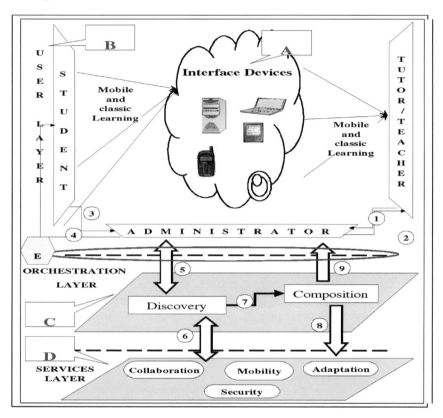

Figure 1: Architecture of SOLEIL

5. General framework for LMS adaptation to mobility

The architecture of our work (Figure 2) is based on an existing LMS platform. It is a prolongation with traditional LMS and provides services adapted for the mobile users; to be adaptable for various devices portable telephones, PDAs and others. ". There are many dimensions of adaptation in m-learning systems essentially: user model, user context, devices and connectivity.

The following figure shows the proposed framework. This framework assembles different adaptation dimensions (user's model, user's context, devices and connectivity) [6], the functionalities offered by LMS [5] as Web services and the functionalities offered by the adapted LMS as M-Services.

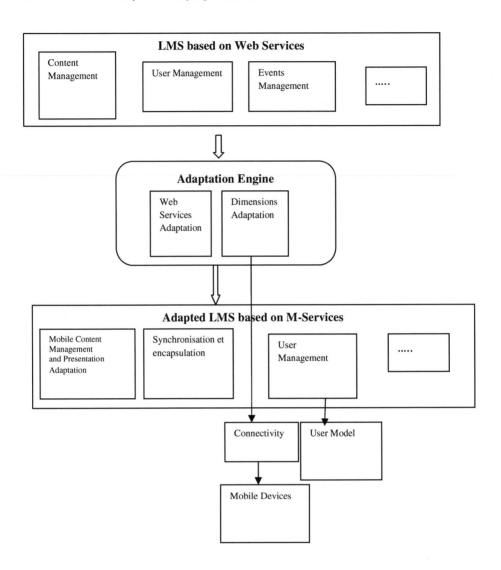

Figure 2: General Framework for LMS Adaptation to mobility

6. Our Proposition

After presenting a framework of adaptation

The first part is that the mobile device should reach the functionalities of LMS following a specific application or a navigator of Web/WAP (i.e; tthe system should be able automatically to detect the capacities of the devices and their limits (software and hardware)), known as "discovered context"

The second part should be to adapt the dimensions on the better manner for the used device. Indeed the adaptation will depend on the characteristics of mobility:

• Type of Connectivity: Several technologies can be used for an Internet accession in the mobiles like GPRS, UMTS, and WAP…

• Characteristics of the mobiles: operating system, resolution of the screen…

• The user model dimension : Location and general context are new features to be considered. Indeed, some environments take the user's location or some aspect of the general context into account, in order to present information or provide an interaction that's relevant to the learner's situation.

The third part is to select the Web Services proper for the device and adapt them to M-Services.

The solution is, as we see in Figure 3 to use a Web client as intermediary between the client side and Web service.

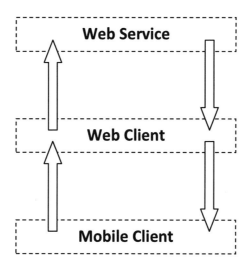

Figure 3 : Architecture of adaptation from Web Services to M-Services

The adaptation of the Web Services to the M-Services. The solution used is to embark an application client/server on three layers on the mobile device:

• Consumer of the service is a mobile client

• Server application where the Web Service will be deployed

• Server of data where the data will be stored.

The dimension chosen for our tests was the « mobile devices dimension »

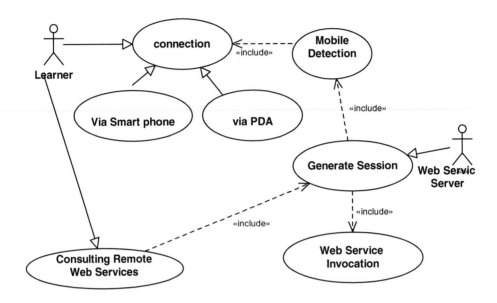

Figure 4 : User Case of adaptation based on the « mobile device dimension »

7. Realization

The choice of Java technology including architecture J2ME is essential. Indeed, it is a solution Open Source, supported by the majority and the most famous mobile devices such as. It will be supplemented by the use of the Services Web developed in Java too.
Java 2 Micro Edition (J2ME) [18] is Sun's version of Java aimed at machines with limited hardware resources such as PDAs cell phones, and other consumer electronic and embedded devices. J2ME is aimed at machines with as little as 128KB of RAM and with processors a lot less powerful than those used on typical desktop and server machines. J2ME actually consists of a set of *profiles*. Each profile is defined for a particular type of device cell phones, PDAs, microwave ovens, etc. -- and consists of a minimum set of class libraries required for the particular type of device and a specification of a Java virtual machine required to support the device. The virtual machine specified in any profile is not necessarily the same as the virtual machine used in Java 2 Standard Edition (J2SE) and Java 2 Enterprise Edition (J2EE).

The Problem encountered in the SOLEIL adaptation is the adaptation of the Web services the mobile devices. Indeed the Generation of Stub poses a problem of incompatible types of data between the Server side and the client side, and it was the case in our mobile application.

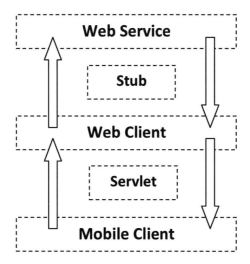

Figure 5: Communication web / mobile

The server side acts as a steering wheel to the Java mobile application, where all user interface items including menu items and how they are displayed are decided on the server side.

For the client side, we will use NetBeans which is an open project source, it currently one of the best IDE Java, they are development tools very rich and understanding, It integrates a Tomcat waiter and packs WTK, it supports new Struts technology and JSF. The goal is to provide a modular tool able to collaborate and communicate with the various waiters of applications, such as Tomcat, Sun AppServer, Jboss and Weblogic.

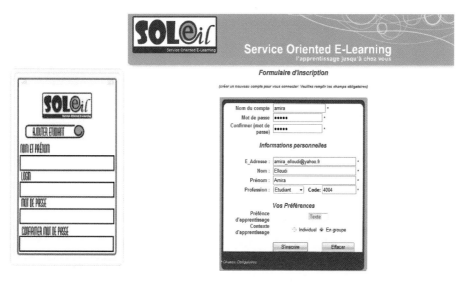

Figure 6. Snapshots from SOLEIL, View (a) show the authentification step in J2ME mobile client and View (b) show the authentification step on PC.

8. Conclusion and Future Work

In this paper, we presented M-Services and their use, We proposed, then a general framework to support adaptation from LMS based on Web Services in the context of mobility with the adaptation. framework assembles different adaptation dimensions (user's model, user's context, devices and connectivity) [Dri06] and the functionalities offered by LMS [Tri03] as Web services and the functionalities offered by the adapted LMS as M-Services. After, we propose and an approach of adaptation of Web Services. Future work includes more study more of the adaptation aspects. One of them is the loss of network connectivity in mobility when the service is not available if there is no connection and the question how a system should recover from a failed web service stays open.

References :

[1] A. Holzinger, ,(2004), "Usability Engineering und Prototyping, Beispiel Mobile Computing," OCG Journal (Forschung und Innovation), vol. 29, (in German) pp. 4-6.

[2] G. D. Abowd and E. D. Mynatt, 2000, "Charting Past, Present and Future Research in Ubiquitous Computing," ACM Transactions on Computer-Human Interaction (TOCHI). Special Issue on HCI in the new Millenium, pp. 29-58.

[3] A. Holzinger, Basiswissen (2004) IT/Informatik, Band 1:Informationstechnik (IT). Würzburg: Vogel, (in German). http://www.basiswissen-it.at]

[4] H. Maurer, (1998), "Web-Based Knowledge Management," IEEE Computer, vol. 31, pp. 122-123.

[5] Trifonova A., Ronchetti M. (2003). Where is Mobile Learning Going?. Proceedings of the World Conference on E-learning in Corporate, Government, Healthcare, & Higher Education (E-Learn 2003), Phoenix, Arizona, USA, November 7-11, 2003. pp. 1794-1801.

[6] Lopez-Velasco C, Villanova-Oliver M, Gensel J, Services Web adaptés aux utilisateurs nomades Deuxièmes Journées Francophones: Mobilité et Ubiquité 2005 Grenoble, Mardi 31 mai - Vendredi 3 juin 2005

[7] Leal Musa .A, Palazzo Moreira de Oliveira .J, June 8, 2004, Sharing Learner Information through a Web Servicesbased Learning Architecture, WISM Workshop co-located with the CAiSE Conference, Riga, Latvia,.

[8]Balke W-T, Wagner M, May 20-24, 2003,Towards Personalized Selection of Web Services, *WWW 2003*, , Budapest, Hungary.

[9] SOAP Protocol. http://www.w3.org/2000/xp/Group.

[10] UDDI. The UDDI Technical White Paper. http://www.uddi.org.

[11] E. Christensen, F. Curbera, G. Meredith, and S. Weerawarana.(2001) Web Services Description Language (WSDL) 1.1.http://www.w3.org/TR/2001/NOTE-wsdl-20010315,.

[12] Robson,R, Learning & Training Innovations, May/Jun (2003), Vol. 4 Issue 4, p 10 - 11 (http://ltimagazine.com)

[13] Maamar, Z., Benatallah, B. and Sheng, Q. (2002) 'Towards a composition framework for e/m-services', Proceedings of the UbiAgents Workshop'02, Bologna, Italy.

[14]Eija Kaasinen, Matti Aaltonen, Juha Kolari , Suvi Melakoski and Timo Laakko, June 2000, Two approaches to bringing Internet services to WAP devices ,Computer Networks Volume 33, Issues 1-6, , Pages 231-246

[15]Chen M, Zhang D and Zhou ,L , 2005, Providing web services to mobile users: the architecture design of an m-service portal Int. J. Mobile Communications, Vol. 3, No. 1.

[16]Berger S, McFaddin S, Narayanaswami C, Raghunath M, (WMCSA 2003) Web Services on Mobile Devices – Implementation and Experience, Proceedings of the Fifth IEEE Workshop on Mobile Computing Systems & Applications

[17] Hadjouni M, Tirellil I, Laroussi M. (2005), Collaborative Platform for mobile learning based on e-services, ML 2005 (Mobile Learning), Malta.

[18]http://www.onjava.com/pub/a/onjava/2001/03/08/J2ME.html,

Techniques and Applications for Mobile Commerce
C. Branki et al. (Eds.)
IOS Press, 2008

Genetic Sequencing Research Approach for users' satisfaction in grid environments

Y. BEN HALIMA, Y. JAMOUSSI, H. BEN GHEZALA, National School of Computer Science

Abstract—Nowadays, the satisfaction of the users' requirements of a composition process execution in a grid environment remains a difficult task to be accomplished. It is done by brokers or using simple mechanisms of matchmaking. There users must express their needs in the grid language and then the grid determines the way to execute. In this article we propose a genetic sequencing approach for the research of the best way to execute a composition of services in a grid environment satisfying the user's need. This paper presents the genetic sequencing approach and then presents how to adapt this approach for the determination of the best time to execute the service composition.

Keywords

Grid computing, web services, composition, genetic sequencing, users' requirements, satisfaction

I. INTRODUCTION

Recently, there has been much interest in Computational Grids, which provide transparent access to large scale distributed computational resources. One important problem in such environments is the efficient allocation of computational resources. Over the past years, economic approaches to resource allocation have been developed [1] and the question arises whether they can be applied to resource allocation on the Grid. They satisfy some basic requirements for a Grid setting as they are naturally decentralised, as decisions about whether to consume or provide resources are taken locally by the clients or service providers, as the use of currency provides incentives for service providers to contribute resources, and as clients have to act responsibly and cannot afford to waste resources due to their limited budget.

Indeed, a number of systems [5] have been built to make a composition of web services. But all of them didn't take into consideration the real requirements of the user in term of reliability, Average Execution Time, Hardiness, Fault Tolerance, etc.

In this paper we propose a model that take into consideration que real requirements of the user and apply them over a web service composition in a grid environment.

We will start in the first section with a description of the gene sequencing approach and we will find basic steps and then elements of this approach. Next, we will expose the

Manuscript received September 21, 2007. This work was supported in part by the computer science Department of the National School of computer science.
Youssef BEN HALIMA is with the National School of Computer Science ENSI Manouba Tunisia 2010 (phone: 00216 22 541523; e-mail: youssef.benhalima@riadi.rnu.tn).
Yassine JAMOUSSI is with the National School of Computer Science ENSI Manouba Tunisia 2010 (e-mail: yassine.jamoussi@ensi.rnu.tn).
Henda BEN GHEZALA is with the National School of Computer Science ENSI Manouba Tunisia 2010 (e-mail: henda.bg@cck.rnu.tn).

way to apply the gene sequencing research approach to satisfy user's requirements in a non stable grid environment.

II. THE GENE SEQUENCING RESEARCH APPROACH

In this section we will present the way biologists make comparison between two sequences of genes.

II.1. Maxam-Gilbert sequencing

In 1976-7, Allan Maxam and Walter Gilbert developed a method of DNA sequencing based on chemical modification of DNA followed by its subsequent cleavage at specific bases[2]. Although this is contemporaneous with the development of Sanger sequencing, Maxim-Gilbert sequencing was initially more popular since purified DNA could be used directly, while the initial Sanger method required each read start be cloned for production of single-stranded DNA. However, as the chain termination method has been developed and improved, Maxam-Gilbert sequencing has fallen out of favour due to its technical complexity, the need for use of hazardous chemicals, and difficulties with scale-up.

In brief, the method requires purifying a particular DNA fragment, radioactively labelled at one end. Chemical treatment generates breaks at a small proportion of one or two of the four nucleotide bases in each of four reactions (G, A+G, C, C+T). Thus a series of labelled fragments is generated, from the radio labelled end to the first 'cut' site in each molecule. The fragments are then size-separated in a gel, with the four reactions arranged side by side. The gel can then be exposed to photographic film, yielding an image of a series of 'bands', from which the sequence may be inferred.

Also sometimes known as 'chemical sequencing', this method originated in the study of DNA-protein interactions (footprinting), nucleic acid structure and epigenetic modifications to DNA, and within these it still has important applications.

II.2. Chain termination method

In chain terminator sequencing (Sanger sequencing), which is possible because of the availability of clones and/or thermal cycling DNA amplification, extension is initiated at a specific site on the template DNA by using a short oligonucleotide 'primer' complementary to the template at that region. The oligonucleotide primer is extended using a DNA polymerase, an enzyme that replicates DNA. Included with the primer and DNA polymerase are the four deoxynucleotide bases (DNA building blocks), along with a low concentration of a chain terminating nucleotide (most commonly a di-deoxynucleotide). Limited incorporation of the chain terminating nucleotide by the DNA polymerase results in a series of related DNA fragments that are terminated only at positions where that particular nucleotide is used. The fragments are then size-separated by electrophoresis in a slab polyacrylamide gel or, more commonly now, in a narrow glass tube (capillary) filled with a viscous polymer.

The classical chain termination method or Sanger method first involves preparing the DNA to be sequenced as a single strand. (The single-band preparation guarantees one band per nucleotide, whereas a double-strand preparation guarantees two bands, and makes sequence prediction impossible.) The DNA sample is divided into four separate samples. Each of the four samples has a primer, the four normal deoxynucleotides (dATP, dGTP, dCTP and dTTP), DNA polymerase, and only one of the four dideoxynucleotides (ddATP, ddGTP, ddCTP and ddTTP) added to it. The dideoxynucleotides are added in limited quantities. The primer or the dideoxynucleotides are either radiolabeled or have a fluorescent tag.

As the DNA strand is elongated the DNA polymerase catalyses the joining of deoxynucleotides to the corresponding bases. The bases available to the polymerase are a mixture of normal and tagged/terminating nucleotides. So if the appropriate dideoxynucleotide happens to be near the polymerase, it is incorporated into the elongating DNA strand. The tagged/terminating base prevents further elongation because a dideoxynucleotide lacks a crucial 3'-OH group. So a series of DNA fragments are produced with random length and (base-nonspecific, hence the four separate reactions) tags. Unfortunately, only short stretches of DNA can be sequenced in each reaction. The polymerase chain reaction(PCR) technique is limited to 10,000 base-pairs and the maximum length of extension is dictated by the concentration of tagged/terminating nucleotides.

The DNA is then denatured and the resulting fragments are separated (with a resolution of just one nucleotide) by gel electrophoresis, from longest to shortest. Each of the four DNA samples is run on one of four individual lanes (lanes A, T, G, C) depending on which dideoxynucleotide was added. Depending on whether the primers or dideoxynucleotides were radiolabeled or fluorescently labelled, the DNA bands can be detected by exposure to X-rays or UV-light and the DNA sequence can be directly read off the gel. In the image on the right, X-ray film was exposed to the dried gel, and the dark bands indicate the positions of the DNA molecules of different lengths. A dark band in a lane indicates a chain termination for that particular DNA subunit and the DNA sequence can be read off as indicated.

There can be various problems with sequencing through the Sanger Method. The primer used can also be annealed to a second site. This would cause two sequences to be interpreted at the same time. This can be solved by higher annealing temperatures and higher G and C content in the primer. Another problem can occur when RNA contaminates the reaction, which can act like a primer and leads to bands in all lanes at all positions due to non specific priming. Other contaminants can be from other plasmids, inhibitors of DNA polymerase, and low concentrations in general. Secondary structure of DNA being read by DNA polymerase can lead to reading problems and will be visualized on the readout by bands in all lanes of only a few

positions. In short, the problems of this method are the standard problems one would encounter in PCR.

There are two sub-types of chain-termination sequencing. In the original method, the nucleotide order of a particular DNA template can be inferred by performing four parallel extension reactions using one of the four chain-terminating bases in each reaction. The DNA fragments are detected by labelling the primer with a base-nonspecific label, radioactive phosphorus for example, prior to performing the sequencing reaction. The four reactions would then be run out in four adjacent lanes on a slab polyacrylamide gel.

The Sanger method can be done using primers that add a non-specific label on the 5' end of the PCR product. Instead of the label being included in the terminating nucleotide, the label is in the primer. The difference between this and the radioactive Sanger method is that the label is at the 5' end instead of the 3' end. Four separate reactions are still required, but the dye labels can be read using an optical system instead of film or phosphor storage screens, so it is faster, cheaper, and easier to automate. This approach is known as 'dye-primer sequencing' [1].

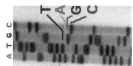

Figure 1: Part of a radioactively labelled sequencing gel

II.3.   Gene sequence comparison [4]

Sequence comparison is a type of substring matching operation where sequence similarity is scored based on biological criteria. Pairs of sequences that match with a higher score are considered to be more similar, potentially sharing common function and origin. The score of a sequence match increases for each matching item, known as an identity, and decreases when elements are substituted, inserted, or removed.

The score associated with each substring pair is a function of biological interaction based on mutation and not necessarily knowledge of English language, the words friend and fiend would seem quite similar, and the words friend and friendly less so. Simple rules based on minimum structural difference would make the comparison of friend and fiend yields a higher score than friend and friendly. Using rules based on the semantics of the words, a better scoring is possible. Such rules exist for comparing proteins. One of these rules is based on a table called Point Accepted Mutation (PAM) matrix. This matrix describes the likelihood of substitution of one amino acid by another, and was derived by examination of the small variations between known related sequences. This matrix is then used to determine the scoring penalty for a mismatched element.

It is likely that many of the matching pairs of sequences share little function or origin, or attempting to separate these from relevant matches by parameter tuning is generally worthwhile. FASTA is just one fast heuristic method used to compare sequences. Others include Smith-Watermann [3] and BLAST [2]. Choosing a particular algorithm and tuning its parameters effects the trade-off between sensitivity (finding distantly related sequences), selectivity (discriminating unrelated sequences), and speed.

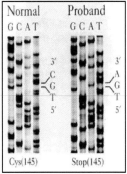

Figure 2 : comparing normal and proband sequences

II.4.   Basing elements of the sequencing approach

Here are general steps for the sequencing approach:

- The first step is to find the normal sequence from the database
- The second step is to determine the proband sequence to compare with the normal sequence.
- The third step is to compare two sequences: normal and proband via their PAM matrix.
- The fourth step is to pick up differences or similarities between them.

Those four steps will be cloned to get the user's satisfaction of web services composition executed over the grid.

III.   THE GSR APPROACH FOR USER'S REQUIREMENTS SATISFACTION

Here are details for the Gene Sequencing Research approach (GSR approch) used to satisfy user's requirements in a grid environment.

III.1.   The Unified Time Unit (UTU)

The UTU is a unified unit of time. This unit depends on the grid and the machines. For example:

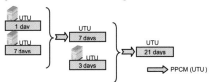

Figure 3 : example of definition of the UTU

The UTU represents the common unit of time that defines the availability of the machines in the grid.

III.2.   Grid modelling approach

III.2.1.   Grid characteristics

Every machine in the grid is associated with a number of characteristics. Some of them are given by the service provider and others are defined automatically by the application.

TABLE 1 : GRID CHARACTERISTICS

Resource type	characteristic	Abbreviation	Type	Possible values
network	Throughput	TP	Quantitative	-
Machine	Processor	SP	Quantitative	-
	Storage	ST	Quantitative	-
	Memory	MR	Quantitative	-
	Failure frequency	BF	Quantitative (probability)	-
	working	WK	Quantitative	{True, False}
	others	OTR	-	-

III.2.2.   The machine availability modelling approach

We can give for the hole UTU of the machine the values of the differents characteristics.

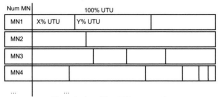

Figure 4: the machine modelling approach

III.2.3.   The grid availability modelling approach

Figure 5 : the grid modelling approach

If there are n machines in the grid we can defines the grid availability model for using n layered machine availability models.

III.3.   Web service composition

We adopt the notation presented in [5], and here is and abstract of this notation with a detailed example.

III.3.1.   The map formalism for service goals composition

We use the map as service composition formalism.

We define two kinds of clients, executive clients and design client. The design clients are persons who make the composition based on intentions and the executive client express their needs by intentions and try to execute the composition. And here is the way based on the MAP model [6] to describe a composition:

A map is a labelled directed graph (see Figure 6) with intentions as nodes and strategies as edges between intentions. The directed nature of the graph shows which intentions can follow which one. An edge enters a node if its strategy can be used to achieve the corresponding intention. Since, there can be multiple edges entering a node; the map is capable of representing the many strategies that can be used for achieving an intention.

An intention is a goal to be achieved by the performance of the process. Each map has two special intentions, Start and Stop, to respectively start and end the process.

A strategy is an approach, a manner to achieve an intention.

A section is the key element of a map. It is a triplet <Ii, Ij, Sij> and represents a way to achieve the target intention Ij from the source intention Ii following the strategy Sij. The strategy Sij characterizes the flow from the source intention Ii to the target intention Ij and the way Ij can be achieved once Ii has been achieved. Thus, each section of the map captures the condition to achieve an intention and the specific manner in which the process associated with the target intention can be performed [6].

Sections of a map are connected to one another:

(a) when a given intention can be achieved with different strategies. This is represented in the map by several sections between a pair of intentions. Such a map topology is called a multi-thread.

(b) when a task can be performed by several combinations of strategies. This is represented in the map by a pair of intentions connected by several sequences of sections. Such a topology is called a multi-path. In general, a map from its Start to its Stop intentions is a multi-path and may contain multithreads.

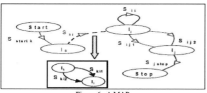

Figure 6 : A MAP

In a multi-thread, strategies are usually related by an AND/OR relationship; one or several of the set being applicable in a given situation. In cases of an exclusive OR relationship, it is possible to bundle the set of alternative strategies as shown in Figure 1 above with the section <Ik, Ii, Ski> (the bold dotted line). This section is a bundle of <Ik, Ii, Ski1> and <Ik, Ii, Ski2> as shown in the Figure 4. This allows us to (a) make explicit alternative threads in a multi-thread and (b) make the graphical representation easier to understand. [6].

Every Strategy in the graph can be represented by two ways. We can represent a Strategy by another MAP and we can use context to represent a Strategy. A context can be a plan context with a graph of dependencies or choice context with conditions or executable context.

We are going to use this model to represent the composition of services. A service is considered like an executable context.

III.3.2. Example of the map composition goals level
This is an example of a web service based composition designed by the MAP model. The example consists of

subscription in a school made by a service composition through internet:

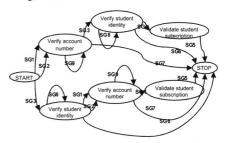

Figure 7 : Example: the Map of the subscription composition

And here are different strategies:

- SG1: introduce account number
- SG2:introduce money account number
- SG3:introduce student identity number
- SG4: validate inscription if account number and identity number are correct
- SG5: print subscription certificate
- SG6: verify student identity number and leave
- SG7: verify account number and leave
- SG8: reinsert student identity number
- SG9: reinsert account number

We suppose that strategies steering to the same intentions are the same.

III.3.3. The execution formalism
An abstract of the execution formalism is presented here and other details will be presented in later works.

Basing elements:

TABLE 2 : DIFFERENT ELEMENTS OF THE SERVICE COMPOSITION

Element	Graphical description
A simple service	S_i^j
A node	—◖❚❚◗→
An obligatory step	·····▶·····
Start point	▶·····
End point	·····▶◀
Service variants	S_i^1 S_i^2 S_i^3 S_i^4 .... S_i^n
Parallel execution	S_i^l S_c^k S_s^l S_t^n .... S_u^d
Sequential organized execution	

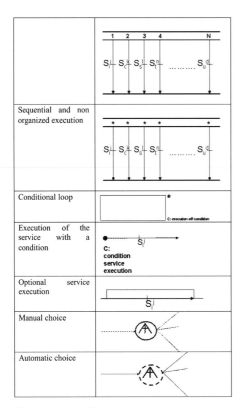

Sequential and non organized execution	
Conditional loop	
Execution of the service with a condition	
Optional service execution	
Manual choice	
Automatic choice	

III.3.4. Example of the composition execution level

And here an instance of this formalism with the same example of student subscription service composition.

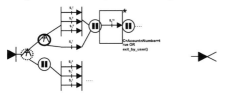

Figure 8 : A part of the execution level of the map of the figure 4

III.3.5. Service characteristics

Every service is associated with a number of characteristics. Some of them are given by the service provider and others are defined automatically by the application.

TABLE 3 : SERVICE CHARACTERISTICS

Resource type	characteristic	Abbreviation	Type	Possible values
Service	Average Execution Time	AET	Quantitative	-
	Hardiness	HR	Qualitative	{high, average, few}
	Reliability	RT	Qualitative	{high, average, few}
	Fault Tolerance	FT	Qualitative	{high, average, few}
	Cast	CT	Quantitative	-
	Availability	AV	Quantitative	{True, False}
	Abandon Rate	ABR	Quantitative	-
	Average Speed to Answer	ASA	Quantitative	-
	others	OTRS	-	-

III.3.6. The service execution model

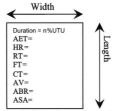

Figure 9 : the service execution modelling approach

This is an example of a service execution model. The width of the rectangle is equal to the value given by the characteristic duration. This model is equal to the PAM matrix in the gene sequence comparision section 2.3.

III.3.7. The service composition execution model

We can generate from the variability model the general execution of the composition with different values of the characteristics. Every service in the Grid-V2SC is presented with a rectangle defined in the section 3.1.9.

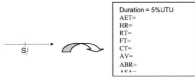

Figure 10 : the service equivalence

And then we can build the whole variability model like figure 11.

S_1^2			
S_1^8			
S_1^9			
S_2^1			
S_3^4			
S_3^7			
S_3^5	S_3^5		

Figure 11 : the composition execution model

Services of the same columns can be executed of the same time. For example the variants of the same service or two different services but executed in the same time.

The width of every rectangle depends of the duration of the service and the Length is the same length used for the machine availability model.

III.4. User requirements

The users' requirements are given by agreements defined in the beginning of the execution. The user defines an SLA [8]. In her thesis [7], S. BENNASRI presents a way to capture the user requirements into the Map formalism. We will present in later works how to transform user requirements into SLA agreements. The user requirements will be presented from the SLA agreement to the service execution model.

In conclusion the user requirements are values of some characteristics of the machines in the grid and services. For example if the user need to execute services with the value of the cast characteristic is null, we present it:

```
Duration = 5%UTU
AET= NA
HR= NA
RT= NA
FT=NA
CT=0
AV= NA
ABR= NA
ASA=NA
```

Figure 12 : values of the service

We assign the value NA to the characteristic not defined by the user. This means that the user don't have any requirement concerning this attribute.

III.5. The GSR approach for user requirement satisfaction

We can now present the user requirements satisfaction approach using the genetic sequencing research method.

TABLE 4: THE GSR APPROACH IN REQUIREMENTS SATISFACTION

Step	Genetic Sequencing Approach	Grid-V2SC
Step 1	Definition of the sequence to search	Definition of the service execution model. Values of the characteristics are defined by the user requirements
Step 2	Definition of the sequence to compare to. http://gdbwww.gdb.org, http://research.marshfieldclinic.org, http://www.chu-rouen.fr/ssf/strucgen/banquegenes.html	Definition of the grid availability model. Values of the characteristic of the machine and the services here are given by the service provider of the grid administrator.
Step 3	Compare the two sequences	Compare the two models
Step 4	Get similarities or differences	Get the similarities to show the best way to satisfy the user requirements

This is an example of the execution of the GSR algorithm to get the best way to execute the service composition.

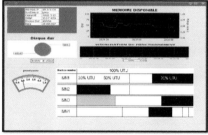

Figure 13 : best execution for user requirements satisfaction

In the first execution we search for the whole set of "best times" to execute our service composition. The system propose to the user the set of time and when the user choose his execution time, another simulation will proceed exactly at the same time to find the last service execution done and to proceed at this one. We can use the Hansdorff Distance method to validate the GSR approach. This will be presented in later works.

IV.   THE DEVELOPED ENVIRONMENT

Here is the environment developed to execute the approach presented in this paper. We develop an environment with java to get the best portability level because the grid may be implanted on different machines

IV.1. The framework

This is the framework of the whole developed environment:

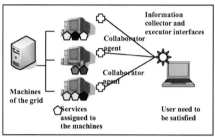

Figure 14 : Developed framework

IV.2. The resource characteristics tools

In this print screens we show how to get the availability of resources in a defined period of time.

Figure 15 : Ressource availability and characteristics

IV.3. Services on the grid

In this screenshot we show how to assign a service to a machine by having available services and available machines.

Figure 16 : Assign services to machines

IV.4.   The model execution tools

In this picture we show how to make the execution of a service composition by a user on a real environment.

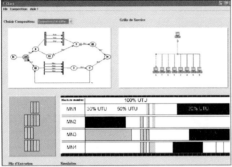

Figure 17 : Execute composition

V.   CONCLUSION

In this paper we have presented our approach to get the best set of time to execute a service composition and to satisfy the user requirements: functional and non functional requirements. This approach is based on the genetic sequencing method used in the biology to determine similarities of specific sequences of genes.

This work will be completed by the integration of developped tools in the Tunisian grid platform called GTRS.

REFERENCES

[1]   http://en.wikipedia.org/wiki/DNA_sequencing 21-3-2007
[2]   S. Altschul, W. Glish, W. Miller, E. Myres, and D. Lipman. Basic local alignement search tool. Journal of molecular biology 215, 403-10, 1990
[3]   T. Smith and M. Waterman. Identification of common molecular subsequences. Journal of molecular biology, 147:195-197, 1981
[4]   Neil Spring, Rich Wolski, Application level scheduling of gene sequence comparison on metacomputers, International Conference on Supercomputing, Proceedings of the 12th international conference on Supercomputing, Melbourne, Australia, 41 – 148, 1998,ISBN:0-89791-998-X
[5]   Sébastien Mosser, Mireille Blay-Fornarino, Michel Riveill
      Orchestrations de Service Web : vers une évolution par composition
[6]   Rim Samia Kaabi, Carine Souveyet, Colette Rolland, Eliciting Service Composition in a Goal Driven Manner,

ICSOC'04, November 15–19, 2004, New York, New York, USA.
[7]   S. BENNASRI, intentional approach for representation and realization of the variability in un software system « approche intentionnelle de représentation et de réalisation de la variabilité dans un système logiciel » thesis work, 9 February 2005
[8]   Akhil Sahai, Anna Durante, Vijay Machiraju, Towards Automated SLA Management for Web Services,HP Laboratories, 1501 Page Mill Road, Palo-Alto, CA 94034,2002

Part III

AutoMoCo: Autonomic Computing and Mobile Commerce

Techniques and Applications for Mobile Commerce
C. Branki et al. (Eds.)
IOS Press, 2008

141

A Scalable Governance Model for Autonomic M-Commerce

Martin RANDLES and A. TALEB-BENDIAB
School of Computing and Mathematical Sciences
Liverpool John Moores University, Byrom Street, Liverpool, L3 3AF, UK
{m.j.randles a.talebbendiab}@ljmu.ac.uk

Abstract: The pervasiveness of computational systems capable of accomplishing electronic commerce over the Internet is rapidly increasing with devices routinely embedded in many everyday household objects. This in itself causes very complex network dynamics. When these devices or associated agents, programme code etc. are liberated from a set geographical location, through laptop computers and mobile phones for example, the control of such systems more than outstrips the capability of any human or currently conceived artificial system to provide all but the simplest features of self-governance as exemplified by autonomic management. This work addresses the need for autonomic type self-governance for these systems by seeking a scalable specification of autonomic systems/networks that is applicable to m-commerce scenarios. This involves the initial realization that the representation is best accomplished through cognitive systems portrayed in mathematical logic with the power to detect and characterize system properties at run time. The system hierarchy can then be viewed through ambient representation for appropriate monitoring leading to sensing and observation overlays that can achieve grounded definitions of system signals for run time self-governance and autonomic response.

1. Introduction

Electronic commerce (e-commerce) continues to grow through the rise of Internet business transactions. Following this phenomenon there is an emerging interest in mobile computing and the additional business opportunities offered through wireless technologies. Mobile e-commerce may be defined as the set of activities performed through the process of a commercial transaction model or implementation conducted through communications networks that interface with wireless or mobile devices [1]. These mobile devices may take a number of forms, including; mobile/cellular phones, wireless enabled handheld computers, laptop computers, in vehicular devices and paging devices. Additionally e-commerce may become mobile through the use of portable non-wireless devices such as computer laptops and Personal Digital Assistants (PDAs). This presents a new set of issues, which are specifically related to *mobile* e-commerce (m-commerce).

The purpose of this paper is to examine some of these issues in ensuring that the system can benefit from the provision of autonomic type self-governance [2] in an environment that permits both code and user/device mobility. The difficulties with m-commerce governance, on the Web, are not created directly by mobility; rather the problems lie in the crossing of domains and the entering of distinct isolated Internet partitions through rigorously controlled paths that are enforced by firewall constraints, for example. Policies are set regarding what is allowed through firewalls and by what means the mobility can occur. In moving a commerce process, for example, it is necessary to ensure that all the supporting services and applications required for the transaction to complete also move with, or are available to, the m-commerce process executing on a new host device. The m-commerce process must also tailor its operation to the new host device's environment. It is for this reason that an approach based on specifying a bounded, moveable computational space that may contain or be contained by other such spaces called *ambients* [3] will be used in this work. Additionally the complex interactions that occur in the mobile domain and the potential scale of the systems themselves make it infeasible to produce a design time model of all the system events and states that may result. Indeed the systems are subject to unpredictable emergent outcome and may self-organise in ways not discernable at design time [4]. Thus the specification will be made through mathematical logic with dedicated monitoring assigned to the *computational ambients* whereby sensed knowledge is utilised at run time by cognitive observation systems. In this way the autonomic governance system does not require a preconceived state and transition model but rather holds sentences of what is true in the domain and the causal laws that apply. Hence no state space enumeration is required at design time.

The structure of this paper takes the following form: Section 2 defines and gives background to the notion of an *ambient* and its associated observation/monitoring system. Section 3 introduces the mathematical logic formalism and associated techniques necessary to ground definitions and provide governance at run time through the observer based monitoring model. Section 4 details a case study in mobility and e-commerce with Section 5 concluding the paper.

2. Modelling Mobility with Ambients

Ambients arose as a solution to describe all aspects of mobility within a framework encompassing mobile agents, the bounded regions, called ambients, where the agents interact and the mobility of these ambients themselves [3]. As described in [3] ambients are named bounded areas of computation. The ambient name controls access to the ambient that contains computational entities realised as agents, processes, threads, etc., which in effect control the ambient and may enter, exit or communicate with other ambients. The central notion is that of the ambient boundary: To provide mobility for m-commerce it is necessary to define the entities that are required to move. This prescribes the ambient boundary to be the enclosure for all the computational resources necessary to complete the m-commerce transaction. For instance, when a user logs on to complete any m-commerce transaction the mobile device ought to adapt itself to the users preferences and have available all computational resources to conclude the transaction.

Ambients may be nested inside each other allowing a modular hierarchical structure to be maintained. Thus an application (ambient) running on a particular machine, comprising an ambient, can be moved to another machine representing a separate new enclosing ambient. The ambient is moved as a whole so that an application moved from one machine to another automatically has its local data moved as part of the ambient.

2.1. The Monitoring and Observation System.

In order to provide self-governance facilities to m-commerce systems it is proposed to organize the system into ambient entities with appropriate observer modules overlaid. The proposed Observer System is built around the deployment of appropriate monitoring and sensing modules, with guards to bound ambient autonomy and describe the boundary of the ambient ensuring legitimate operation, for the system ambients and their components. These ambients may be further reduced to sub-ambient level with appropriate monitoring, guard and boundary facilities. The behaviour of the ambients is thus viewed at a reductionist level for the purposes of modularisation but the interactions can be assessed at the global (containing) super-ambient level. This gives the hierarchical reductionism of the collectivist case where the global behaviour of the containing system is not necessarily a linear combination of the comprised component behaviour. Figure 1 gives a view of two levels, at a particular point, in a system.

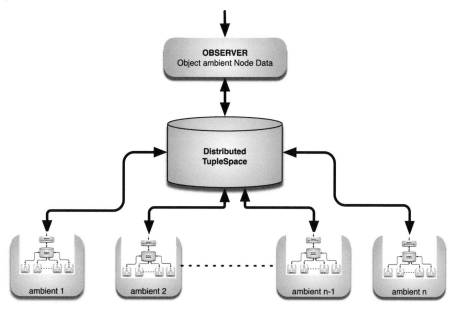

Figure 1: A Monitoring System for Ambient Observation

Each ambient at the illustrated level of the system, has its own domain specific observing module that reasons over the intrinsic knowledge contained within the ambient. This is relayed and stored in a distributed tuplespace where the observer of the containing system can reason on the state of individual ambients and more importantly the behaviour that emerges from the interactions of the n ambients, in this case. Also norms can be passed down the system, through the observers, to bound the autonomy of the individual ambients. The distributed tuplespace is an application of adaptive middleware for co-ordination, such as SwarmLinda [5], which can utilise features of self-organisation [6] to ensure monitored data from the ambients is stored close to the appropriate observer. Through this representation the formal account can be expressed from any reasonable perspective: The norms for individual ambients and their contained components can be stated as well as the deliberative mechanisms for the observers, for instance.

The flexibility of this Observer Model lies in its self-similar structure at each hierarchical level of the system. Each, separated out, observer monitors a set of ambients, which may themselves consist of or comprise ambients with separate Observer Systems. Thus the system is open-ended in either direction through the hierarchy and may be followed upwards, where more high-level goals may be set, or downwards to ever-smaller components, where more low level functional goals will be satisfied. At each hierarchical ambient level in the system the Observer System takes the same structure although the detail would differ according to context with the deployment of the most appropriate probes for the part of the system being monitored. In this way data emanating from a low level component can be passed up the observer hierarchy until a level is reached where the data has intrinsic meaning for that particular observer. This may even result in human intervention, as any observer system is necessarily bound to culminate in human level assessment. This allows each ambient in its the hierarchy, autonomy of operation bounded by the purpose of the enclosing ambient as defined and enforced by the associated Observer System. Furthermore cooperation and coordination is achieved between components at the same or different levels through the abstract communication facilities provided by the distributed tuplespace with the Observer System permitting deliberation on the entry, exit or communication between ambients.

2.2. Example

Various arrangements of ambients have been tested using the Netlogo simulation environment [7]. Here ambients are arranged hierarchically with observers attached to monitor configuration and control access (entry, exit and communication) between individual ambients to conform to set topologies. Figure 2 shows a particular ambient and its boundary containing sub-ambients with their sub-ambients shown as connections.

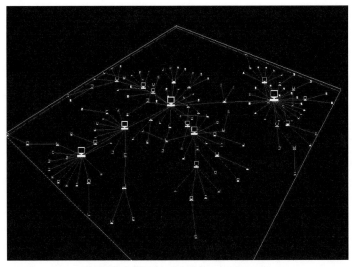

Figure 2. A Simulated Ambient Arrangement

The Observer System overlay, which reasons over the topology of this particular arrangement, detects the emergence of certain high activity ambients within this ambient, as denoted by the larger depiction size in Figure 2. Such a scenario models ambients in an m-commerce setting where a users profile enters a retail space as a buyer. The user's profile, modelled as an ambient, is much more likely to enter a retailer's purchase process ambient space to complete a purchase transaction if that retailer already possesses a high volume of traffic. Barabási and Albert [8] have previously noted that these dynamics of preferential attachment lead to scale free connectivity amongst participants giving a power law distribution [9]. This in turn leads to the formation of a small number of high activity ambient hubs as shown by the graphical analysis of the number of ambients that contain each number of sub-ambients in Figure 3.

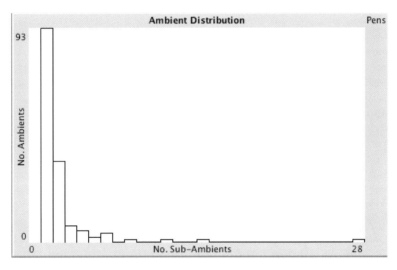

Figure 3. Scale-Free Ambient Distribution

Thus upon detection or construction of this topology the observer system can provide autonomic protection to its most vulnerable ambients, direct entering ambients to the source most likely to fulfil their request or generally utilise the topology of the ambients to achieve run time autonomic governance.

3. Specifying the Cognitive Observation System

The mathematical logic approach to the specification of the ambient observation system is needed to enable run time deliberation on the observed state of the ambient hierarchy. Other approaches rely on design time knowledge of all states and transitions, which is not feasible in the complex, interactive and large-scale environment comprising the setting for most m-commerce scenarios [10]. The formalism used here is based on the situation calculus first proposed by John McCarthy in 1963 [11]. Furthermore a cognitive robotics approach, detailed in [12], has led to the refinement of the formalism to be more a calculus of situations with no reliance on state based representations at all. The main difference, in using situation calculus, from alternative approaches is the concentration on cognition as the driver for ambient behaviour and observer system autonomic function. The fully formal description of the situation calculus is given in [12], briefly stated, however, the main concepts consist of situations and actions. A situation provides a snapshot of the world that is changed by an action occurrence: Actions are the cause of situation transitions which are themselves composed of a sequence of actions or action history, forming the major objects in the calculus. Each of these situations will have a set of fluent values dictated by the initial situation, termed S_0 and the action history. There is a primitive binary operation do; $do(a,s)$ denoting the successor situation to s resulting from performing the action a. Actions are generally denoted by functions and situations (action histories) are first order terms. In seeking to represent a domain actions must have preconditions; necessary conditions that must hold before the action can be performed. The predicate *poss* is used with *poss(a,s)* meaning that it is possible to perform the action a in a world resulting from the execution of the sequence of actions s. In order to address the frame problem, effect and frame axioms are combined into one Successor State Axiom [13]: A successor state axiom for a fluent is TRUE in the next situation if and only if an action occurred to make it TRUE or it is TRUE in the current situation and no action occurred to make it FALSE, with the precondition axiom *poss*(a, s) meaning it is possible to perform action a in the situation s. These form the simple, yet highly expressive, primitives of the Situation Calculus.

The representation of knowledge and beliefs in the Situation Calculus is achieved by seeing the world states as action histories or situations with the concept of accessible situations [14]. So if s_1 and s_2 are situations then (s_1, s_2) □ K_i means that in situation s_2 agent i considers s_1 a possible situation with K_i an accessibility relation for agent i. That is all fluents known to hold in situation s_2 also hold in s_1. So an accessibility fluent may be specified: $K_i(s_1, s_2)$ meaning in situation s_2 agent i thinks s_1 could be the actual situation.

So knowledge for agent i ($knows_i$) can be formulated in a situation as:

$$knows_i(\varphi, s) \equiv \forall s_1(K_i(s_1, s) \rightarrow \varphi(s_1)) \text{ [alternatively } \forall s_1 (\neg K_i(s_1, s)(\varphi(s_1))]$$

However to make any axiom complete it is necessary to establish whether a sensing action has taken place [15]. That is if the action that occurred, to change the situation to its successor, was the perception of the value of a fluent. So the change was a change in the epistemic state of the agent. Thus it is necessary to distinguish sensing actions by writing SR($sense\varphi$,s) to denote that the action produced a result for φ.

SR($sense\varphi$, s) $=r=$ value of φ in s.

Thus a successor state axiom for K can be stated:

$$K(s_2, do(a, s)) \Leftrightarrow \exists s_1(s_2 = do(a, s_1) \wedge K(s_1, s) \wedge poss(a, s_1) \wedge SR(a, s) = SR(a, s_1))$$

3.1. Example: Ambient Concurrency

In order to represent actions that occur in time, for a certain duration or at the same time it is necessary to consider the ways in which time may be represented within the situation calculus, as stated up to this point. The formulisation described so far only conceives of actions occurring sequentially and without timing constraints. Actions may occur together and have the same duration; the duration of one may completely envelope the duration of the other or their durations may just overlap. The representational device used within the situation calculus to address these problems is to consider instantaneous actions initiating and terminating action durations with a relational fluent representing the extent of the action. For instance instead of the monolithic action to move an m-commerce ambient, A, from some location l_1 to another location l_2: *move(A,l_1,l_2)* the instantaneous actions *startMove* and *endMove* may be used and the procedure of moving represented by the relational fluent *moving(A,l_1,l_2,s)*: The *startMove* action causing the *moving* fluent to become true with the *endMove* action making it false. Similarly the *communicate* action can be represented by the pair of instantaneous actions *startCommunicate* and *endCommunicate* with the relational fluent *communicating(s)*. It is then quite simple to represent these actions and fluents in the Situation Calculus, as defined:

$$poss(startMove(A,l_1,l_2),s) \Leftrightarrow \neg \exists (l_3,l_4) moving(A, l_3,l_4,s) \wedge location(A,s)=l_1$$
$$poss(endMove(A,l_1,l_2),s) \Leftrightarrow moving(A, l_1,l_2,s)$$
$$moving(A, l_1,l_2,do(a,s)) \Leftrightarrow a=startMove(A,l_1,l_2) \vee [moving(A, l_1,l_2,s) \wedge$$
$$a \neq endMove(A,l_1,l_2)]$$
$$location(A,do(a,s))=l_2 \Leftrightarrow \exists l_1\ a=endMove(A,l_1,l_2) \Leftrightarrow \vee [location(A,s)=l_2 \wedge$$
$$\neg (\exists l,l')\ a \neq endMove(A,l,l')]$$

With this representation complex concurrency can be handled. For example for a particular process:

$$\{startMove(l_1,l_2), startBroadcast\},\{endBroadcast,startReplication(l_3)\}, \{endMove(l_1,l_2)\}$$

forms the sequence of actions commencing with simultaneously starting to move an ambient from l_1 to l_2 and broadcasting from the ambient, followed by simultaneously ending the broadcast and starting to replicate the ambient at location l_3, followed by ending the move at l_2 whilst the replication is still proceeding.

This gives a particularly neat representation for interleaved concurrency: Two actions are interleaved if one is the next action to occur after the other. Thus an interleaved concurrent representation can be given for ambient moving and broadcasting, for instance:

$$do([startMove(l_1,l_2),startBroadcast,endBroadcast, endMove(l_1,l_2)],S_0)$$

Where broadcasting is initiated after a move is started and terminated before the end of the move. Alternatively it might be the case that:

$$do([startBroadcast, startMove(l_1,l_2), endBroadcast, endMove(l_1,l_2)],S_0)$$

Thus any overlapping occurrences of moving and broadcasting, except for exact co-occurrences of the initiating or terminating actions, may be realised in the formalism. This is achieved without having to extend the formalism in any way.

3.2. Example: Stochastic Ambient Actions

In reality most stochastic actions revolve around the success or failure of action occurrences. For example if there is an action of ambient X entering ambient Y, denoted by *enter(X,Y)*. The *enter* action is a stochastic action, in that the action may succeed or fail so can be decomposed into two deterministic actions: *s_enter(X, Y)* and *f_enter(X,Y)* (meaning the action succeeds or fails respectively). The action *enter* is assumed to be under the cognitive systems autonomous control. If the system elects to perform the action then non-determinism arises and exactly one of either *s_enter(X, Y)* or *f_enter(X,Y)* is enacted with associated probabilities. Thus it may be written:

$$choice(enter(X,Y),a) \equiv a{=}s\_enter(X,Y) \vee a{=}f\_enter(X, Y)$$

with

$$prob_0(s\_enter(X,Y),enter(X,Y),s) = p$$
$$prob_0(f\_enter(X,Y),enter(X,Y),s) = 1{-}p$$

where p is a probability distribution for the action occurrence and $prob_0$ is the probability given that the action is possible in the particular situation.

The associated successor state axioms for the domain and the action precondition axioms can then be stated in the usual manner. To provide a decision theoretic position into the account, to in effect assess the importance of actions, a real valued reward function, *reward(a,s)*, may be introduced. This denotes the reward a component may gain by performing action *a* in situation *s*. For instance:

$$reward(s\_enter(X,Y),s){=}r \equiv [(ambient(X) \vee (ambient(Y)) \wedge r{=}80] \vee$$
$$[(process(X) \wedge ambient(Y)) \wedge \neg (ambient(X)) \wedge r{=}30]$$
$$reward(f\_addLink(X,Y),s){=}r \equiv [(ambient(X) \vee ambient(Y)) \wedge r{=}{-}60] \vee$$
$$[(process(X) \wedge ambient(Y)) \wedge \neg (ambient(X)) \wedge r{=}{-}10]$$

There may also be costs involved with performing actions. For instance it is costly to move an ambient from its present location *loc(s)* to a new location *l*:

$cost(move(l),s) = 0.2|(loc(s),l)|$ where $|(x,y)|$ is some domain measure of a distance between x and y, the coordinates of *l*. It is possible to eliminate the cost function by incorporating it into the reward function. The domain usually determines the approach taken: If resources are consumed in the performance of actions it is usually more intuitive to retain the cost function. In this way Markov Decision Processes (MDP) may be specified in this situation calculus: The representation, in situation calculus of a dynamic probabilistic domain. In general an MDP consists of a state (situation) space, a set of actions, a transition function over the space and a reward function that maps a state (situation) and action to a real value. The goal is to find a policy that maximises the value function. In the simplest case, for a situation calculus account of an MDP, a cost function, *cost(a,s)*, and a reward function, *reward(a,s)*, are defined for each deterministic outcome *a* of a stochastic action and the value function becomes a linear combination of these:

$$value(do(a,s)) = value(s) + reward(a,s) - cost(a,s)$$

4. Case Study

This case study was completed as part of an Engineering and Physical Sciences Research Council (EPSRC) funded project [16]. It involved the provision of a commercial decision support system for the use of clinicians. It was necessary for the system to possess a separated cognitive observation meta-system to reason on the behaviour of the system as a whole enclosing ambient, including the clinician's actual decision. Thus, in order to process a decision for a clinician, an ambient representing the profile and data from the user enters the decision system ambient to participate in the computation of a best practice decision. This facilitated the three stated aims of the project: Supporting the clinician's decision within the National Institute for Health and Clinical Excellence (NICE) guidelines; the analysis of historical data to produce new rules for treatment choice and a combination of the previous two notions to provide a decision support system that is adaptive to clinicians' needs and changing environments. Thus, in presenting this case study, the proposed situation calculus formalism is shown to be equally useful for defining application system rules with the decision calculating ambient as well as specifying meta-system operational procedures for the ambients.   The specification describes a centralised; observation controlled decision support system, which nevertheless may also be considered as an enclosing ambient subject to monitoring by a higher-level observer. Through this case study the specification of a separated observer system is demonstrated for the establishment of self-governance norms with deliberation based on reward and cost functions for norm adaptations.

The decision support system considered in this case study was required to output treatment options based on rule sets with patient data as inputs. Additionally, however, the system was also required to exhibit self-governing features. Thus, for instance, a simple treatment rule, in the decision calculating ambient, for using the drug tamoxifen, which is recommended in the guidelines for postmenopausal patients with positive oestrogen receptors, can be formally stated as:

$$NICEtreatment(patient, tamoxifen, do(a,s)) \Leftrightarrow [NICEtreatment(patient, tamoxifen, s) \wedge$$
$$\neg \exists treatment(a = nice\_treament\_decision(patient, treatment) \wedge$$
$$(treatment \neq tamoxifen))] \vee [a = nice\_treatment\_decision(patient, tamoxifen)]$$

with

$$poss(nice\_treatment\_decision(patient, tamoxifen), s) \Rightarrow$$
$$(oesreceptor(patient, s) = pos) \wedge (menostatus(patient, s) = post)$$

Similar rules can, trivially, be stated for the other options, within a NICE ambient environment, or any other set of guidelines. These rules are, however, irrelevant for the purposes of this work; merely forming an ambient decision calculation environment to be managed by the autonomic meta-system observer. The main concerns of the autonomic system requirement are the maintenance of quality in service and process.

Quality of Process: The rules governing the meta-system are required to reason over the operation of the ambients. A quality of process concern, applicable to the user profile ambient may involve assessing the clinician's adherence to a specified guideline treatment:

$$compliance(patient, treatment, service\_decision, do(a, s)) \Leftrightarrow$$
$$[compliance(patient, treatment, service\_decision, s) \wedge$$
$$a \neq treament\_decision(patient, treatment1)] \vee$$
$$[a = treatment\_decision(patient, treatment) \wedge$$
$$service\text{-}decision(patient, s) = treatment]$$

In order to express the efficacy of the treatment decisions for the quality of the ambient process it is obviously appropriate to consider the outcomes of courses of treatment. These courses of treatment occur over a period of time and it is thus necessary to employ the situation calculus technique that deals with the duration of actions. Therefore the treatment duration is covered by two instantaneous actions *startTreatment* and *endTreatment* with a fluent *treating* through the duration of the treatment. So, for a patient ambient type *p,* continuing with the example of tamoxifen treatment given above, there may be a reward function such as:

$$reward(treatment(p,tamoxifen), do(a,s)) = r \Leftrightarrow a = endTreatment(p,tamoxifen) \wedge$$
$$[(r=100 \wedge living(p,s)) \vee$$
$$(r=-500 \wedge \neg living(p,s))]$$

with

$$fitness((treatment(tamoxifen) \wedge menostatus(p,s) = post \wedge oesreceptor(p,s) = pos), do(a,s)) =$$
$$fitness((treatment(tamoxifen) \wedge menostatus(p,s) = post \wedge oesreceptor(p,s) = pos), s) +$$
$$reward(treatment(p,tamoxifen), do(a,s))$$

In this way the success of each rule occurrence can be assessed including previously untried treatments instigated by the clinician, communicated through the user profile ambient entering the decision calculation ambient, and flagged for non-compliance. Thus less successful treatments will be deleted from the decision options whilst the decisions that lead to more favourable results will be chosen, improving the quality of process and adapting the decision calculation ambient.

Quality of Service: Quality of service concerns can be dealt with by the meta-system through monitoring demand against system capacity. If response time is too slow, for instance, it may be necessary to generate the ambient at a location closer to areas of higher demand. The ambient location may be specified as:

$$at(location,ambient,do(a,s)) \Leftrightarrow (at(location,ambient,s) \wedge (a \neq move(ambient,location1) \vee$$
$$a \neq delete(ambient,location))) \vee$$
$$(a = generate(ambient, location))$$

To facilitate the generation of an ambient due to high demand requires the specification of a procedure to detect the behaviour and prescribe the action to take to rectify the potential failure. The CPU load can be monitored:

$$cpuload(do(a, s)) = n \Leftrightarrow [cpuload(s) = n \wedge a \neq sense_{CPULOAD}] \vee$$
$$[a = sense_{CPULOAD} \wedge SR(sense_{CPULOAD}, s) = n]$$
$$heavyload(do(a, s)) \Leftrightarrow [heavyload(s) \wedge ((a \neq sense_{CPULOAD}) \vee$$
$$\neg(a = sense_{CPULOAD} \wedge SR(sense_{CPULOAD}, s) < 60))] \vee$$
$$[a = sense_{CPULOAD} \wedge SR(sense_{CPULOAD}, s) > 60]$$

with response time given as

$$roundtriptime(do(a, s)) = n \Leftrightarrow [roundtriptime(s) = n \wedge a \neq sense_{ROUNDTRIPTIME}] \vee$$
$$[a = sense_{ROUNDTRIPTIME} \wedge SR(sense_{ROUNDTRIPTIME}, s) = n]$$

$$unresponsive(do(a,s)) \Leftrightarrow [unresponsive(s) \wedge ((\ a \neq sense_{ROUNDTRIPTIME}) \vee$$
$$\neg (a = sense_{ROUNDTRIPTIME} \wedge SR(sense_{ROUNDTRIPTIME},\ s) < 1000))\ ] \vee$$
$$[\ a = sense_{ROUNDTRIPTIME} \wedge SR(sense_{ROUNDTRIPTIME},\ s) > 1000]$$
$$generated(ambient,\ location,\ do(a,s)) \Leftrightarrow generated(ambient, location,\ s) \vee$$
$$a = generate(ambient,\ location)$$

with

$$poss(generate(ambient,\ location),\ s) \Rightarrow heavyload(s) \vee unresponsive(s)$$

The representation describes a centralised control structure, where the observer acts as the system controller. The ambients, within the system, are mandated to act within the normative position of the system as monitored by the Observer System. A full implementation of this system was completed as part of the EPRSC project; this is, however outside the scope of the work presented in this paper. Further details may be found in [17] and [18]. The decision support system component produced in this way may also form part of a wider distributed ambient.

5. Conclusions

This paper has proposed a novel approach to provide autonomic governance in m-commerce applications based on the concept of ambients represented in mathematical logic. The use of mathematical logic is required to handle the extreme complexity of the domain whilst the notion of an ambient captures a number of features relevant to mobility. This is necessary because of the wide scope of mobile e-commerce definitions: Ngai and Gunasekaran identify five categories of m-commerce research [19]: m-commerce theory and research, wireless network infrastructure, mobile middleware, wireless user infrastructure, and m-commerce applications and cases. The work presented here is concerned primarily with the systems' governance so may be termed mobile middleware. The governance (monitoring and observation) of the ambients, however, also requires research from entire scope of m-commerce research issues. This is most easily captured by the abstract concept of the ambient, which may be hardware or software or may describe computation on the move or the mobility of code, agents, etc. Liang and Wei classify m-commerce into six areas of concern [20]: Time critical services, location based functionality, identity and access control, ubiquitous communications for the promotion of m-commerce business, improving the efficiency of business processes and mobile office integration. It is evident that the ambients described through this paper have relevance to each of these six topics.

The ambient concept is given a thorough rigorous treatment in a process algebra setting in [3]. This work has sought to gain additional applications to more unpredictable dynamic domains through the use of situation calculus. As such this is a proposal to encourage work on defining scalable methods for autonomic systems to be applied to complex m-commerce systems. There remains much to do in terms of ambient negotiations, efficient and relevant data collection, characterization and detection of ambient topologies to name but a few. Work is ongoing in all these areas.

References

[1]   P. Tarasewich, R.C. Nickerson, M. Warkentin (2002) Issues in Mobile E-Commerce. *Communications of the Association for Information Systems* 8, pp: 41-64.

[2]   M. Randles, A. Taleb-Bendiab, P. Miseldine, A. Laws (2005) Adjustable Deliberation of Self-Managing Systems. *Proceedings of IEEE International Conference on the Engineering of Computer Based Systems (ECBS 2005)* pp: 449-456, Maryland, USA.

[3]   L. Cardelli, A.D. Gordon (1998) Mobile Ambients. *Proceedings of the First International Conference on Foundations of Software Science and Computation Structure*. M. Nivat (ed) LNCS 1378, pp: 140–155. Springer-Verlag.

[4]   Martin Randles, Hong Zhu, A. Taleb-Bendiab (2007) A Formal Approach to the Engineering of Emergence and its Recurrence. *Proceedings of The Second International Workshop on Engineering Emergence in Decentralised Autonomic Systems (EEDAS 2007)* at the IEEE International Conference on Autonomic Computing (ICAC07) Jacksonville, Florida, USA.

[5]   A. Charles, R. Menezes, R. Tolksdorf. (2004) On the Implementation of SwarmLinda. *Proceedings of the 2004 ACM Southeastern Conference,* pp: 297-298.

[6]   Matteo Casadei1, Ronaldo Menezes, Mirko Viroli1, Robert Tolksdorf (2007) A Self-organizing Approach to Tuple Distribution in Large-Scale Tuple-Space Systems. *LNCS 4725,* pp: 146-160. Springer-Verlag.

[7]   U. Wilensky (2007) NetLogo Simulation Software Version 4beta1 http://ccl.northwestern.edu/netlogo Center for Connected Learning and Computer-Based Modeling, Northwestern University, Evanston, IL.

[8]   A.-L Barabási,. and R. Albert (1999), Emergence of Scaling in Random Networks, *Science* 286, pp: 509–512.

[9]   R. Albert, A.-L. Barabasi (2002) Statistical Mechanics of Complex Networks. *Reviews of Modern Physics* 74, pp: 47-98.

[10] Kun Chang Lee, Namho Lee (2007)   CARDS: Case-Based Reasoning Decision Support Mechanism for Multi-Agent Negotiation in Mobile Commerce. *Journal of Artificial Societies and Social Simulation* 10(2) pp: 4.

[11] J McCarthy (1963) Situations, Actions and Causal Laws. *Technical report, Stanford University*, 1963. Reprinted in Semantic Information Processing, ed: M. Minsky, pp: 410-417, MIT Press, Cambridge, Massachusetts, 1968

[12] H. J., Levesque, F. Pirri and R. Reiter (1998) 'Foundations for the Situation Calculus'. *Linköping Electronic Articles in Computer and Information Science*, http://www.ep.liu.se/ea/cis/1998/018/.

[13] R. Reiter (1991) The Frame Problem in the Situation Calculus: A Simple Solution (sometimes) and a Complete Result for Goal Regression. *Artificial Intelligence and Mathematical Theory of Computation: Papers in Honor of John McCarthy*, ed: V. Lifschitz, pp: 359-380, Academic Press, San Diego, California.

[14] R.C. Moore (1985) A Formal Theory of Knowledge and Action. In J.B. Hobb, R.C. Moore (Eds.) *Formal Theories of the Commonsense World*, pp: 319-358, Ablex Publishing Corporation, Norwood, NJ.

[15] R..Scherl, H.J. Levesque (1993) The Frame Problem and Knowledge Producing Actions. In the *Proceeding of the 11th National Conference on Artificial Intelligence (AAAI-93)*, Washington DC, USA, pp: 689-695

[16] 2nrich Project (2006) Towards a Disciplined Approach to Integrating Decision-Support Systems for Breast Cancer Care Activities. http://www.cms.livjm.ac.uk/2nrich/

[17] P.Miseldine, A. Taleb-Bendiab (2005) An Empirical Study into Governance Requirements for Autonomic E-Health Clinical Care Path Systems. In *Proceedings of the 1st International Workshop on Requirements Engineering for Information Systems in Digital Economy* (REISDE 2005) within ICETE05, pp: 171-178.

[18] A Taleb-Bendiab, D. England, M. Randles, P. Miseldine, K. Murphy (2006) A Principled Approach to the Design of Healthcare Systems: Autonomy vs Governance. *Reliability Engineering and System Safety Journal* 91(12), pp: 1576-1585.

[19] E W T Ngai A Gunasekaran (2007). A Review for Mobile Commerce Research and Applications, *Decision Support Systems*, 43(1), pp: 3-15.

[20] T P Liang, C P Wei (2004), Introduction to the Special Issue: Mobile Commerce Applications, *International Journal of Electronic Commerce*, 8(3), pp: 7-17.

Techniques and Applications for Mobile Commerce
C. Branki et al. (Eds.)
IOS Press, 2008

Semantic Transaction Processing in Mobile Computing

Fritz LAUX [a], Tim LESSNER [b], and Martti LAIHO [c]

[a] *Reutlingen University, Germany*
[b] *University of Duisburg-Essen, Germany*
[c] *Haaga-Helia University of Applied Sciences, Finland*

Abstract. Transaction processing is of growing importance for mobile computing. Booking tickets, flight reservation, banking, ePayment, and booking holiday arrangements are just a few examples for mobile transactions. Due to temporarily disconnected situations the synchronisation and consistent transaction processing are key issues. Serializability is a too strong criteria for correctness when the semantics of a transaction is known. We introduce a transaction model that allows higher concurrency for a certain class of transactions defined by its semantic. The transaction results are "escrow serializable" and the synchronisation mechanism is non-blocking. Experimental implementation showed higher concurrency, transaction throughput, and less resources used than common locking or optimistic protocols.

Keywords. transaction processing, semantic knowledge, classification of transactions, abort-replay reconciliation, disconnected operation, reread validation

Introduction

Mobile applications enable users to execute business transactions while being on the move. It is essential that online transaction processing will not be hindered by the limited processing capabilities of mobile devices and the low speed communication. In addition, transactions should not be blocked by temporarily disconnected situations. Traditional transaction systems in LANs rely on high speed communication and trained personnel so that data locking has proved to be an efficient mechanism to achieve serializability.

In the case of mobile computing neither connection quality or speed is guaranteed nor professional users may be assumed. This means that a transaction will hold its resources for a longer time, causing other conflicting transactions to wait longer for these data. If a component fails, it is possible that the transaction blocks (is left in a state where neither a rollback nor a completion is possible).

The usual way to avoid blocking of transactions is to use optimistic concurrency protocols.

In situations of high transaction volume the risk of aborted transaction rises and the restarted transaction add further load to the database system. Also this vulnerability could be exploited for denial of service attacks.

In order to make mobile transaction processing reliable and efficient a transaction management is needed that does not only avoid the drawbacks outlined above but also fits well into established or emerging technologies like EJB, ADO, SDO. Such technologies enable weakly coupled or disconnected computing promoting Service Oriented Architectures (SOA).

These data access technologies basically provide abstract data structures (objects, data sets, data graphs) that encapsulate and decouple from the database and adapt the programming models. We propose a transaction mechanism that should be implemented in middle tier between database and (mobile) client application. This enables to move some application logic from the client to the application server (middle tier) in order to relief the client from processing and storage needs. Validation, eventual transaction rewrites, reconciliations or compensations are implemented in the middle tier as shown in Figure 1.

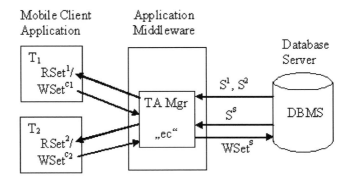

Figure 1. Three tier architecture for mobile transaction processing

0.1. Motivation

The main differences between mobile computing and stationary computing are temporary loss of communication and low communication bandwidth. However increased local autonomy is required at the same time. Data hoarding and local processing capability are the usual answers to achieve local autonomy. The next challenge is then the synchronisation or reintegration of data after processing [1,9,20]. As pointed out above, blocking of host data is not an option.

The challenge is to find a non-blocking concurrency mechanism that works well in disconnected situations and that is not leading to unnecessary transaction cancellations.

We need a mechanism to reconcile conflicting changes on the host database such that the result is still considered correct. This is possible if the transaction semantic is known to the transaction management. In this paper we propose to automatically replay the transactions in case of a conflict.

We illustrate the idea by an example and defer the formal definition to the next section. Assume that we have transactions T_1 and T_2 that withdraw € 100 and € 200 respectively from account a. If both transactions start reading the same value for a (say € 1000) and then attempt to write back $a := $ € 900 for T_1 and $a := $ € 800 for T_2 then a serialization conflict arises for the second transaction because the final result would lead to a lost update of the first transaction.

However, if in this case the transaction manager aborts the transaction, re-reads a (= € 900 now) and does the update on the basis of this new value then the result (= € 700) would be considered as correct. In fact, it resulted in a serial execution from the host's view. Clearly this transaction replay is only allowed if it is known that the second transaction's subtract value does not depend on the account value (balance). This precondition holds within certain limits for an important class of transactions: Booking tickets, reserving seats in a flight, bank transfers, stock management.

There are often additional constraints to obey: A bank account balance must not exceed the credit limit, the amount on stock cannot be negative, etc.

We will introduce a transaction model based on this idea that allows higher concurrency for a certain class of transactions defined by its semantic. The transaction results are "escrow serializable" and the synchronisation mechanism is non-blocking.

0.2. Related Work

For making transaction aborts as rare as possible essentially three approaches have been proposed:

- Use the semantic knowledge about a transactions to classify transactions that are compatible to interleave.
- Divide a transaction into subtransaction.
- Reconcile the database by rewriting the transaction in case of a conflict.

Semantic knowledge of a transaction allows non serializable schedules that produce consistent results. Garcia-Molina [2] classifies transactions into different types. Each transaction type is divided into atomic steps with compatibility sets according to its semantic. Transaction types that are not in the compatibility set are considered incompatible and are not allowed to interleave at all. Farrag and Özsu [3] refine this method allowing certain interleaving for incompatible types and assuming fewer restrictions for compatibility. The burden with this concept is to find the compatibility sets for each transaction step which is a $\mathcal{O}(n^2)$ problem.

Dividing transactions into subtransaction that are delimited by breakpoints does not reduce the number of conflicts for the same schedule but a partial rollback (rollback to a subtransaction) may be sufficient to resolve the conflict. Huang and Huang [4] use semantic based subtransactions and a compatibility matrix to achieve better concurrency for mobile database environments. Local autonomy of the clients may subvert the global serializability. The solutions proposed by Georgakopoulous et al. [5] and Mehrotra et al [6] came for the prize of low concurrency and low performance. Huang, Kwan, and Li [7] achieved better concurrency by using a mixture of locking to ensure global ordering and a refined compatibility matrix based on semantic subtransactions. Their transaction mechanism still needs to be implemented in a prototype to investigate its feasibility.

The reconciliation mechanism proposed in this paper attempts to replay the conflicting transactions and produce a serializable result. This method has been investigated in the context of multiversion databases. Graham and Barker [8] analysed the transactions that produced conflicting versions. Phatak and Nath [9] use a multiversion reconciliation algorithm based on snapshots and a conflict resolution function. The main idea is to compute a snapshot for each concurrent client transaction which is consistent in terms of isolation and leads to a least cost reconciliation. The standard conflict resolution function integrates transactions only if the read set $RSet$ of the transaction is a subset of the snapshot version $S(in)$ into which the result needs to be integrated. In the case of write-write conflicts this is not the case, as $RSet \nsubseteq S(in)$.

We illustrate this by an example using the read-write model with Herbrand semantics (see [10]). Assume we have two transaction: $T_1 = (r_1(a), w_1(a), r_1(b), w_1(b))$ transfers € 100 from account a to account b and $T_2 = (r_2(b), w_2(b))$ withdraws € 100 from account b. If both transactions are executed in serial, the balance for account b will end up with its starting value. Now assume, that snapshot version $V(0) = \{a^0, b^0\}$ is used and both transactions start with the same value b^0. Assume the schedule $S = (r_1(a^0), r_2(b^0), r_1(b^0), w_1(a^1), w_2(b^1), c_2, w_1(b^1), c_1)$. S is not serializable and no other schedule either if both transactions use the same version ob b. The last transaction attempting to write account b will produce a lost update and should abort.

The multiversion snapshot based reconciliation algorithm of Phatak and Nath [9] will not be able to reconcile T_1 as $RSet(T_1) = V(0) = \{a^0, b^0\} \nsubseteq V(1) = \{a^0, b^1\}$. $V(1)$ is the result of transaction T_2.

If no snapshot would have been taken and making sure that the update (read-write sequence) of b is not interrupted (interleaved) the result would have been the serializable schedule $R = (r_1(a), w_1(a), r_2(b), w_2(b), c_2, r_1(b), w_1(b), c_1)$. This shows the limitations of snapshot isolation compared to locking in terms of transaction rollbacks. On the other hand the schedule R leads to low performance because no interleaving operations for the read-write sequence are allowed.

Our approach is to abort a conflicting transaction and automatically replay the operation sequentially. The isolation level should be read committed to avoid cascading rollbacks or compensation transactions. To ease the reconciliation processing we classify transaction in terms of its semantic.

1. Transaction Model

A database D may be viewed as a finite set of entities $a, b, \cdots, x, y, z$ (see [11]). If there exists more than one version of an entity, we denote it with the version number, e.g. x^2. These entities will be read (read set $RSet$) and modified (write set $WSet$) by a set of transactions $\mathbf{T} = \{T_1, T_2, \cdots, T_n\}$. The database D at any given time exists in a particular state D^S. A snapshot of D is a subset of a database state D^S (see [12]).

Our mobile computing system consists of a database server, an application middleware with mobile transaction management, and a mobile client with storage and computing capabilities as sketched out in Figure 1. A mobile transaction is a distributed application that guaranties transactional properties. We assume that the data communication is handled transparently by a communication protocol that can detect and recover failures on the network level. Mobile client and server have some local autonomy so that in case of network disconnection both sites can continue their work to some extent.

The data base consists of a central data store and snapshot data (at least the $RSet$) on the mobile client for each active transaction. From a transactional concept's view the transactions on the client are executed under local autonomy. The local commit is "escrowed" along with the changes to the server. The transaction manager tries to integrate all escrowed transactions into the central data store. In case of serialization conflicts reconciliation can be achieved if the semantic of the transaction is known and all database constraints are obeyed.

1.1. Escrow Serializable

For the sake of availability we want to avoid locked transaction as far as possible. One approach is to use optimistic concurrency, the other way is to relax serializability. Optimistic concurrency suffers from transaction aborts when a serialization conflicts arises [13]. The multiversion based view maintenance could minimize that risk but it requires a reliable communication at all times [14].

Much research was invested to optimize the validation algorithms [15,16,17,18] for serialization. We prefer to allow non-serializable schedules that produce consistent results for certain types of transactions similar to [19].

A transaction T transforms a consistent database state into another consistent state. This may be formalized by considering a transaction as a function operating on a subset of consistent database states $\mathbf{D}$, i.e. $D^2 = T(D^1)$ with suitable $D^1, D^2 \in \mathbf{D}$, where $RSet \subseteq D^1$ and $WSet \subseteq D^2$. If we want to make the user input u explicit we write $D^2 = T(D^1, u)$.

Definition 1 (escrow (ec) serializable) Let Q be a history of a set of (client) transactions $\mathbf{T} = \{T_1, T_2, \cdots, T_n\}$ that are executed concurrently on a database D with initial state D^0. For each transaction T_i the user input is denoted by u_i. The history Q is called *escrow serializable* if

1. there exists a serial history S for $\mathbf{T}$ with committed database states $\mathbf{D^S} = (D^1, D^2, \cdots, D^n)$, where
2. $\exists r \in \{1, 2, \cdots, n\}$ with $D^1 = T_r(D^0, u_r)$ and
3. $\exists s \in \{1, 2, \cdots, n\}$ with $D^k = T_s(D^{k-1}, u_s)$ for each $k = (2, 3, \cdots, n)$

Please note that this kind of serializability is descriptive as it is not based on the operations but on the outcome (semantic) of the transactions. Escrow serializability means that the outcome is the same as with a serial execution using the same user input.

The name *escrow serializable* stems from the idea that a mobile client "escrows" its transaction to the server. On the server site the transaction manager reconciles the transaction if all database constraints are fulfilled. This can be achieved by analysing the conflicting transactions and producing the same result as a serial execution would have done. We demonstrate this with the following example:

Example 1 (withdraw) Let T_1 and T_2 be two withdraw transactions that lift-off € 100 resp. € 200 from account a. We denote by c_i (resp. a_i, ec_i) the commit (resp. abort, escrow commit) command. The history

$$S^c = r_1(a)r_2(a)w_2(a' := a - 200)ec_2w_1(a'' := a - 100)ec_1$$

normally produces a lost update, but it is escrow serializable. The transaction manager on the server will detect the conflicting transaction. T_1 is aborted and automatically replayed with the previous input data. The resulting history on the server will be

$$S^s = r_1(a)r_2(a)w_2(a' := a - 200)c_2w_1(a - 100)a_1r_1(a')w_1(a' - 100)c_1.$$

Schedule S^s is equivalent to the serial execution (T_2, T_1).

If there exists a constraint, say $a > 0$ any violating transaction has to abort. Assume that $a = 300$ and take the same operation sequence as in schedule S^c then transaction T_1 has to abort because $a' - 100 \not> 0$.

ensure: set of transactions $\mathbf{T} = \{T_1, T_2, \cdots, T_n\}$
ensure: actual database state D^s, set of constraints $C(D)$
ensure: only committed data in read set $RSet(i)$ of T_i
ensure: $T_i = (op_{ik}, i = 1, 2, \cdots, k_i)$
for $\forall ec_i \in \{ec_1, ec_2, \cdots, ec_n\}$ received **do**
    // test if T_i conflicts with D^s
    if $RSet(i) \subseteq D^s$ and $\forall c \in C(D): (c = true)$ **then**
        commit T_i
    else // abort and replay transaction
        abort T_i
        ensure: serial execution
        for each $op_{ik} \in op(T_i)$ **do** op_{ik}
        if $\exists c \in C(D)$ with $(c = false)$ **then** // c violated
            abort T_i
        else
            commit T_i
    end if
end for

Figure 2. Reconciliation algorithm for ec serializability

1.2. Escrow Reconciliation Algorithm

Escrow serialization relies on reconciling transaction in such a way that the outcome is serializable. This is only possible if the semantic of the transactions including the user input are known. The idea is to read all data necessary for a transaction and defer any write operation until commit time. If a serialization conflict arises at commit time this means that a concurrent transaction has already committed. In this case the transaction is aborted and automatically replayed with the same input data.

Our transaction model is divided into two phases:

(client phase) During the processing on the client site, data may only be retrieved from the server. It is important that the read requests are served in an optimistic way. Technically a read set of data, a data graph or any other snapshot could be delivered to the mobile client. The client transaction terminates with an escrow commit (ec) or an abort (a).

(server phase) When the server receives the ec along with the write set and no serialization conflict exists the transaction is committed. In case of a conflict the transaction is aborted. The replay is done automatically with pessimistic concurrency control or serial execution. This prevents the starvation [12] of a transaction. If no constraints are violated the replayed transaction is committed.

A possible reconciliation algorithm using the abort-replay mechanism is presented in Figure 2.

Care has to be taken with transactions not using the abort-replay mechanism. In this case the database should work in isolation level "serializable".

If the abort-replay mechanism is always used to integrate the transactions on the server there is no need for a certain isolation level as the read sets only contain consistent results. Any competing transactions will not alter the database until the server integrates the result. As the transaction results are integrated one-by-one, no read phenomena may occur and serial results are ensured.

We describe an implementation using SDO technology later in section 3.

So far we have illustrated the model with transactions that produce a constant change for a data item (see Example 1). The model is valid for any transaction with a known semantic (see Theorem 1). For instance the transaction $T_3 = (r_3(x), w_3(x := 1.1x), ec_3)$ increases the prize x of a product by 10%. If the first read of x and the reread differ $(r_3'(x) \neq r_3(x))$, then the replay will produce a 10% increase based on the actual value.

For an automatic replay it is is essential to know which transactions are "immune" or depend in a predicted manner of from the read set. These are the candidates for escrow serializability.

There is a technical issue for the banking example. Here we do not really need the actual withdraw amount of the transaction to replay it. It is sufficient to know three database states since the new value can be calculated by $a := a^1 + a^c - a^0$ where a^1 is the actual balance, a^c is the new balance calculated by the client transaction, and a^0 is the basis on which the value a^c was computed. This observation gives reason to find classes of transactions that are ec serializable without knowing the actual user input.

2. Semantic Classification of Transactions

To facilitate the task for the reconciliation algorithm we shall classify the client transaction according to their semantic, in particular the dependency of the input from the read set.

Definition 2 (dependency function) Let T be a transaction with $RSet = \{x_1, x_2, \cdots, x_n\}$ and $WSet = \{y_1, y_2, \cdots, y_m\}$ on a database D. The function $f_i : \vec{x} \to y_i$ with $\vec{x} = (x_1, x_2, \cdots, x_n)$ and $y_i \in WSet$ is called *dependency function* of y_i.
Let $x_k \in RSet$ and $y_i \in WSet$ be numeric data types for all k. If f_i is a linear function then y_i is called *linear dependent* and we can write

$$y_i = f_i(\vec{x}) = \vec{a_i}^T \vec{x} + c_i \quad (i = 1, 2, \cdots, m) \tag{1}$$

with $\vec{a_i}^T$ being the transposed vector $a_i = (a_{i1}, a_{i2}, \cdots, a_{in})$.
If all functions f_i are linear dependent, then

$$\vec{y} = A\vec{x} + \vec{c} \tag{2}$$

with $m \times n$-Matrix $A = (a_{ik})$ and m-dimensional vector $\vec{c}$. We call the corresponding transaction T *linear dependent*.
If $f_i(\vec{x}) = \vec{1}^T \vec{x} + c_i$ then f_i is called *linear dependent with gradient 1* ($\vec{1}$ is the identity matrix).
IF $f_i(\vec{x}) = \vec{b}^T \vec{x} + c_i$ then f_i is called *linear dependent with gradient $\vec{b}$*.

In our banking example the accounts are linearly dependent with gradient 1. The 10% price increase is an example for a transaction that is linearly dependent with gradient $b = 1.1$.

If the values of the $WSet$ however depend in an non-formalized user dependent manner from the $RSet$ then there is no way to reconcile the transaction automatically. The escrow serializable execution of a transaction depends on the fact that the outcome does change in a known functional manner.

Theorem 1 Let **T** be a set of transactions where each transaction T has known dependency functions f_i (i = 1,2, ..., m). Then the concurrent execution of **T** is escrow serializable using the abort-replay algorithm of Figure 2.

Proof Let D^0 be a consistent state of a database with transactions $\mathbf{T} = \{T_1, T_2, \cdots, T_n\}$. Let H be a history of **T** and let w.l.o.g. the commit order be the same as the transaction index. We construct a serial transaction order that matches the definitions of escrow serializability using the abort-replay algorithm. Any write operations of the transactions T_i are postponed until commit time. The read set of T_1 is a subset of database state D^0. Then we have $S^1 = T_1(D^0)$ after the first commit c_1. When a subsequent transaction T_k tries to commit and $RSet_k \cap D^{k-1} = \emptyset$ then there is no serialisation conflict and the commit succeeds. In case of a conflict, the transaction is aborted and replayed with the same user data. During the replay the algorithm ensures serial execution, so further commits are queued. Finally we have $D^k = T_s(D^{k-1}, u_s)$ for $k = 1, 2, \cdots, n$. QED

Let $\{r_1, r_2, \cdots, r_n\} \subseteq D^c$ be the read set values of a client transaction and let $\{s_1, s_2, \cdots, s_n\} \subseteq D^s$ be the read set values on the server when the transaction tries to commit. Then the abort-replay mechanism produces $WSet(T) = T(D^s, \vec{u}) = A\vec{s} + \vec{u}$. The value of any numerical data item $x \in WSet$ for a linear dependent transaction is computed as

$$
\begin{aligned}
x^T &= \Pi_x T(D^s, \vec{u}) = \vec{a}^T \vec{s} + u \\
&= \vec{a}^T \vec{s} + (\vec{a}^T \vec{r} + u) - \vec{a}^T \vec{r} \\
&= \vec{a}^T(\vec{s} - \vec{r}) + \Pi_x D^c \\
&= \Pi_x A(\vec{s} - \vec{r}) + \Pi_x D^c
\end{aligned}
\tag{3}
$$

From the above equation we see that the reconciliation for transactions with a linear dependent write set may be simplified. For the transaction manager it is sufficient to know the client state D^c, the read set D^s at commit time and the state produced by $T(D^c, u)$.

Corollary A linear dependent transaction can be reconciled (replayed) in a generic way, if client state D^c at begin of transaction, the read set D^s at commit time and the state produced by $T(D^c, u)$ are known.

The corollary statement is similar to the reconciliation proposed by Holliday, Agrawal, and El Abbadi [20].

2.1. Quota Transaction

In many cases the semantic of a transaction has well known restrictions. We can guaranty the successful execution of certain transactions if the user input remains within a certain value range.

Assume a reservation transaction. If the transaction is given a quota of q reservations then the success can be guarantied for reservations within these limits. It is the responsibility of the transaction manager to ensure that the quota does not violate the consistency constraints. For example if there are 10 tickets left and the quota is set for 2 tickets, then only 5 concurrent transactions are allowed. As soon as a transaction terminates with less than two reservations the transaction manager may allow another transaction to start with a quota that ensures no overbooking.

Quota transactions in this sense are similar to increment or decrement of counter transactions with escrow locking (see [10]).

Definition 3 (quota transaction) Let T be a transaction with $WSet = \{y_1, y_2, \cdots, y_m\}$ on a database D. For each y_i there is a value range $I := [l, u]$ associated. T is called *quota transaction* if the success of the transaction can be guarantied in advance if the result values y_i do not exceed the quota, i.e. $y_{i(old)} + l \leq y_{i(new)} \leq y_{i(old)} + u$.

Setting quotas is a mean to guaranty success for a transaction by reserving sufficient resources without locking the resources. Caution has to be taken when using quotas as resources are reserved that finally should be taken or given back. Therefore a time out or a cancel operation is required on the server site.

3. Example Implementation of the ec Model with SDO

Service Data Objects (SDO [21,22]) are a platform neutral specification and disconnected programming model, which enables dynamic creation, access, introspection, and manipulation of business objects.

Our implementation (see Lessner [23]) of the transaction manager (TM) uses SDO graphs and resides between the data access service (DAS) and the client. This way, the TM fits well into SDO's vision of being independent of the data source.

A snapshot of each delivered graph is taken by the TM and each SDO graph associates a change summary that complies with the requirements for optimistic concurrency control (see section 1). To assert "escrow serializabilty" (provided by the reconciliation algorithm) an association between a transaction and the semantic of this transaction is needed[1]. This association results in a classification of the transaction (e.g. "linear dependent").

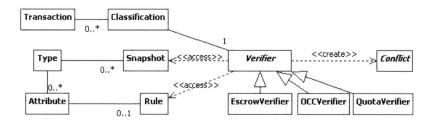

Figure 3. Abstract design of the transaction manager

---

[1]In heterogeneous environments an additional data object could be used to describe the semantic of a transaction, SDO uses XML as protocol

An association between a classification and a verifier (see Figure 3) enables a semantic transaction level (e.g. optimistic concurrency control (OCC), escrow concurrency (EC)).

Assume that we have an incoming transaction (T-Level=EC) with a changed data graph. The transaction handler delivers the transaction to the verifier. To ensure EC, OCC is checked first. This means, two verifier implementations come into play (Step 1, Figure 4) and the order is relevant (OCC → EC).

Each changed attribute is OCC validated against the snapshot (Step 2, Figure 4). If an OCC conflict exists and the attribute associates a "withdraw rule" for example, then reconciliation is possible and a conflict object is instantiated that represents the transaction rewrite (withdraw correction). If an OCC conflict occurs for an attribute that is not corrigible, the transaction has to abort. In a second step the EC verifier tries to resolve the conflicts (e.g. to reread the balance from the latest snapshot). If any conflicts exist after the EC verifier has finished (e.g. the withdraw amount would exceed the credit limit), the transaction has to abort, too. Each time a conflict is eventually resolvable (each verifier ensures the changes) the modification is sent to the replay manager (Step 3, Figure 4). The replay manager determines the snapshot's modifications and the graph's changes (Step 4, Figure 4).

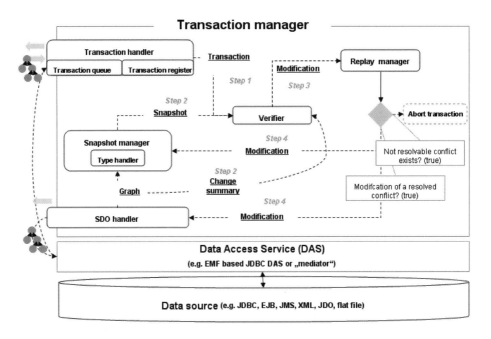

Figure 4. Architecture of the transaction manager

The snapshot is data centric, which means that there exist a snapshot version of each delivered data object related to a transaction. Therefore the knowledge about the type's schema is necessary. To acquire this knowledge we decided to implement a separate meta schema. Another possibility would be, to use the schema provided by the implementation of the SDO Data Access Services (DAS). The first possibility fits better into a general usage of the TM but causes schema redundancy. In both cases a type handler module is needed, either for accessing the schema of the SDO DAS or for accessing the additional schema.

4. Conclusions

Mobile transactions have special demands for the transaction management. We propose a transaction model that is non-blocking and is reconciling conflicting transactions by exploiting the semantic of the transaction. A simple abort-replay mechanism can produce reconciliation in the sense of escrow serializability. The abort-replay algorithm detects conflicts by rereading the data. The mechanism is easy to implement and can make use of update operation when read - and write set overlaps.

If all writes are postponed until the commit is issued and the reread and write operations during reconciliation are executed serialized or serial, then no inconsistent data will be read. A further option is to use consistent snapshots. Independent from the mechanism the read phase should be executed with optimistic concurrency control.

In contrast, the reconciliation phase should run in a pre-claiming locking mode. This ensures efficient sequential processing of competing transactions without delays as user input is already available and starvation is avoided. With this marginal condition the escrow serialization algorithm has the potential to outperform other mechanisms.

For the class of linear dependent transactions it is sufficient for reconciliation to know the client state at begin of transaction, the state produced by the client transaction on the client site, and the database server state at commit time.

Acknowledgements

This paper was inspired by discussions with the members of the DBTech network and the ideas presented during the DBTech Pro workshops. The DBTech Project was supported by the Leonardo da Vinci programme during the years 2002 - 2005.

References

[1] J.H. Abawajy, M. Mat Deris; *Supporting Disconnected Operations in Mobile Computing*, The 4th ACS/IEEE International Conference on Computer Systems and Applications (AICCSA-06) , 911–918 (2006), American University of Sharjah, UAE.

[2] Hector Garcia-Molina; *Using Semantic Knowledge for Transaction Processing in a Distributed Database*, ACM Transactions on Database Systems, Vol. 8, No. 2 (1983), 186–213.

[3] Abdel Aziz Farrag and M. Tamer Özsu; *Using Semantic Knowledge of Transactions to Increase Concurrency*, ACM Transactions on Database Systems, Vol. 14, No. 4, (1989), 503–525.

[4] Shi-Ming Huang and Chien-Ming Huang; *A semantic-based transaction model for active heterogeneous database systems*, IEEE Conference on Systems, Man, and Cybernetics **3** (1998), 2854–2859

[5] D. Georgakopoulous, M. Rusinkiewicz, and A. Sheth; *On Serializability of Multi-database Transactions through Forced Local Conflicts*, Proceedings of the 7th Conference Data Engineering, IEEE publication (1991), 314–323

[6] S. Mehrotra et al; *Non-serializability Executions in Heterogeneous Distributed Database Systems*, Proceedings on the 1st International Conference Parallel and Distributed Information Systems, IEEE publication (1991), 245–252

[7] Shi-Ming Huang, Irene Kwan and Chih-He Li; *A Study on the Management of Semantic Transaction for Efficient Data Retrieval*, SIGMOD Record **31** (3) (2002), 28–33

[8] Peter C. J. Graham, Ken Barker; *Effective Optimistic Concurrency Control in Multiversion Object Bases*, Object-Oriented Methodologies and Systems, International Symposium ISOOMS '94, Palermo, Italy (1994), 313-328, Lecture Notes in Computer Science, Springer

[9] Shirish Hemant Phatak and Badri Nath; *Transaction-Centric Reconciliation in Disconnected Client-Server Databases*, Mobile Networks and Applications **9** (2004), 459–471, Kluwer Academic Publisher, The Netherlands.

[10] G. Weikum, G. Vossen; *Transactional Information Systems: Theory, Algorithms, and the Practice of Concurrency Control and Recovery*, Morgan Kaufmann Publishers, San Francisco, CA, 2002

[11] Hector Garcia-Molina, Jeffrey D. Ullman, Jennifer Widom; *Database Systems: The Complete Book*, Prentice Hall, New Jersey, 2002.

[12] Avi Silberschatz, Hank Korth, S. Sudarshan; *Database System Concepts, 5th ed.*, McGraw Hill, New York, NY, 2006.

[13] SongTing Chen, Bin Liu, and Elke A. Rundensteiner; *Multiversion-Based View Maintenance Over Distributed Data Sources*, ACM Transactions on Database Systems, Vol. 29, No. 4 (2004), 675–709.

[14] JuhnYong Lee; *Precise serialization for optimistic concurrency control*, Data & Knowledge Engineering, Vol. 29, Issue 2 (1999), 163–179, Elsevier Science B.V., The Netherlands.

[15] K. A. Momin, K. Vidyasankar: *Flexible Integration of Optimistic and Pessimistic Concurrency Control in Mobile Environments*. ADBIS-DASFAA, 346–353 (2000), Prague, Czech Republic

[16] Stefano Ceri, Susan S. Owicki; *On the Use of Optimistic Methods for Concurrency Control in Distributed Databases*, Berkeley Workshop (1982) 117-129

[17] Ho-Jin Choi, Byeong-Soo Jeong; *A Timestamp-Based Optimistic Concurrency Control for Handling Mobile Transactions*. ICCSA (**2**) 2006, 796-805

[18] Adeniyi A. Akintola, G. Adesola Aderounmu, A. U. Osakwe, Michael O. Adigun; *Performance Modeling of an Enhanced Optimistic Locking Architecture for Concurrency Control in a Distributed Database System*, Journal of Research and Practice in Information Technology 37(4): (2005)

[19] D. Agrawal, J.L. Bruno, A. El Abbadi, V. Krishnaswamy; *Relative Serializability: An Approach for Relaxing the Atomicy of Transactions*, SIGMOD/PODS 94 (1994), Minneapolis, Minnesota, USA.

[20] Joanne Holliday, Divyakant Agrawal, Amr El Abbadi; *Disconnection Modes for Mobile Databases*, Wireless Networks **9** (2002), 391–402, Kluwer Academic Publisher, The Netherlands.

[21] M. Adams, C. Andrei et al; *Service Data Objects For Java Specification*, BEA Systems, Cape Clear Software, IBM, Oracle, et al, (2006), http://www.osoa.org/download/attachments/36/Java-SDO-Spec-v2.1.0-FINAL.pdf

[22] J. Beatty, S. Brodsky, M. Nally, R. Patel; *Next-Generation Data Programming*, BEA Systems, IBM, (2003), http://www.bea.com/dev2dev/assets/sdo/Next-Gen-Data-Programming-Whitepaper.pdf

[23] Tim Lessner; *Transaktionsverarbeitung in disconnected Architekturen am Beispiel von Service Data Objects (SDO) und prototypische Implementierung eines Transaktionsframeworks*, Diploma Thesis (2007), Department of Business Informatics, Reutlingen University, Germany

Techniques and Applications for Mobile Commerce
C. Branki et al. (Eds.)
IOS Press, 2008

Support for M-Commerce Software Autonomy

Thar BAKER, A. TALEB-BENDIAB, Martin RANDLES
Department of Computing and Mathematical Sciences,
Liverpool John Moores University, Byrom Street, Liverpool, L3 3AF, UK
t.shamsa@2007.ljmu.ac.uk , a.talebbendiab@livjm.ac.uk, m.j.randles@ljmu.ac.uk

Abstract: Recently there has been a flurry of research inspired by social and biological models for achieving software autonomy. This has been prompted by the need to automate laborious administration tasks, recover from unanticipated systems failure, and provide self-protection from security vulnerabilities, whilst guaranteeing predictable autonomic software behaviour. However, runtime assured adaptation of software to new requirement in a mobile setting, where there is code mobility in the form of mobile agents as well as the presence of mobile devices, is still a major outstanding issue for research. This paper presents a language support for the programming of autonomic software in mobile environments and m-commerce environments in particular. The paper starts by a review of the state-of-the-art into runtime software adaptation and mobility. This is followed by a developed Neptune framework and language support applied to mobile ambients, which is here described via an illustrative example based on a commercial decision support system that automatically updates according to a newly developed run time code editor. The paper ends with a discussion and some concluding remarks leading to suggested further works.

1. Autonomic Computing

By mimicking the autonomous behaviour exhibited by living organisms, research into autonomic computing is exploring ways to imbue software systems with self-managing capabilities [1]. Much research development already exists including autonomic middleware frameworks targeting grid-based computing [2] to promote analogous self-management. ReMMoC [3] focuses on service discovery for mobile clients across heterogeneous platforms and protocols, whilst the authors' Cloud Architecture can be applied to disparate, localised networks [4] for self-organisation. Other works focused on code base analysis adaptation such as Toskana [5] and similar approaches use AOP as a basis for adaptable change. These changes, however, are enabled by specific modifications to one or more OSI layers, such that with Toskana, for example, an operating system kernel is made adaptable. Thus, for complete autonomy, components must be built to support the kernel. In dynamic domains, including mobile applications, this is not always possible.

Further holistic paradigms for autonomic software have emerged based on software agent theory [6] that treat a complete system as a series of agents, each of which processes their own behaviour models to collectively perform set tasks and behaviours. Effectively arranging co-ordination and providing communication between agents for unified, directed behaviour [7] remains a challenge in mobile environments.

Other approaches to software autonomy in mobile settings are based on service-oriented architecture and service hot-swapping, in that, for instance adaptive middleware marshals and re-routes calls to alternative services [8]. There is however little or no support to permit the deployment of autonomic systems within mobile e-commerce (m-commerce) scenarios to encompass cross-device/platform and multi-location commerce transactions with heterogeneous commerce components including such non-functional requirements as their associated enactment, governance and assurance constraints. The mobility to be considered here is not solely confined to computation on the move but also applies to mobility of code and services; leading to highly complex and dynamic systems. Hence, the task of provisioning and managing such systems far outstrips the capabilities of human operatives, with most adaptations to operational circumstances requiring the system to be taken offline reprogrammed, recompiled and redeployed.

A systematic approach to the adaptation of software at runtime for new or emergent requirements that occur through mobility is still an outstanding issue for research. In addition, providing adaptation of an m-commerce system based on assured, bounded governance requires knowledge of not only what should be adapted, but also its impact on other components and the safety of producing such adaptation within its defined boundaries. In effect, knowledge of the construction and the meanings behind the formation of an m-commerce system is vital for bounded autonomy through adaptation to be accomplished.

This paper presents a language support for the programming of autonomic software in an m-commerce environment. The paper starts with a review of the state-of-the-art into runtime software adaptation. This is followed by a description of a developed Neptune framework and language support, which is applied to mobile ambients through a run time code editor. This is further described via an illustrative example using a commercial medical decision support system. The paper concludes with a discussion and concluding remarks leading to suggested further works.

In short this paper presents a developed Neptune method and language to enable full runtime adaptation of a distributed, component-based mobile application. The full description of the language is outside the scope of this paper but can be found in [4].

2. Proposed Solution

Introducing autonomic components to mobile applications is very difficult to achieve due the highly dynamic nature of the domain. Updates to introduce new products, refine business models or adapt processes, for example, are difficult to accomplish at run time. This paper proposes a new solution based on performing the updates through a run time (Wiki) code editor using the Neptune language applied to a mobile bounded computational entity called an ambient [9].

2.1. Ambients

An ambient is a bounded computational entity. To perform mobile computations it is necessary to define all the required elements that need to move in order for the mobile entity to execute successfully. If computations are to be moved in an assured way it must be possible to determine what should move; a boundary specifies deterministically the scope of the required mobility: Everything within the boundary moves with the computation. Ambients are also hierarchical in nature so that sub-ambients may be nested inside super-ambients. There are just three actions applicable to ambients; they may enter or leave containing ambients and communicate with other ambients. When ambients move, they move as a whole entity including all the resources required to complete the task. For example if a laptop computer, as the boundary of an ambient, is disconnected from a network and moves to another network all of its address space and file system should move with it.

2.2. Neptune

An authoring environment, Neptune has been developed that can facilitate the deployment of a self-governing m-commerce applications based on ambients. Whilst discussion of Neptune is out of the context of this paper, what follows is a brief discussion regarding its principal features.

Neptune produces an object form of logical connectives that can be inspected, modified and deliberated upon at run time. The Neptune objects encapsulate the logical model and assignments expressed within the script in object notation, allowing it to be inspected, modified, recompiled, and re-evaluated at runtime. Neptune allows the modification and enhancement of an m-commerce process during any point in its lifetime, allowing the ambients to adapt after being deployed. Such adaptation requires co-ordination. The m-commerce application itself acts as a software agent within a grid based architecture designed to execute Neptune objects at runtime, based on an ambient framework similar to the cloud architecture [10]. The ambient can be thought of as a federation of services and resources controlled by the system controller and discovered through the system space to facilitate all resource requirements for the ambients computational function. The system space provides persistent data storage for service registration and state information giving the means to coordinate the application service activities. The system controller controls access to and from the individual services and resources within an ambient. It brokers requests to the system based on system status and governance rules, in Neptune objects, derived from the logical normative deliberative process. The system controller acts as an interface to the ambient. It can function in two roles, either as an abstraction that inspects calls between the system space and services, or as a monitor that analyses the state information stored within the system space.

2.3. The Wiki Editor

For a mobility purposes, Neptune encoded process "intention" models are represented in XML, a generic storage format that can be stored and retrieved by a wide variety of other software systems [11]. Thus, the intention model can be distributed with the ambients and retrieved via the Internet, a database, or a network, allowing multiple users to make use of the same intention process. The Wiki editor, described here, deals with the intention model of the system directly, unlike more traditional Wiki Editors, which deal with simple text; providing the software with a high level of assurance to ensure the correct interpretation of the intentions it is automating. The Intention model can be thought of as consisting of both flow and aspect models: The flow model of the intention set provides the order in which decisions for adapting the ambient are made and the links between them, as well as directing which path through the flow model should be taken based on the inputs from the user for the adaptation update. Thus

Neptune deployed ambients are adaptable at run time through a user controlled interface with the underlying logical model, encoded in the Neptune objects, being responsible for maintaining safety assurrance.

In this case, as illustrated in the Figure 1, the Intention model will be connected directly with the Parser that is responsible for interpreting the flow model (via the Process Model Interpreter) and the logic rules (via the Logic Interpreter), as well as including the Execution manager that decides whether the next required process is to the Semantic linker or the Execution engine depending on the user intentions.

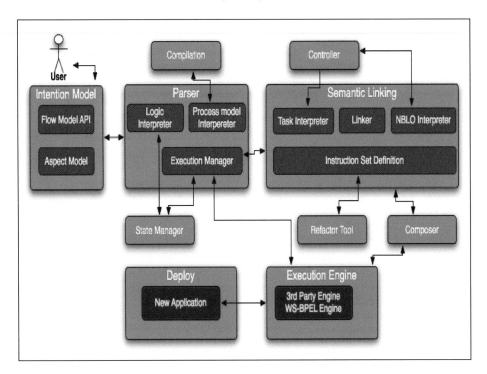

Figure 1. Wiki editor for ambient adaptation

2.4.   Implementation

It is necessary for Neptune to be deployed across heterogeneous systems programmed in any language. The solution should sit above and be separate from any single language used to produce language components in the m-commerce application. In effect, the components are hidden from Neptune by way of a semantic interface: Neptune need only be able to dispatch calls defined within the semantic interface, rather than needing to directly host and manage the component itself. In this way, a bridge between Neptune and a base language is required both to facilitate communication between the base language and Neptune so that the language can instruct Neptune and interpret results from it, but also Neptune can dispatch a call that is required to be handled by the base language.

It is also clear from the discussion that Neptune requires a form of expression to be defined such that it is capable of representing the ontological model desired to fulfil the ambient requirements and ensure integrity including maintaining the requisite resource/service selection within the ambient boundary. Neptune presents information using a context-free language NeptuneScript. Figure 2 shows a schematic view of the method in which Neptune communicates with base language components. The Base Language Connector's are written within the base language rather than with NeptuneScript, and encapsulate the structure and communication methods needed to interact fully with Neptune and to be able to interpret and write NeptuneScript. Neptune itself provides numerous interfaces using standardised protocols such as COM, SOAP, and RPC forms such as Java RPC or .NET Remoting to enable a base language connector to dispatch a call to Neptune, and receive responses from it. These calls are marshalled either directly to the higher Neptune Framework for processing, or situated as Neptune Base Language Objects (NBLOs), a reified semantic form that describes the intentions and conditions needed by a base language component [10]. The NBLO itself is written within NeptuneScript. In addition, the NBLOs contain the requisite information to determine how to interoperate with the appropriate base language connector to marshal a call to the base language component. This information is used by the Neptune framework to invoke the behaviour described in the NBLO.

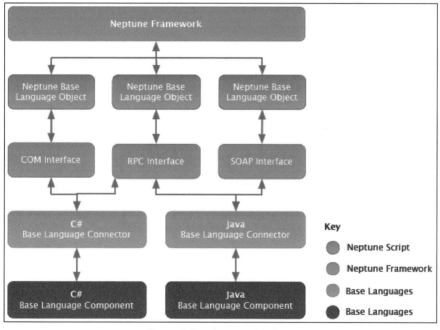

Figure 2. Base language interface.

2.5. Example

A Service Selection Software (S3) web application is used to combine different web services based on an intention model. S3 uses two methods for invoking web services depending on the number of the web services that the user wants to combine; *AJAX* or *WSDL*.

Assuming that "*S*" represents the number of web services and "n" is any number greater than or equal to two, if "*S=1*" then the *AJAXnblo* will be used, otherwise if "*S=n*" the *WSDLnblos* for the n web services will be used. The system will not be able to use AJAX to invoke more than one web service at a time in the same placeholder because there should be one and only one instance for the ScriptManager in the application, where each web service has its own script manager.

As is evident from the discussion above, the Logic Rules Algorithm will as shown in Figure 3.

Input: [S]- {the number of the required web services}.
Input: [n]- {any number >= 2}.
Output: {Either *Ajaxnblo* Or *WSDLnblos*}
1:      **if** S= 1:
2:          **then**
3:              **do** Semantic Linking **then** // to find the required web service
4:              **execute** (*AJAXnblo*) //to execute the selected *AJAXnblo*'s web service
5:          **end if**
6:      **else**
7:          **then**
8:          **if** S=n:
9:              **then**
10:                 **do** Semantic Linking **then**
11:                 **do** Composition **then** // to combine the selected web services together
12:                 **execute** (*WSDLnblos* (S))
13:             **end if**
14:         **end else**

Figure 3: The logic rules algorithm

The authors' Neptune Studio 2.0 was used to form the Flow model of the system depending on the described rules as shown in Figure 4.

Here, the logic rules form the basis of the required adaptation and flow is transferred to either *AJAXnblo* or *WSDLnblos* depending on this decision. However, the logic rule itself has no reference to either *AJAXnblo* or *WSDLnblos*. Instead, the logic rules return a result (1 or n), which is interpreted by the flow model to produce an action (choose *AJAXnblo* or *WSDLnblos*). Consequently, without change to the logic rule, the flow model can adapt so that *WSDLnblos* would be considered, rather than the *AJAXnblos, for example*. Indeed, any number of adaptations can occur in the flow model by using the Intention Editor, shown in Figure 5, without impacting on the logic rules. This level of independence between the models means that both can be written and adapted separately, allowing the logic that powers the decision process to remain assured and tested, though the actions and consequences of the decision open to change. This also means that those familiar with programming and writing abstract, logical statements can be committed to the logic model, whilst the more concrete and understandable flow model can be formalized and updated by either the user or the administrator themselves due to its recognizable format.

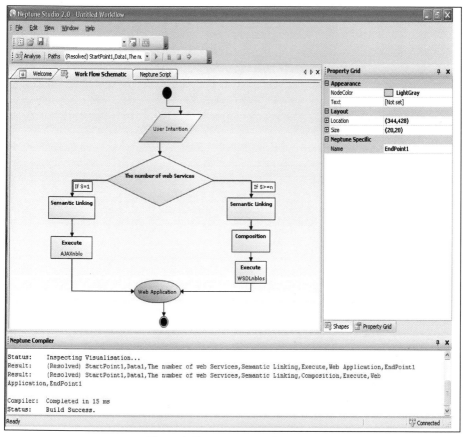

Figure 4: The Neptune IDE (flow editor)

If the user has adapted the intention model so that an ambient requires a service that does not exist within its defined boundary then the governance structure inherent in Neptune intervene to assure the quality and safety of the adaptation. *Concept Aided-Situation Prediction Action* (CA-SPA) is introduced to this system to enable it to inspect its own operation and available functionality to produce its own plan of action, or resolution to a provided intention, The full description of the language is outside the scope of this paper but can be found in [12]. This would translate into the high level Neptune CA-SPA policy shown in Figure 6.

Thus, when the value of the service is not equal to the value of one of the available NBLOs (as defined in the situational state) the *ChoiceList for the available NBLOs* appears as a service to be used, then the user can choose the required NBLOs (defined within the action). The prediction state determines the desired behaviour.

Thus, the system, without prior instruction, has produced an optimised response for the ambient that conflicted with a requirement expressed and represented in the governance of the system.

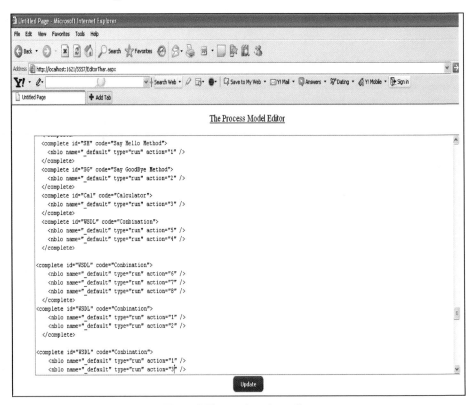

Figure 5: The user intentions editor

```
situation s
{
    if (S.Value != nblo.Value)
        {
            return false;
        }
}
prediction p to a
{
    if (S.Value == nblo.Value)
        {
            return true;
        }
}
action a as s
{
        S.Value == ChioceList for the available nblos;
}
```

Figure 6. CA-SPA policy

3. Case Study

This case study focuses on a commercial decision support system based on reaching decisions based on medical guidelines. Users of the system carry out their work at multiple locations and the guideline models are themselves mobile and subject to amendment or replacement. Thus the profile of a user is viewed as a mobile ambient, itself containing ambients representing the resources required for the user, which may enter the decision calculation ambient when required.

When a new decision model becomes available it is necessary for all ambients representing user profiles, requests, etc. to be updated with the decision model based on their requirements. Thus the system may be updated at run time through the 'Wiki' editor with the Neptune language supplying the logical procedures to ensure system integrity and maintain the mobile user with the most up to date system features. Such a system has been fully implemented: Although full details are outside the scope of this paper further information can be found in [11] and [13].

3.1. Editing the Operational Model for the Mobile Ambient

Based on a scenario in [14] the following circumstance is considered. The distributed network of the organisation has a server used by a certain number of clinicians to execute critical requests. This could be represented as an implementation using the grammar:

$$SYS_2 = Serv[PORT|PORT|PORT|Exec] \mid Cl[REQ] \mid Cl[REQ]$$
$$PORT = P[\text{in } Req.\text{in } Exec]$$
$$REQ = !Req[\text{out } Cl.\text{in } Serv.\text{open } P.DATA]$$

A client *Cl* asks the server to execute a decision process by sending a request. Details of requests are contained in *DATA*. The ambient *Req*, implementing a request, leaves the client and goes into the server decision process ambient. Once there, *Req* uses one of the available data structures used by the server to execute the requests at a particular "PORT". The port *P* moves the request to some process *Exec* which executes the request in *DATA* (returning *P* to *Serv*). Server capacity, however, is limited; the decision process server can only accept a limited amount of requests at the same time. It can occur that the finite number of internal data structures (ports *P*) is consumed in pending requests not yet completed. This can result in an overflow and the server must be rebooted while — in the meanwhile —urgent or critical requests are denied. Predicting the likely number of requests is inherently difficult as the probability density functions, in such cases, operate according to many variable parameters. Thus the safety of such systems is dependent on the *number* of requests that the server has to deal with at any particular time. It is essential that the property no-overflow (NO) holds, i.e. *at any point in time the server has to deal with a number of requests smaller or equal to the size of its data structures (in this case 3 ports)*.

To expand the system and accommodate new clients it is necessary to implement some strategy to avoid overflows. In this case the Wiki editor is utilised: the server sends a message to the administrator saying there is a new client ambient added to the system requiring to enter a decision process ambient and all the PORTs are engaged. Depending on this message, the administrator should amend the data structure of the system (the number of PORTs) according to the number of the new clients so that, for, in this case one new client, the implementation would be realised with the following grammar:

$$SYS_2 = Serv[PORT|PORT|PORT|Exec] \mid Cl[REQ] \mid Cl[REQ]$$
$$PORT = P[\text{in } Req.\text{in } Exec]$$
$$REQ = !Req[\text{out } Cl.\text{in } Serv.\text{open } P.DATA]$$
$$NEW = Serv[NewPORT]$$

In this way the no-overflow (NO) property holds and the run time adaptation of the system and relevant ambients has been achieved.

3.2. Adaptation at Run Time

The implementation of a model autonomic control service based in the middleware is based in this instance on a control service or administrator for the ambients. It should be noted that this administrator may be a separated autonomous, automated application. The control service incorporates three core services, embedded in a three-layered model comprising: an ambient manager for each ambient reporting to the distributed shared system space service and the system controller, as shown in Figure 7. The architecture is based on a control service model that continuously monitors the specified ambient for non-ideal behaviour, to identify conflicts and errors, prescribing repair plans and performing reconfiguration.

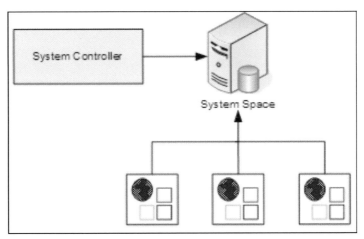

Figure 7. System controller monitors system space

For instance, a report of an unavailable service reported in the system space by the ambient triggers a situation whereby the role of service reconnect is activated in the system controller: When the system detects a failure to connect to a service that is defined within an ambient boundary, it automatically retries as a responsibility to the connecting ambient. On failing a predetermined number of times it then attempts to connect to an alternative service and/or starts a diagnostic process assembled from its available resources resulting in a repair strategy committed intention.

For example an availability rule is defined together with resolution strategies in the case of a service being unavailable. This specifies that if the service is not available for calling, then the system status is queried to see if a service instance alternative is available to enter the ambient. If no instance is found, the repair strategy is service regeneration within the ambient. Calls are then rerouted to the newly generated service, or the alternative service instance if located. This is shown in Figure 8.

```
define service s
if (service.availableServices.likeMe.count = 0)
     service.s = regenerate(me,machineID)
else

     service.s = services.availableServices.likeMe[0]
end if
rerouteCalls(s)
```

Figure 8. Neptune repair script

4. Conclusion

This work has sought to reconcile autonomic computing with m-commerce. In this way assured models of mobility may be established that enable m-commerce systems to be updated at run time and perform self-governance. This has been achieved using the concept enshrined in the Neptune scripting language. This means that, subject to strict logical prescriptive rules, code adaptation may be performed throughout run time either to update the system through code editing or to automatically adapt the system to respond to some perceived failing. The basic constructs that this adaptation has been applied to have been termed mobile ambients. It was necessary to introduce the notion of an ambient in order to capture the nature of mobility, both in terms of code and user location variability, for m-commerce processes. The boundary of an ambient allows the specification of a coherent computational entity that may be moveable: The extent of the m-commerce process dependencies is specified by the ambient boundary and captured in the encoded system logical model.

The associated computational costs of this approach are being assessed at the time of writing. First results indicate quite a high initial overhead dependent upon the range, frequency and scope of the adaptation. It has, however, been observed that this can be more than offset by a reduction in future system down time as the system evolves away from its initial deployed state. Work is still ongoing in this area with various types of system including large-scale m-commerce applications.

Additional work is required to assess the scalability of these methods and tools. A propositional account of the ambients and their domains will be investigated to move away from the state-based approach evident in decision and control theory, for example. Hence, instead of enumerating states and their transition functions, logical descriptions of the system its ambients and domain will be used together with the causal laws for that environment. Thus behaviour will be mediated by what is true in the system and the laws governing that system. In this way it is hoped to further refine the Neptune language to address outstanding issues whilst also gaining more representative and flexible expressions for ambient analysis. Thus allowing a scaleable approach to specifying, designing, deploying and maintaining autonomic systems in any size of m-commerce application.

Acknowledgement

The authors wish to thank and acknowledge the work of Philip Miseldine. His initial contribution forms the basis of the continuing work detailed in this paper.

References

[1] M. Parashar, S. Hariri (2005), 'Autonomic, Computing An Overview', Springer Verlag.
[2] A,Sajjad, H Jameel, , U Kalim, , Y Lee, & S Lee (2005) 'A Component-Based Architecture for an Autonomic Middleware Enabling Mobile Access to Grid Infrastructure., EUC Workshops, pp.1225–1234.
[3] P.Grace, G. Blair, S. Samuel (2005) 'A Reflective Framework for Discovery and Interaction in Heterogeneous Mobile Environments, SIGMOBILE Mob', Comput. Commun. Rev. No. 1, pp.2–14.
[4] P. Miseldine, A. Taleb-Bendiab (2006) 'Retrofitting Zeroconf to Type-Safe Self-Organising Systems', Proceedings of the 17th IEEE International *Conference on Database and Expert Systems Applications (DEXA'06) (Los Alamitos, CA, USA)*, IEEE Computer Society, pp. 93–97.
[5] M. Engel, B. Freisleben (2005) , 'Supporting Autonomic Computing Functionality via Dynamic Operating System Kernel Aspects', AOSD '05: *Proceedings of the 4th international conference on Aspect-oriented software development (New York, NY, USA)*, ACM Press, pp. 51–62.
[6] C. Castelfranchi (1995) 'Guarantees for Autonomy in Cognitive Agent Architecture', ECAI-94: Proceedings of the workshop on agent theories, architectures, and languages on Intelligent agents (New York, NY, USA), Springer-Verlag New York, Inc., pp. 56–70.
[7] K. Kurbel, I.Loutchko (2003) 'Towards Multi-Agent Electronic Marketplaces: What is there and What is Missing?', Knowl. Eng. Rev. 18, no. 1, 33–46
[8] Y. Caseau (2005)'Self-Adaptive Middleware: Supporting Business Process Priorities and Service Level Agreements', Advanced Engineering Informatics 19, no. 3, 199–211.
[9] L. Cardelli, A.D. Gordon (1998) 'Mobile Ambients'. *Proceedings of the First International Conference on Foundations of Software Science and Computation Structure*. M. Nivat (ed) LNCS 1378, pp: 140–155. Springer-Verlag.
[10] P. Miseldine, A. Taleb-Bendiab (2007) 'Neptune: Supporting Semantics-Based Runtime Software Refactoring to Achieved Assured System Autonomy' In the 4th International Conference on Autonomic and Trusted Computing (ATC-07), IEEE organization.
[11] P. Miseldine, A. Taleb-Bendiab, D. England, M. Randles (2007) 'Addressing the Need for Adaptable Decision Processes Within Healthcare Software', Medical Informatics and the Internet in Medicine, Taylor and Francis, 37(1), pp. 35-43.
[12] P. Miseldine, A. Taleb-Bendiab (2006) ' CA-SPA: Balancing the Crosscutting Concerns of Governance and Autonomy in Trusted Software' International Workshop on Trusted and Autonomic Computing Systems (TACS-06), The IEEE 20th International Conference on Advanced Information Networking and Applications (AINA 2006), pp. 471-475.
[13] 2nrich Project (2006) Towards a Disciplined Approach to Integrating Decision-Support Systems for Breast Cancer Care Activities. http://www.cms.livjm.ac.uk/2nrich/
[14] D. Distefano (2005) 'A Parametric Model for the Analysis of Mobile Ambients' K. Yi (Editor) APLAS 2005 LNCS 378, pp: 401-417.

Techniques and Applications for Mobile Commerce
C. Branki et al. (Eds.)
IOS Press, 2008
177

Author Index